LATINOS IN THE UNITED STATES

Latinos in the United States

The Sacred and the Political

David T. Abalos

UNIVERSITY OF NOTRE DAME PRESS
NOTRE DAME, INDIANA 46556

Library of Congress Cataloging-in-Publication Data

Abalos, David T.
  Latinos in the United States.

  Bibliography: p.
  Includes index.
  1. Hispanic Americans—Ethnic identity. 2. Hispanic
Americans—Cultural assimilation. I. Title.
E184.S75A63 1963   305.8′68073   85-41010
ISBN 0-268-01277-6

Manufactured in the United States of America

FOR CELIA, DAVID, VERONICA, AND MATTHEW
MY FELLOW SOJOURNERS ON THE WAY OF TRANSFORMATION

Contents

Foreword

This book brings us a radically new understanding of the political choices facing Latino men and women living in the United States. Politics here means all that we can and need to do together. Understanding the threats and opportunities that face Latinos is here grounded upon a theory of transformation.

Why a theory—and therefore also a practice—of transformation? The idea of theory first came into being in Greece to describe the compassionate act of meditating upon the dying and rebirth of a god, and therefore of all human beings for whom this god constituted their force of life. Each year Greek cities sent a representative to an enactment of this drama of dying and being reborn. Each representative upon his return had to report in public on his experience of this transformation.

Theory first arose, and always arises, out of the same beginning as transformation. Both begin with a great dying—with the death of what was once held to be sacred, empowering, and secure. Both renew our questioning and our compassion. Both demand our participation, personally and politically, in a drama of rebirth. Theory constitutes our shared understanding of how the cosmos of human relationships can be nourished, destroyed, and re-created with love and justice. But such a shared theory of practice is transforming only if it liberates each individual to make his and her own creative contribution, which is always—as a proof of freedom—unique in its actual, concrete practice, even while it expresses underlying patterns that (theory shows) we share by virtue of our species-being.

The theory of transformation which David Abalos here pioneers in applying to Latino communities in the United States is both a critical and a creative theory. It is concerned with our participation in changing both underlying forces and their concrete manifestations in human relationships when they have become unbearable or fruitless as well as in nourishing them knowledgeably and lovingly as we help to make them just.

The chief difficulty in understanding this theory of transformation stems from the fact that it deals not only with the concrete and the particular. It takes the sensuously concrete with utmost seriousness: everyone needs their daily bread and each particular child needs our daily care. But this theory also sees every concreteness as the manifestation of underlying patterns that it recognizes and analyzes as living forces with real powers of their own. None of the concepts of this theory are to be understood as mere abstractions. Instead they point to real underlying, patterning forces in our life. The wondrous, confusing, miserable, boring, exciting, inspiring immediacy and specificity of our life is one real face of our being. It also symbolizes and (if we are theoretically informed) reveals the other real face of our being: its transpersonal depths.

Let us take a roundabout road in discovering the nature of this theory. If we take what looks like the straightest and quickest road, we are likely to mislead ourselves. Rushing into the first chapter or browsing in the middle of this work, we might suppose that the theory of transformation offers us a catalogue of eight relationships and three paradigms, or ways of life, as a system of classification that one or two social scientists thought instrumentally useful for a particular purpose at hand. This supposition would be entirely mistaken. It is true that this theory offers about a dozen new concepts. That is the least of it. What is being offered here is an entirely new way of seeing and living.

The eight archetypal relations and three archetypal paradigms—or ways of life—which David Abalos puts to use for re-visioning Latino life are discoveries about the range of fundamental choices open to any and all of us. This theory of transformation is different from most theories in the modern social sciences, philosophy, and psychology in that it is empirical and normative at the same time. It helps us analyze what practical choices we have and also whether they are just or unjust. We are not accustomed to such theories. Most of us suppose that the analysis of what is and the evaluation of whether it is just is the business of two distinct, indeed separated, realms of life. Especially since the seventeenth century we have come to accept a gap between what we call the "is" and the "ought," politics and religion, practical life and philosophy, the objective and the subjective. This theory of transformation rejects and overcomes such distinctions, not by returning to old dogmas or offering new ones. It is founded instead on the discovery of archetypal patterns of human relationships and ways of life which any human being can examine and validate in her and his own life. Why are we to bother with archetypes and thus with our participation in the patterning forces of the transpersonal—or sacred—realm of being?

I never planned to go in that unfamiliar and strange direction. After I had published *The Politics of Social Change in the Middle East and North Africa* (Princeton, 1963) analyzing the revolutions in progress from Morocco to Pakistan—the forces, groups, ideas, and institutions dissolving or emerging—a fundamental question still baffled me. Muslim society had persisted for nearly fourteen hundred years (more than twice as long as the Roman Empire), able to cope with conflicts and changes, assuring collaboration over a large area while giving rise to two radically different experiences of justice— one orthodox, one transforming. Muslims during that long period contributed greatly to world civilization.[1] Why is it that Muslim societies today—whether rich or poor, parliamentary or authoritarian, traditionalist or socialist, tribal or nationalist—cannot deal with continuity or change, collaboration or conflict, or the achieving of justice?

I returned to the Middle East and North Africa with what seemed to me in the 1960s a straightforward social-science type of question: Suppose one wishes to experience (or observe) all five of the following issues *simultaneously* at stake in any human relationship: continuity as well as change, collaboration as well as conflict, and also the achieving of justice. How many qualitatively different ways of enacting these five faces of relationship are there? I discovered that human beings have altogether eight different ways of structuring such relationships. David Abalos' first chapter will spell out these eight ways, which are the same in underlying structure whether I relate to myself, to other persons or groups, or to ideas or values or problems. I thought then that these eight forms of relationships were the most useful abstractions possible for inquiring why relationships were dissolving among Muslims (and all other peoples around the world) and also why relationships were breaking between individuals and groups and their inherited concepts and norms.

Then it dawned on me that I had missed an essential dimension in the inquiry into a great dying. The despair, demoralization, and confusion of Muslims was a response not only to the breaking of the concrete, inherited manifestations of their repertory of relationships—or to the crippling effect of trying to maintain old relationships in the face of new challenges. An entire way of life was disintegrating. To Muslims it felt as if a sacred force that had for long infused all aspects of being was being shattered. How can we grasp a way of life?

To discover our way of life we need to ask, Why, ultimately, am I enacting this (or any other) relationship? Why, ultimately, am I doing what I am doing? It turns out that to this "Why?" there are only three answers, that is, only three underlying patterns or paradigms for organizing life. One can answer that I ultimately do what I do because a mysterious and overwhelming source ordained how life hangs together and what we must do to keep it that way. Orthodox Muslims, Catholics, Jews, and most peoples in the past answered thus, whatever their concrete manifestation of the paradigm of emanation. Or, as more and more people reply today, we say that there is no answer to such an ultimate why: no way of discovering it; no way of proving it; no way of getting people to agree on it. Thus we live in a paradigm of incoherence. Individuals in this paradigm, therefore, know no ultimate limits to the pursuit of self-interests. And there is a third answer: to discover the ultimate structures and choices of the cosmos of human relationships and lovingly choose what is most just. This means living in the service of the paradigm of transformation. These brief hints concerning paradigms David Abalos will elaborate upon in chapter one and throughout his work as constituting the most basic choices open to us.

At this point of the inquiry I came to recognize that I was not developing intellectually convenient abstractions but discovering archetypes—underlying, transpersonal forces that pattern all concrete manifestations of our lives. That there are eight archetypal relationships (when those five issues cited earlier are simultaneously at stake) and three archetypal paradigms (or ways of life) is a discovery about the reality of human nature both in its concreteness and its ultimate depths. It is an empirical discovery: anyone can test our report on the quality of each and the number of all in his and her own life. And it is an empirical discovery as well about the justice that is intrinsic to each relationsip and each way of life as we enact it. No external judgment is imposed afterward from a subjective, ideal, pragmatic, or dogmatic position. David Abalos' elaboration and analysis will make this clear.

Within any archetype the pattern necessarily hangs together the way it does. Within any archetype (and we always live within an archetype) its living forces will move all the concrete manifestations of our life according to its underlying pattern. But we can free ourselves to choose among archetypes and to participate as well in creatively giving shape to its particular expressions. That freedom is fully ours, however, only within the paradigm of transformation.

To explain this last statement further requires one more turn into the depths of our being. Since we mean by transformation the persistent creation of fundamentally new and better relationships, the question we must now ask is, Where is such a new relationship to come from? When I suddenly say, "I never thought of that before!" where was that thought before?

To the question regarding the source of the fundamentally new and better, philosophers throughout the ages have produced four possible answers. One answer is that there is in fact nothing ever fundamentally new under the sun. What we call new is the old rearranged. Such modifications are certainly possible, but Christ did not merely rearrange Judaism; Buddha did not merely rearrange Hinduism; Picasso did not merely rearrange representational art. A second answer is that the new comes into being by random movements. No doubt accidents happen, some for the better, some for the worse; but we cannot spend our lives waiting only for a lucky accident. A third answer is: do not ask this question. This answer has two different forms. One is the response of orthodox religion, reflecting the paradigm of emanation: only god in his own infinite wisdom brings forth the new and better; it is not for us to ask how or why. The other is the response of conventional science, reflecting the paradigm of incoherence: scientists have not yet discovered how the fundamentally new comes into being, and they will never be able, as scientists, to answer any question regarding what is ethically better. That, in our dire personal and political need, leaves us with the fourth answer.

The fourth answer begins by pointing to the right direction—into mysterious depths. What is now newly differentiated and conscious for us—a new thought or feeling or image—was a moment ago undifferentiated and unconscious. "Un" in both words states a truth to be taken seriously: initially we do not know. Philosophers as Plato (d. 347 B.C.) started millennia ago to inquire into this mysterious source of the new. They recognized that most of their neighbors—living in the paradigm of emanation—regarded this source not only as mysterious but also as overwhelming. However, the philosophers of the countertradition of transformation—such as Avicenna (d. 1037), Meister Eckhardt (d. 1327), Moses Maimonides (d. 1204), Giordano Bruno (d. 1600), and Hegel (d. 1831)—saw that we can also experience this source as one of continual creation in our life, and they asked how we might lovingly and justly participate in continual creation. Lovingly and justly: they (and we) know from our daily experience that the deepest sources of our life can also spring forth destructively. Our task is never a merely simple obedience to the transpersonal depths, never a merely shrewd, conscious translation of whatever pours forth into practice; but rather a conscientious, creative collaboration with the depths and with our neighbors.

In their investigations the philosophers of the countertradition of transformation realized long ago that this transpersonal source of our being gives form to the particular through underlying patterns, that is, through archetypes. In our own time Carl Gustave Jung explored the sacred realm of archetypes. The work of identifying archetypal patterns is far from complete. This present theory of transformation is only the most recent contribution to this inquiry. But we are building upon one of the oldest insights when we say that it is the archetypal paradigm of transformation that gives us the deepest understanding of the process of creating fundamentally new and better relationships and the greatest freedom to share in such work.

However much we suffer, however much we desire to return to an old security or move on to a new salvation, nothing will change if we merely believe in this transpersonal source of creation, worshipping it obediently as a god of a fixed and final revelation. However much we fight for change, nothing will come of it if we, because we are secular revolutionaries, reject all knowledge and experience of the transpersonal because others have for so long worshipped it as god. I arrived at the realization that we must become conscious of our link to the transpersonal depths, not because I had been a believer in god (I was not), but because there are no other good answers to the question that arises out of a great need around the world: Where are fundamentally new and better relationships to come from?

This answer is also a radically democratic answer. We can all free ourselves to participate with the transpersonal depths in the work of creation. We share these transpersonal depths by virtue of being human. They are transpersonal in the sense that they move through each person. We face fundamental choices. We can, as in the paradigm of emanation, become uncritical embodiments of these sources in the depths, that is, of the archetypes, as well as of the source of all sources, whom we have usually called god. We can, as in the paradigm of incoherence, fantasize that there are no such sources and turn the inspirations that nonetheless well up within us into merely subjective drives for pursuing our self-interest. Or we can, as in the paradigm of transformation, recognize that this transpersonal realm of living sources and underlying patterning forces is the realm of the truly sacred. It follows that each of us, as a concrete manifestation of that realm, is also sacred. Each of us is for that reason precious, and each of us, as an image of these creative sources, is also free to help ourselves and each other to be transforming beings with understanding and love and justice.

David Abalos' work is devoted above all to this transformation. My own manuscript on this subject, *Transformation: Its Theory and Practice in Personal, Political, Historical, and Sacred Being*, will still need a couple of years to be completed. But it is entirely right that David Abalos should pioneer even now in applying this theory to the destiny of what is soon to be—or may already be—the largest minority in the United States. Because he was for many years a student for the priesthood but did not join it, he knows the established past and its emanational inheritance, yet is free to evaluate its present meaning. Because he grew up of Mexican parentage in Detroit but has returned on frequent study trips to Mexico, he knows Latino culture in its origins and in its migrations. Because he has taught students at both Catholic and Ivy League universities, and also educated workers, nurses, and priests, he has a wide and deep comparative grasp of the problems of transformation.

David Abalos became a student of mine more than fifteen years ago, just as the theory of transformation was beginning to take shape. As a colleague, he has ever since been one of the most concerned and fruitful contributors, critics, teachers, and practitioners in the development of this theory.

In November 1970 he wrote to me that the majority of Catholics and Latinos who are not yet breaking with their traditional roots are like India's Untouchables. They *are* India. Gandhi needed to embrace his past if he were to participate lovingly in changing the past. David Abalos then added: "A similar awareness came to me. Unless I could transform my own prejudices, destructiveness, and hatred towards my own past, I would not be able to help others to change their consciousness. . . . Thus I am once again redefining my life and searching my past for continuities and yet recognizing that the discontinuities were necessary for me to have even asked the questions that changed my consciousness."

David Abalos has not ceased to ask ever anew what the past of his religion and culture symbolizes in terms of deep insights and of turning points arrested and not yet taken into transformation. His present work opens doors never opened before.

Manfred Halpern
Professor of Politics
Princeton University

September 20, 1985

NOTE

1. To speak of Muslim society is to speak of a culture which deeply and directly influenced Spanish culture for about six hundred years. The orthodox experience of Islam may well have helped to develop or reinforce Spanish devotion to masculine heroism, patriarchalism, patron-client dependencies, and the repression of the feminine. The transforming forces in Muslim society—for transformation is not a modern discovery, but rather has become now a more desperate and widespread need in the face of growing incoherence—also bore early and splendid fruit in Spain. As almost nowhere else, Christians, Jews, and Muslims in Spain collaborated from the tenth to the twelfth century in developing the theory, art, and practice of transformation—material which has much influenced this present work. To destroy this transforming movement was the principal task which the Inquisition set for itself.

To apply the theory of transformation to Muslims or to people of Spanish or any other origins is simply to exemplify the application of a theory that applies as well to you and me and her and him, without exception.

Acknowledgments

First of all my wife Celia brought this book to life with her loving encouragement and expertise. Celia transformed the scrawl of my inadequate penmanship into a beautiful new reality by her prowess on the word processor. This gave the ideas in my head and in script a concreteness that inspired me to bring forth more ideas so that they could come to life on the monitor screen and in print.

My friend and colleague Manfred Halpern gave me the confidence to be bold enough to write the following: "Manfred had a heart like the heart of God; and God had a heart like the heart of Manfred." Each of us in our own way completes God.

My Mexican parents, Luis Jose and Luz Gil de Avalos, Luis and Celia Dorantes, and my grandparents on my wife's side, Jose and Maria Hernandez, all taught me the importance of the journey of transformation by taking the risk of loving enough to create new generations of Latinos in a new land.

I owe much to my brothers and sisters, Angie and Jim, Vicki and Leroy, Marge and Bill, Sal and Louis, for their love and support through the years.

A special recognition is owed to all of my students during the past twenty years and especially to my Chicano/Latino students like Myrna Santiago, Roberto Barragan, Mike Montoya, Michael Lopez, Luz Calvo, Susan Villalon, Joel Barrera, Rene Flores, Miriam Lopez, Jacqueline Rodriguez, Luis Cordero, Maria Montanez, David Cordero, Rickey DeLeon, Adolph Falcon, and Jose Adames who contributed to the writing of this book with their ideas and constant support.

To my colleagues in the Religious Studies and Sociology/Anthropology Departments at Seton Hall University, and to others at the University like George and Paula Tzannetakis, Frank Morales, who helped me so much in returning me to my Latino/Chicano heritage, Ann Rebhan, and Helen Hamilton, I am very thankful for their invaluable help and encouragement. I am very grateful to Frank Sullivan and Dick Scaine who inspired me as a young faculty member with their dedication to excellence in teaching and their compassionate concern for others; they helped me to be a better teacher and human being. I am also indebted to Martha Chavez Brummel, a former Dean of Yale University, who never tired in her efforts to help me and other Chicano/Latino students and teachers to achieve academic and personal growth.

I would also like to acknowledge the support which I received throughout the writing of this book from the staff in the Dean's Office in the College of Arts and Sciences, and I especially appreciate the help of dedicated men like Deans Bernhard Scholz and Peter Ahr.

There are many who toil daily in our Latino communities who were both a source of inspiration and of valuable resource material in the writing of this book. Among the many, I wish to especially thank Dr. Hector P. Garcia, the founder of the GI Forum, and his sister Dr. Clotilde Garcia; Dr. Jose Rosario, the founder and Executive Director of Focus; Tony and Ruben Bonilla of Corpus Christi, the backbone of the League of United Latin American Citizens; Ms. Dolores Huerta of the United Farm Workers; Ms. Lourdes Soto of Talent Search; and Dr. Hilda Hidalgo of Rutgers University; Sr. Carla Barr and Brother Miguel Campos of the Archdiocese of Newark.

Finally, I would like to thank my editor Mr. John Ehmann for his encouragement and genuine friendship throughout the writing of the manuscript.

Grateful acknowledgment is made to *Democracy* and the *Journal of Dharma* where earlier versions of chapter two and chapter five respectively were published.

Introduction

I hate objectivity. I am convinced it's a Western, white, male
plot to rob the rest of us of our experience by negating our
point of view and thus invalidating our being.

—*Myrna Santiago*

This comment on the poverty of objectivity that excludes the
subject, the person, was written by a young Chicana/Latina sadly com-
plaining about how all of us have been wounded by our socialization
in this culture. In a similar vein Elizabeth Dreyer, a Jungian analyst,
reminds us to resist "the allure of the abstract at the cost of the concrete." Evelyn Waugh's character Sebastian in *Brideshead Revisited*
is scolded by his cousin for not upholding the family honor and the
tradition of scholarship at Oxford. Sebastian comments that his
cousin unfortunately will never know what he has learned this semester: "That to know and love another human being is the beginning of wisdom."

I want to offer a different kind of book, a book which addresses
all of these contemporary issues with the close-up lens of the self,
myself. In the midst of such general/abstract concerns as undocumented workers and Simpson/Mazzoli; the growing political power
of Latinos, the soon-to-be largest minority in the nation; the debate
over bilingual education; the rise of an upwardly mobile Latino class;
the wars of liberation in Central and South America coupled with
a conservative United States foreign policy in Latin America to stem
the tide of communism, I want to begin with the personal, the autobiographical, the subject, the self; the self is the center of all revolution whether it be in the social, political, or religious realm. Furthermore, I believe that what I am experiencing as an individual Chicano/
Latino is being experienced by a growing number of Puerto Ricans,
Cubans, Chicanos, Colombians, Dominicans, and other Latinos. But

1

when we look around for direction, myself included, we find little to comfort us. Thus I write this book as a source of guidance for myself and other Latinos. By relating and reflecting upon our personal lives and searching for a meaningful theoretical framework we can better explain what is happening to us. Too often our own best scholars are seduced by their academic training. To be accepted into the circles of university life they end up doing statistical studies and other detached, neutral scholarship. They thus turn themselves and us, their fellow Latinos, into abstractions. To be objective such a method abstracts from the concrete and then relates the conceptual abstractions to other concepts abstractly until we have "pure," distilled objective truth. In this context the personal becomes the residual category. Descartes in his famous treatise *On Method* spoke of liberating the student from all cultural baggage in order to purify them so that they could bring to their studies an objective self. And this point of view is precisely the issue: the emphasis on abstraction, objectivity, methods, and techniques moves us away from the concrete, the subject, the personal, the touchstone of reality. Anything that cannot be quantified—such as love, truth, beauty, and justice—are regarded as purely subjective categories that blur the objective search for truth. Each person's views are just as good as another, that is, almost worthless. This attitude severs our soul and fragments us into the empirical versus the normative, the abstract concept versus feelings, and object versus subject.

Some Latinos anguish over their inability to merge the private world of their poverty-stricken background and shy Spanish-speaking parents with their newfound public existence that finds them drinking orange juice and eating croissants while discussing the arcane value of medieval literature with Ivy-League colleagues. They feel fragmented; they are. When a person or cultural group is cut off from its own feelings, personal sources, and intuitions, it is also cut off from its creative depths. Thus some Latinos gain an identity by holding on to a past, by romanticizing it out of all proportion, which leads to an ethnic chauvinism or a strident nationalism. Other Latinos attempt to forget their past by assimilation, which implies self-alienation and self-hatred. Assimilation is a question never of both/and but of either/or, with the element of power dictating the choice of the predominant culture. Assimilation creates fragmentation. Deprived of our personal feelings and emotions, Latinos accept the real, "objective" world of the others. This creates the guilt-ridden schizophrenic/amnesiac walking-wounded who have dropped out of their consciousness their own emotional heritage. The therapy of the Chicano, Boricua, and other Latino movements is intended to lift such suppressed consciousness back into place. Latinos are angry because they now know that their oppression is more than political or economic; it is cultural. We were all deprived of more than money or position; we were stripped of a self. Without a self there is no basis by which a person can resist what is being done to them. I agree with Rousseau when he wrote that the peasants were not born dull; they were made that way. Rousseau would disagree with Spiro Agnew regarding a silent majority. There has never been a silent majority by choice; people were *silenced*, somebody violated them so that their dissident voice would not lead to a destabilizing of democracy for the few. Similarly, Paulo Freire refuses to accept the stereotype of Latinos as passive or fatalistic, as if we chose to be violated. Freire correctly points out that perceived fatalism is the result of particular historical and sociological conditions. The truth of the matter is that one group had a vested interest in *making* others passive so that they could control them.

Beginning with the personal leads me to the social and political realms, however, because to be a person is to be political and social. We become who we are by being interdependent with others. Yet if the others in the greater society reject us until we become like unto them or assimilated, we enter into society as lesser beings. In addition, we are depoliticized or deprived of being political, that is, we cannot shape our environment and lives on a basis of equality with others. Every individual has the inherent right to participate in creating an environment to nurture and enhance society but also to dismantle or destroy institutions that have turned against the creators by taking on a destructive life of their own. One turn in the spiral is complete when an alternative creation is substituted for the old. This understanding of revolution, politics, and the intimate relationship between being personal and political demonstrates that not only Latinos are victimized; all of us in this society are deprived of shaping our private and public lives through an alarming trend toward a hierarchical society. Many white ethnics or Anglos do not realize when they feel threatened by our participation that the health of the whole system is based on a declining participation by all groups, including whites. American voters do not participate; we unfortunately help to legitimate the growing inequality every two or four years. This is largely because many of us define wealth as consuming more and more and not as participating with others to take risks in building new institutions or consciously sustaining the old.

Thus, when/if Latinos consciously take themselves back from

a society and culture that wants to redefine them as honorary whites (provided they "behave"), it is viewed as both a personal and political act. It is a personal act because it presupposes an act of resistance that can only come from a center, a self, which is capable of imagining alternatives and of acting to implement a different life. It is a political act because it is the rejection of having "superior" others shape life, attitudes, and values for us. As self-conscious political beings, we insist that we can establish institutions that incarnate our reality. This is revolutionary stuff. This desire and inherent right to shape one's own life and environment together with others is largely behind the transformation of Mexican-Americans to Chicanos, of Puerto Ricans to Boricua, and of Spanish Americans to Latinos. It is the desire to define oneself, to shape oneself anew, to make oneself over according to a new vision. Al Pacino, playing the role of Tony Rome in *Scarface*, tells us what United States society is all about. Tony crudely figures out the philosophy of life in his new home. By constantly using the four-letter expletive for "making" somebody, what he is saying is that you have to get somebody before they get you. Unfortunately, such a statement only masks rebellion; it is stark capitulation to the power games of United States society. What one cannot do is shape, make, or love your own selfhood and demand respect for your person *as* a person. For Tony the whole society is a brothel, and whoever moves fast achieves the prize. Everybody is a threat, and so to win you have to be better at the game than those who devised it. He outsmarts his tutors but tragically comes to ask, "Is that all there is?" This is the ultimate question for all of those who at the cost of the self are successful at assimilating. Nothing new is created, only the affirmation that the system is right. What I, and I believe many others, seek is not power over others but the capacity to change not only our lives but the system of power itself.

To be personal and political is also to participate in the sacred drama of completing creation. The Muslim mystical tradition names every person as a spark of the divine. This is an ontological statement, an affirmation of our own sacredness since we participate in the being and thus in a sense share in the divinity of the Creator. Such a philosophical understanding adds an urgency to our being full selves who participate in re-creating our world. The new cannot come from carbon copies of the roles that others play and give to us. To repeat the orthodox world whether of religion or politics is to impoverish ourselves, the world, and the sacred.

Latinos have always been a deeply religious people. Certainly our indigenous forebearers recognized the presence of the sacred as is witnessed by the pyramids, gods and goddesses, and prayers to the divinity found throughout Latin America. The Spaniards did not introduce the sacred. They simply contributed a particular, historical, although very important, manifestation of the sacred as found in the Catholic/Christian religion. The sacred is always more than its manifestations and has to be pursued and struggled with in whatever way the Source of all Sources chooses to reveal itself. Both the Spaniards and the Aztecs, for example, attempted to domesticate the sacred by preserving formulas, rituals, an official priesthood and theology. Such institutionalization, although a necessary part of the process of culture-making, often malfunctions through relating *recipients* not to the sacred but to mediators who claim that the ultimate truth was already delivered to them. Rather than leading us to inner selfhood to experience the sacred, which is the ground of our being, priests and ministers often pointed us toward a religion that was outside of ourselves. Such alienation from the sacred is also an alienation from the self. A disconnection from one's sacred sources and from one's self leaves others to play god. And this they do with a vengeance. Social and political arrangements are no longer the domination of a class or oligarchy but god's will. After generations of this kind of religious indoctrination, people internalize their own perceived inadequacy as sinfulness, powerlessness, and a sense of uselessness: "No sirvo para nada" (I am not good for anything).

Most Latinos have for historical and cultural reasons been Catholics. From the time of the Conquest the Church became an institutionalized buffer for the Indian and mestizo population. Eventually this became a negative relationship, because the Church considered it a duty to protect the Indian from greed and cruelty without questioning the hierarchical system that oppressed the peasants. Thus the Church never challenged the legitimacy of the system itself, only its excesses. In this way the Church became part of the problem. At different times due to internal political upheavals liberal groups turned against the Catholic Church. These conflicts occurred after the wars of independence that ended Spanish rule. New political groups fought against the Church because it controlled much of the land and education and exercised a heavy influence on the law courts. This was not an antireligious or antisacred position, but it was anticlericalism. There was a refusal to allow the cleric to be the final arbiter in the realm of the state. I see a similar trend today. Latinos in this country are not antireligious or antichurch, but there is a growing anticlericalism aimed at resisting the desire of the clergy to consider themselves as final arbiters of the sacred.

Recently there has been a series of attempts on the part of the Catholic Church to evaluate the condition of Latinos in various dioceses throughout the United States. These studies have a very pragmatic basis; one-quarter of Roman Catholics in the United States are Latinos. That number will continue to grow, so that by the year 2000 it will be fully one-third. All of a sudden the Catholic hierarchy has discovered "a problem." We have always been here but not so vocally or in such numbers. In fairness we wish to say there were countless parish priests who devoted their lives to serving the Latino missions, as they were named as recently as the mid-1960s, even in Texas. The official Church through the hierarchy gave rhetorical service and some funds to the numerous Spanish-speaking apostolates. However, they significantly failed to develop an indigenous clergy, sisterhood, and hierarchy. Thus, no matter how hard they tried, the missions mentality still remained largely paternalistic and condescending. Another factor in the recent interest in Latinos of the Catholic Church has been the growing success of evangelical Protestantism among Latinos. There are many reasons for their appeal to Latinos, but suffice it to say that the ministers invariably come from a Latino background, speak Spanish, share the daily hardships of the community, and have more of an egalitarian church service based on Scripture. I believe that Catholics are now competing for their "fallen" members with these groups.

The U.S. Catholic Bishops' pastoral letter on "The Hispanic Presence: Challenge and Commitment" was issued in January 1984. It is a very mild, almost apologetic statement that can charitably be considered a beginning. In speaking to one of the writers of the document regarding its timidity, I received the answer that they did not want to be too bold or outspoken lest the rest of the bishops be disturbed, hesitate, and reject the draft of the letter. This attitude exposes the very effect that the Church has had on Latinos. We do not demand or speak of struggle or political rights because we have been socialized to be patient, work through the system, and be thankful for what we get. This socialized passivity and ritualized avoidance is a disservice to our people because it denies the depth of the suffering and the urgency of our needs. We have a right to be filled with *coraje*, anger, and to refuse to defer our needs because of fiscal constraints. I was told that conscious efforts were made to avoid words such as liberation and political, or institutionalized, violence; they were considered too provocative. When the pastoral letter wishes to say political, it uses such traditional ecclesiastical language as "social justice," "social action," and "temporal needs." Voting rights, discrimination, immigration rights, status of farmworkers, bilingualism, and pluralism are referred to as "social concerns." In spite of the fact that since Rerum Novarum Catholics see it as their right to form workers' unions, nowhere do the bishops support the right of Latinos to organize, to struggle for their rights; nor do they urge other Catholics of goodwill to help Latinos empower themselves. I see this letter as condescending because it is not a clear and distinct statement declaring the rights of Latinos to be political in shaping our own lives. Furthermore, two very important issues are entirely ignored: male-female relationships in the Latino culture and the ordination of married men and women. The failure to raise these issues perpetuates the sexism based on machismo in our community and continues the harmful belief that the spiritual/clerical/celibate is superior to the bodily/lay/married life. In this way the pastoral letter badly fragments reality and severs us from ourselves and one another.

Let me offer another example of the intertwining of the sacred and the political. I participated in the study *Hispanics in New York: Religious, Cultural and Social Experiences,* or *Hispanics en Nueva York: Experiencias Religiosas, Culturales y Sociales,* sponsored by the Archdiocese of New York and completed in 1982. The fundamental flaw in the study was the separation of the religious from the political. The writers neglect to focus on the political dimension which flows from a sense of selfhood. This study leaves me with the fear that the real concern of the archdiocese is not for Latinos *as* Latinos but for the institutional Church and its members. The Catholic Church has always been political. Now we as Latinos are asking that the Church stand with the poorest of the poor in terms of actual participation rather than support the *status quo.* Church studies should begin with and conclude with a statement that the Church is willing to identify herself with and to support the struggle of Latinos both as a group and as individuals for jobs, housing, health facilities, bilingual/bicultural education, and legal justice, that is, participation in all the benefits of our society. Latinos do not ask that the Church support particular political parties such as La Raza Unida but that she preach the right of all to *be* political. Furthermore, what we ask is that the Church speak of structural violence and systemic injustice and not just individual sin. We seek not charity in the form of U.S. government-issue cheese but justice. What Latinos are asking for is institutionalized justice for all, not selective charity as a handout that perpetuates dependence. If the Church is to be a carrier of the sacred in the modern age, it cannot neglect such basic issues of how the self comes to be in the community.

It is not enough to assert the relationship between the personal, the political, and the sacred. The quality of the relationship between the person and the sacred must also be addressed. This also has a lot to do with the guides we find in our churches. So the issue is not the name of the church, the theological degrees, or the use of Scripture. The point is whether or not the community, Catholic or Pentecostal, relates the individual to God in a redemptive way. Some Catholics and some Pentecostals seek to give security above all else to Latinos and so relate to us in such a way that they try to possess us and to give us an identity in a harsh world. Herein I shall be distinguishing between three gods who correspond to three fundamentally different ways of living and shaping our lives. Two of these gods, the god of emanation and the god of incoherence, are false gods or idols, and only the god of transformation allows us to fully participate. Thus the god of emanation is a divinity that embraces us and protects us. But we cannot struggle or talk back. We must be perpetual children to be comforted by this mother-god-Church. Others link us to the god of incoherence that will help us to triumph over others if we are good. This is a capitalistic god that urges us to capitalize on our ethnic backgrounds to seek power. It is only the transforming god who asks/needs our participation in completing the creation of divinity, community, world, and our own selfhood. This is why statistics about going to church, or reading Scripture, or receiving the Eucharist are not helpful. I propose that when examining the relationship of Latinos to the sacred, we have to know what god is being related to and the quality of that relationship. This reveals whether human life is being affirmed or oppressed. Surely it makes a difference if one Catholic goes to Mass to hide from his problems and that of the community and another Latino attends Mass in order to gain the courage to help organize a rent strike or a parents' council to monitor the quality of education of their children. These kinds of issues regarding the quality of a relationship a statistical study cannot evaluate.

This is not a book that will blindly celebrate the various Latino cultures. We must not project unto others what we cannot or refuse to face in ourselves. We have to take on the courage to criticize ourselves as individuals and as a group. One of our most immature relationships is that between men and women. What we have done to each other in the name of *cariño*, affection, needs to cease for the sake of our humanity and that of our children. For example, my father related to my mother in a way that was blessed by the culture but detrimental to my mother. My father kept my mother in a state of suspended dependence that made it difficult for her to cope when he died. Much of our family life after my father's death was spent helping my mother to survive. In addition to such sexism, also there is certainly a great deal of racism and classism in our communities. This is partially due to our Latin American heritage. Many of our mothers and fathers and *abuelos*, grandparents, came to this country already lamed by the poverty of a hierarchical class society run largely by white European males who had little use for the *Indios* or mestizos in their societies. Moreover, the Inquisition that rooted out the Moors and Jews for reasons of religious and racial purity followed the Spaniards to the New World. The *indigenos* in our background also organized their societies in a hierarchical manner, with the noble warrior priestly caste at the top. Unfortunately Latinos practice a racism and classism of our own in this country. Upwardly mobile Latinos and professionals often feel superior to lower class Latinos and reject them on grounds of class. Other Latinos are ashamed of or look down upon the *morenos* or darker skinned among us. Latinos with an African heritage are often discriminated against in their Latino community. So there is much in our Latino tradition that we must resist, reinterpret, and struggle with to see if it affirms or oppresses our individual and mutual humanity.

Our families must serve as crucibles that prepare us for selfhood. Too often our families seek to possess us and to give us security by protecting us. But the basic familial experience of our lives must allow the flowering of the self to take place. To keep us in containers is to prevent us from bringing our sacredness to fruition. Affection is essential for liberation, to prepare us to walk away or to stay by *choice*. Love that cripples is not love but possessiveness that feeds on guilt.

One of the central motifs I will use in examining Latino relationships to the sacred and the political will be that of the journey. The archetype of the journey has been central in the lives of all Latinos. Our forebearers came to this country seeking a new life, a better life, at the cost of great personal suffering and risk. They left behind loved ones, a familiar land and culture, to journey into the desert of an unknown land with a strange language and customs. But they came and they endured. So they have witnessed to one of the oldest archetypes of humanity—uprooting, wandering and creating a new life in a new land. The Aztecs were told by means of a vision to travel south into the Valley of Mexico, and they were told that when they saw an eagle perched on a cactus, eating a serpent, that place would be holy ground. They were to stay and settle the land. This is the sacred story underlying the founding of Tenochtitlan, or Mexico City. But the symbolism of the journey does not only point us to a spatiotemporal reality; it is also a myth that points us inward, into the atemporal psychic depths; it is an invitation to travel within the valleys and mountains of the inner world in order to discover a new landscape of the self. This internal voyage is the journey that we are all called upon to endure so as to forge a new connection between the conscious self that we know and the undifferentiated unconscious self that wants to emerge out of the darkness into the light of our consciousness. It is this further linkage to our larger self in the depths that releases an infinite amount of energy in the self and the world.

However, it is not enough to pour out our souls; we need the discipline of a theory to organize and understand what is being revealed. Einstein put it best when he said that it is the theory that allows us to see, to see a new world, to ask new questions. Sheldon Wolin has used the method of Michael Polanyi to remind us of the element of surprise and playfulness in the tacit dimension. Theory is not a bag of tricks by which we capture reality. Theory and its choice is more like a conversion, a turning around of our being by which to receive a fuller view of the world, self, other, and God. Method is not a well-beaten track but a process of taking the next step in our daily task of creating, nourishing, destroying, and recreating the institutions and structures of our personal and public lives. The word theory can also be traced to its Greek roots and be said to be a participation in the life and death of a sacred source. To theorize regarding ourselves-in-process is to struggle with the gods in our midst. In short, we need a theory that will allow us to see, to link together our personal, social, political, and religious worlds. Reality is of a piece. We are personal, social, economic, political, and sacred selves simultaneously. But our education and socialization has fragmented us into many disconnected roles and faces. The theory applied in this work is a theory that allows us to begin with the self and to link ourselves to self, problems, others, the world, ideas, and our sacred sources. It is a theory based on relationships in motion. It is symbolized by a mandala, one of the oldest universal symbols pointing to the ever-expanding search for wholeness in the personal and cosmic realms.

Traditional social scientists always ask us to rearrange what is already present as the only reality. But the fundamentally new arises out of the irrational or dark side of our lives. If it remains dark and nonintegral to our life, it will become our demonic impulses. Our theory, if it is to be a viable alternative to theories that only name the superficial aspects of our life, must address this underlying archetypal dimension. The flow of life can be differentiated by human choices. Thus, a theoretical analysis that enriches our lives is really an attempt to respond in an archetypal or symbolic manner to the fundamentally new that is unknown, undifferentiated, unsocialized. But more importantly, our participation is shaping and directing the fundamentally new, or the process of differentiation, is essential. Traditional social-science analysis based on structures and functions of what is logical, rational, and efficient is inadequate. We also need in our analysis to take into account the opposite: the illogical, the irrational, and the disorderly as we continuously shape life dialectically. To shape life dialectically is to recognize that change emerges out of opposing positions and that to reconcile opposites is to bring about a new reality, synthesis, or transformation. There is no final resting place from this adult process. Our calling is to continuously destroy, create, and nourish.

All of us, then, are experiments of the depths who are in reality temples of the Holy Spirit, crucibles and vessels, carriers of the sacred. There are universal archetypal dramas being played out in all of our inner lives.

It is my friend and colleague Manfred Halpern who has guided me through an extraordinary theory of transformation which he created and taught. But more importantly, by means of the theory and his friendship he led me to myself and in so doing brought me into a new world that I had glimpsed but not really entered. Like Ken Kesey's friend Vik Lovell, he led me to the lair of dragons, and then I had to face the dragons within myself. He has taught me that underlying all of reality are three fundamental choices, three paradigms, or archetypal ways of life: emanation, incoherence, and transformation. Each of these ways of life have a sacred source, the god of emanation, the god of incoherence, and the god of transformation. All of us enact our lives within these overarching and underlying realities. He claims only to have rediscovered a 2,000-year-old tradition that has been witnessed to by every universal religion: life is an unfinished struggle between the self, the world, others, and our sacred sources. When humanity became conscious, evolution was immeasurably affected and accelerated because the undifferentiated side of the Source of Sources was now given conscious direction by human creation and participation. Our vocation as human beings is to respond to the sacred impulse within and complete ourselves, the world, and the Source. All is unfinished. What a marvelous task! This means that all of us have a calling to be makers of the world together with the sacred, to be political and religious and thereby fulfill our humanity.

This is the real meaning of the ancient paradox of spirit seeking to become matter and matter seeking to be spirit. God sought to become human through us as other Christs, and we seek to be God through saving him. We save the sacred in the depths and become more god-like by revealing through our lives the dark side, the undifferentiated side of the underlying depths. The Source of Sources becomes concrete and differentiated by flowing through us.

It is up to all of us to find corresponding connections within our own tradition that point toward the archetypal drama of transformation. We are all socialized in the awareness of good and destruction. But we are often not aware of how we perpetuate or share in the various ultimate choices of life. The root of knowledge means *gnosis*, knowledge of the process of transformation; however, not all transformation is to the good. Therefore, we have to distinguish how we live our lives, the quality of our actions and intentions. The knowledge of archetypal ways of life or paradigms points to a fundamental life's choice dedicated either to (1) the service of emanation, being possessed by eternal once-for-all truths and patterns, or (2) the choice of incoherence, a response to the destruction of a way of life by advocating a pursuit of power which only masks and represses our incoherence without providing better alternatives by which people can live, or, finally, (3) transformation, the creation together with our neighbors and sacred sources of new and fundamentally better relationships.* In regard to the first two ultimate choices, the paradigms of emanation and incoherence, even transformation as one of our eight archetypal ways of relating is misused, and, furthermore, transformation in the service of incoherence thereby becomes deformation, since it is the creation of fundamentally new but worse relations.

Finally, in regard to the theoretical perspective of the book, let me say that the view of life underlying this theory does not belong exclusively to anybody. It cannot be commercialized or copyrighted as property. Whoever hears this theory and listens to the words by which to better explain one's life finds the theory also belongs to him or her. Manfred Halpern has served me essentially as a guide, a rare guide who invited me (via the teaching of this theory in a contemporary context) on a journey that he himself is still traveling. But this is also the journey of our Latino parents and of countless other pil-

---

* Throughout the book "archetypal ways of life" and "paradigm" will be used interchangeably.

grims from many cultures and ages. In this sense we are no longer talking only about Latino patterns, culture, and symbols of transformation but about a universal human task that all are called upon to undertake. My hope is that as Latinos we are still sufficiently unspoiled by assimilation into power to be able to be witnesses to others of what authentic transformation is all about.

Throughout the following chapters the theory of transformation will serve as our guide to help give us direction and continuity through the labyrinth of our personal, political, and religious lives. I will, therefore, devote a specific chapter to the explanation of the theory, and then I will allow the theory to have its impact through an ability to explain our daily lives. We will see how the theory can be employed to organize and give meaning and direction to specific problems, relationships, and institutions such as the family, male-female relations, politics in the community, and concepts such as Chicano, Boricua, and racism. I shall do this by using examples taken from our everyday encounters as Latinos.

A summary of the theory in its main components is found in the first chapter. The chapters that follow are intended to develop and qualify the perspective of life for Latinos that has been raised by these introductory remarks. The second chapter is dedicated to the search for the transpersonal self: the authentic self underlying the social self is the key to any transformation whether in the personal or political realm. If we do not know who we are, we will merely accept the definitions of those around us who seek to turn us into happy consumers. Next, in chapter three, the family as relationships-in-motion is explored as well as male-female relationships. Among Latinos the family, as in all cultures, is of fundamental importance for nourishing and forming the next generation. The politics of the family will prepare us for one of three kinds of participation in the wider society: authoritarian democracy, liberal democracy, or participatory democracy. The kinds of relationships created, nourished, and destroyed by our parents relating to each other and to their children will socialize us in such a way as to shape our connections to authority in the public realm. If we do not learn love and dissent, obedience and disagreement, struggle and cooperation simultaneously, then we will not be prepared to participate in shaping a public environment that is conducive to caring deeply about the individual sacredness of each person.

To be political, to participate in shaping new and better institutions, is the focus of chapter four. We need concrete and specific examples of how as Latinos we can create new kinds of institutions that are responsive to the needs of people. Alternative patterns of relating, such as new forms of institutionalized power in the service of transformation, are necessary because they allow large numbers of individuals and groups to collaborate on a sustained basis in connected roles. This is a new personal and political relationship for Latinos, which makes unions, food co-ops, medical clinics, and other forms of organizing possible. Official United States society is largely organized around bureaucracy for the sake of preserving power and preventing change, and so in order to bring about changes we must create new concrete manifestations of organizations in order to protect our humanity.

In chapter five we will consider the role of the sacred as the ground of our being in renewing our personal, historical, and political lives. We shall consider three gods among whom our community has often not been able to distinguish. All three sacred sources are manifestations of the Source of Sources, or god beyond god, but each has its own characteristics. Each god has its archetypal way of life and values; these three gods are the gods of emanation, incoherence, and transformation. For Latinos the god of emanation is the one usually referred to when we say Ay bendito! O My God!, or Queriendo Dios, God Willing, manifesting a passive stance in the presence of an all-powerful absolute god, the god of sin, shame, and guilt. The second one, the god of incoherence, is the god of "la maquina," or the brutal relentless system that takes on a life of its own, and becomes the god of our life; this is the god of assimilation that says that we have to brutalize each other in order to survive; this is the capitalistic god to whom we pray in order to make more money and to increase our competitive edge over others. Our third god is the god of transformation that invites us to journey again into the depths and by so doing to gain the creative imagination by which to renew history, our self, and our neighbor.

In chapter six the question of how we are to relate to the greater society is pursued. Once we begin to gain success in the greater society, will we struggle to assimilate or to choose the liberation of transforming our lives? Assimilation, in the final analysis, is a form of self-hatred and the deprecation of our ethnic and racial heritage. This is so because assimilation strips us of our selfhood, for it signifies an authentic self is not necessary and, as a matter of fact, is a handicap if people are to dominate others. Stripped of our sacred sources both personal and collective renders our Latino heritage meaningless and a burden because it is stigmatized. Assimilation means to lose ourselves; transformation demands that we be a self with all our particular cultural enrichment. To paraphrase Ralph Ellison, the best way to describe the purpose of assimilation is to have a person mix brown paint into a batch of optic white; the paint does not turn *canela*, or tan; it becomes whiter because the white is even more convinced of its superiority since the brown lost its identity and therefore its ability to assert its own reality.

In chapter seven we shall consider the question What is the task for our educated and professional Latinos in shaping our communities? We shall, in this context, redefine what middle class means and demonstrate that those Latinos who have middle-class skills do not have to accept a personal therapy with which the system embraces those of us who have "made it," only to send us back to our solitude. We have choices other than following or becoming *caciques*, the new, absolute rulers, or *vendidos*, those who sell their goods to the highest bidder. Latino professionals can be part of the transforming class who aggressively step forward with skills to build a more human community. And, finally, chapter eight will address the next moment, the next step, the future. I shall explore four options available to Latinos by which to shape their personal and political lives. The four choices include, first, the traditional model characterized by perpetuating the concrete inherited expressions of the relationships within which they were raised. Second is the assimilationist model that leads Latinos to reject their inherited relationships and culture only to accept the power relationships of United States society; this involves creating new forms of some of their old relationships, but now to pursue power rather than enhance a traditional way of life. The third model is a fragmented one wherein Latinos live dangling between two cultures, unable to be at home in either one. These last two models, assimilation and fragmentation, are actually two expressions of the way of life of incoherence. Finally, we shall look at the transforming model, the only model that expresses the way of life of transformation in which we can be fully Latino *and* American but in a fundamentally new way. This is the strategy of reacquiring ourselves and, in light of this return to our own sources of revisioning and transforming what it means to be a Latino still growing her or his own Latinohood. To be able to accomplish this means that we will also be able to contribute simultaneously to the formation of America as it continues the process of re-discovering its soul.

In writing this book I have been moved by a strong impulse to explain myself to myself, to clarify meanings through writing, and to share with Latinos/Latinas what I have come to know in my depths. There have been many times when I have almost despaired reading the scholarly articles, books, anthologies, and commentaries regarding Latinos. What is available till now has not been very helpful to me, and in many cases I consider material to be misleading and even damaging. Lately I have been developing new courses for Latino students. Almost no courses or serious academic studies are devoted to all the Latino groups in our midst. Latin American studies programs only address our problems in Latin America. Once Latinos arrive here, we are mostly approached as monolithic abstractions in survey courses on race and ethnicity or urban studies or in courses on deviance and crime. This is one way by which we are turned into invisible people. Most Chicano and Puerto Rican studies programs with their corresponding readings are too narrow in scope and at times suffer from certain nationalistic exclusiveness. Many books and articles tell us what *is* but not what can or ought to be. Most of the academic literature has as its underlying assumption that in time Latinos will simply assimilate. This is not the way for me.

I hope that Latinos/Latinas will see themselves in these pages and that they will be able to derive an understanding of and a strategy for their lives. Finally, my further hope is that other minorities along with white ethnic groups will also be able to see themselves as a result of reading this book. If so, we might come to discover that we all need each other in order to be fully human.

1. A Theory of Transformation

In all my borned days I never seed
Nothing unto like this here a-fore!
'Course I ain't really been lookin'
For nothin' like this either.
—*Pogo*, 1955

It is the theory that allows us to see.—*Albert Einstein*

A theory of transformation shall serve as our guide to give both a new perspective by which to view the new ways of life being enacted by Latinos and to provide us with a touchstone such that "The end of all our exploring will be to arrive where we started and know the place for the first time" (T. S. Eliot). It is a politics of transformation that reminds us of our mutual right to participate in a larger drama of life together with our neighbor and our sacred sources. This participation allows us to bring together the personal, political, historical, and sacred aspects of our lives.

A NEW THEORETICAL PERSPECTIVE

We need a theory that will help us go beyond mere descriptions of what is. In this book we shall be asking urgent moral questions concerning what ought to be done so that Latinos will no longer be brutalized. We need not only describe reality but alter it. What *is* does not work. How do we know this? Our lives and experiences reveal to us the ultimate poverty and unworkability of the present state of affairs. What our experiences tell us is that the social bonds of society are certainly breaking for many of us, as they did for others in

17

the past. It was difficult in the days of the Inca, Mayan, and Aztec empires for people of the underclass to continue to give their total loyalty to a society that asked so much and which could no longer convey a feeling of justice, righteousness, or security. This sense of general fear and urgency, both cosmic and personal, is upon us once again. The same archetypal forces are at work: a time of stability and preservation is called into question because stability for some means the destruction of the majority; this questioning begins a period of incoherence or separation from the loyalty linking one to the legitimacy of the way things are; the transition from doubting to action can be either swift or gradual, but it means the destruction of what is. Transformative revolution requires that we refuse to be romantic rebels who are eager to die to bring down a system, but that we affirm the commitment to live for the sake of creating a fundamentally new and better society.

Talk of structures and functions, periods of equilibrium, and systems are of little use in helping us to build new and more fruitful and nourishing lives. None of us has ever seen a system sit down and have a hamburger or walk across a busy street. But we have all seen ourselves or others enact concrete relationships that became systemic or routinized ways of doing things, that is, we all act out roles, or as most often happens, roles enact us. We become a part of the abstract system by allowing ourselves to be made into bloodless extensions who carry out expected behavior.

To take ourselves back is to become conscious of what is being done to us, and to begin to name the linkages and their corresponding logic: that is, What do these relationships or institutions do to us as human beings and, perhaps more importantly, what human capacity do we deprive ourselves of as a result of this way of being, living, and acting? But we are more than external, social beings; we also have a natural self, an undiscovered self, an ontological sacred self that moves us from the depths and that in turn is grounded in and nourished by those underlying realities known as sacred sources, transpersonal being, or archetypal depths which we all share by virtue of our humanity. It is what D. H. Lawrence described as that space of timelessness and unknowing beyond the morning star to which the old gods return and from whence the new gods are born.[1]

What all of us always enact concretely are the faces of eight archetypal relationships. In addition, our theory allows us to point to three fundamentally different ways of life in the depths. These three ways of life determine whether any of the eight relationships is enacted (1) for the sake of a new and fuller life, as in the ultimate service of transformation; (2) for the sake of destroying, because nothing makes sense to us anymore, and therefore we get what we can while the time is ripe, which is the way of life of incoherence; or (3) in the way of life of emanation, to hang on to a web of life that is coming apart and that we consider at its best as having been a golden age in our personal and group life.

The theory that will be applied in this book was developed by Manfred Halpern.[2] It is an extraordinary theory in its ability to recognize the relationships that link us to ourselves, to others, to common endeavors, and to our sacred sources, that is, the theory unites our personal, political, historical, and religious lives. The theory allows us to understand the connection between individual human behavior and what goes on in politics and society. To know archetypal relationships and archetypal ways of life is to know something crucial of how the whole of life hangs together.

We need theory, that is, an interrelated set of testable generalizations, which fulfills the following requirement: It must allow us to deal with problems which are central to all human relations, formulated in terms of concepts that are not culture bound. Such a theory must allow us to use the same concepts and interrelated hypotheses for intrapersonal, interpersonal, and intergroup relations. I propose to sketch the outlines of Halpern's theory here and to apply it to the analysis of the conditions and hopes for Latinos in the United States. I believe that this theory tells us *how* the linkages or polarities connecting Latinos are being used, whether creatively, destructively, or heroically and romantically avoiding incoherence. The theory also makes a fundamental value judgment: the only viable alternative to a way of life that is now dying and to a way of life dedicated to the pursuit of self-interest is transformation, a way of life committed to the creation of fundamentally new and better relationships.

LIVING IN A TIME OF INCOHERENCE

To see reality differently is to experience oneself differently because something has happened inside. What allows people to ask different kinds of questions is that they see reality differently. This begins the crisis of the old order. Usually this crisis, separation, or break is accompanied by confusion and pain. The means by which one ordered one's own experience, relations to others and the world, begin to deteriorate. In such a situation people have choices. They can decide to leave the old containers, live through the anxiety, and seek an alternative that does justice to what they experience. Or people can reject their own feelings for the sake of security and embrace the old order even more vehemently so as to suppress the doubt. Or again one can live in a transient state, never committing oneself to any reality. The choice that I and other Latinos have made is the first one: to break in order to create something else. I believe that our theory of transformation explains what we are experiencing. There is a growing literature on the subject of a new consciousness that rejects powerlessness and seeks to build alternatives. The breakdown of authority throughout our society is symptomatic of a cultural revolution that is taking place. All institutions and authorities, systems of thought and relationships, are in crisis. What the Latino community is experiencing is symptomatic and analagous of what the whole of our society is confronting. To break as Latinos from a society that subjects and excludes us is the same archetypal process as a Latino separating himself from a view of life dominated by a patriarchal father or a Latina rejecting the culturally established definitions of mother and housewife. To point to this universal crisis is to say that there is no conspiracy against established authority. Everywhere there is doubt, searching, and breaking out.

The radical politicization and participation of the human person is asserted and affirmed. It is the participatory self who creates, nourishes, and destroys concrete, outward manifestations of our eight archetypal relationships in order to build anew. We say participatory self because this kind of self is always aware of its connectedness to its own self, the neighbor, and the sacred. Such a self rejects rugged individualism, going it alone, romantic heroism, and the pursuit of power as the meaning of life. The participatory self is always in community in a threefold manner: linked to other forces and aspects within one's self as an intrapersonal community, to others in an interpersonal community, while these two communities are in turn rooted in the community of sacred sources. Thus, persons who enact this age-old drama within a group discover their humanity in and through each other and their work to build a society. Yet individuals, who are tested by the groups, must nevertheless remain free to conflict with the group in order to criticize and act as the conscience of the rest. The group must take care to nourish the possibility for the emergence of such great individuals who are great only because they live and witness to the mystery that is within each person making up the group but that is still unrealized. Consequently, it is never a question of either the community or the individual but of *both* the community and the individual. Great individuals in our midst are those who make creative and open societies possible. To be free is to be able to participate with our neighbors and our sacred sources to create strategies of transformation, that is, the conscious choosing of which institutions to uproot, plant, and nourish. And always the person radically connected to the sacred and others must search and ask on behalf of what ultimate way of life are they uprooting, planting, and watering.

A THEORY OF ARCHETYPAL RELATIONSHIPS AND ARCHETYPAL WAYS OF LIFE

Our analysis is based on a theory of eight archetypal relationships and three archetypal ways of life that sees the encounter between self, other, and the transpersonal with respect to concrete problems as the most fundamental dialectic in human life. According to this view the quality of the connections between individuals, groups, ideas, and our personal and transpersonal sources is what gives us the capacity simultaneously to change, yet continue; to conflict, yet cooperate and achieve justice. What constitutes our first worldwide revolution consists precisely in the breaking of the concrete inherited manifestations of our archetypal relationships. They are breaking because they can no longer give us the capacity to respond to the flow of life, changes that demand a new kind of self, a renewed relationship to those around us, and a mutual creation with our underlying depths.

First of all, here is a drawing that provides us with a symbolic representation of one important part of the theory of transformation.

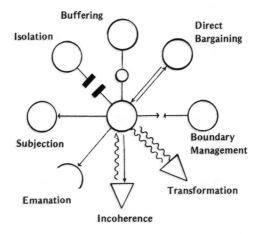

It is a wheel of eight archetypal relationships: emanation, subjection, isolation, buffering, direct bargaining, boundary management, incoherence, and transformation. These are patterns by which we link ourselves to self, others, problems, and our sacred sources. We are in difficulties when the *concrete inherited* manifestations of these underlying patterns no longer give us the ability to deal with the five issues of performance: continuity and change, collaboration and conflict, and justice. Each archetypal form of a relationship gives us a different ability to cope with these five issues of performance. Usually people limit their repertory of archetypal relations to one dominant and two or three subdominant forms in dealing with most problems of life. Our goal is to demystify inherited patterns so that when they break, as they do, people will recognize that they can reject the concrete, inherited manifestations of these underlying patterns and create new combinations of archetypal patterns that restore to us the capacity to renew our world. This is to identify the enemy by naming it clearly as patterns that in their present concrete form cripple the human capacity to re-experience self, other, and our creative sources.

However, the eight archetypal relationships that we shall soon define and give examples of do not stand alone. Each of the eight archetypal relationships in their concrete manifestations derive their deeper meaning and value from a wider matrix—a paradigm or whole way of life. As stated above, there are three fundamentally different archetypal ways of life: emanation, incoherence, and transformation. Though the name is the same for three of our eight archetypal relationships—emanation, incoherence, transformation—these relationships differ from emanation, incoherence, and transformation as a whole way of life. We shall always specify which we mean, the relationship or the way of life.

Each of these ways of life determine the quality of our life; each of these three paradigms is a sacred way of life that is in the service of a particular sacred source or god. Consequently, the eight archetypal relationships are never negative or creative in themselves; their quality or ultimate meaning is given to them by the way of life in which we choose to enact them. For example, our theory allows us to go beyond Weber's discussion of charisma, because Weber could not tell us when charisma was used positively or destructively. Knowing about archetypal ways of life allows us to say that Cesar Chavez, for example, used the attraction of his personality by which to draw others to him so that his fellow Mexican workers could realize or transform their own inner lives and wider society. James Jones in Guyana, on the other hand, used the same power and relationship of being able to attract others for a fundamentally different reason—to possess them as loyal disciples and exalt his own *permanent* leadership. Cesar Chavez used one of our eight archetypal relationships, emanation, which shall be further described below, to lead others to their own selfhood and participation, while Jones and others like him seduced people so that they could be the master. Chavez, therefore, chose to enact relationships in the way of life of transformation, which allows us to create fundamentally new and better relationships; Jones chose an archetypal way of life known as incoherence, which can deepen repression and violence, ultimately leading to fundamentally worse relationships or deformation.

  No polarity is ever enacted in and for itself. It gains its larger content, meaning and purpose by virtue of its contributions to, and derivation from, a larger context. The largest of the contexts—ways at once of asking, seeing, understanding, organizing, working, suffering, and enjoying human relationships—we call archetypal ways of life. Just as it is possible to discover and demonstrate that there are only eight polarities, so it is also possible to discover and demonstrate that all particular and concrete paradigms in human history are manifestations of three ultimate paradigms. These are the paradigms of emanation, incoherence, and transformation. No polarity can be enacted except in the service of one of these three paradigms.[3]

In the paradigm of emanation persons are secure in the traditional container of inherited patterns. This may best be symbolized by a repetitive cycle. Continuity is assured through accepting or cooperating with the mystique of the overwhelming ultimate sacred source which created and sustained this way of life; the cost is the repression of self by avoiding conflict and change. Any new consciousness is impossible, creativity is stillborn, linkages with others beyond one's own way of life is threatening, but one's experience of justice is that of total security. One accepts whatever pain one cannot overcome. One cannot imagine asking new questions. When life shatters this container, there is no continuity or cooperation; all is flux and conflict with no security. To act as if the container has not fragmented is to avoid the problems, to hide the incoherence and the necessity of creating again. Some people then create relations to try to go home again in order to restore the original unity of the container; this is no longer possible, and so we call it a pseudoparadigm of emanation. This actually deepens the incoherence. Others try simply to pursue power and so live with incoherence. Hence our symbol for this paradigm is a broken container. Finally, in the thrid paradigm, that of transformation, persons accept the end of the inherited patterns and see the broken pieces of their lives as an opportunity to create alternatives. In the service of transformation, continuity is no longer purchased at the expense of change; the emergence of self as related to others, the world, and the sources in a fundamentally new way replaces the cooperation with false mystery, and repression gives way to creative conflict. This paradigm is symbolized by a spiral. Since the transforming journey can never be a final state of being but always a process, the spiral with its persistent creativity exposes the poverty of remaining in the other two ways of life: the repetition of the one and flailing of the air in the other. Repeating old formulas, the pursuit of power, and appeals to loyalty are inadequate responses to the new problems and challenges that come with the flow of life.

Therefore, archetypal patterns once broken in their inherited, concrete manifestations in the service of either the paradigms of emanation or incoherence can be re-created in new concrete expressions under the aegis of the paradigm of transformation. Now all eight relationships can be nourished, destroyed, created as they provide us with the means to live our lives creatively. We are no longer at the fringes of our wheel but become the archetypal center as a participatory self that can persistently nourish, destroy, and create new forms of all eight relationships, so that no incarnation of any of the eight ever becomes permanent. We have eight archetypal relationships but an infinite number of possible concrete creations in each pattern. This constitutes our freedom-participation in relationships in motion. Strategies of transformation in the self, other, history, and the source consist of the breaking of the container of emanation and its transcendence, so that the mystery will not be permanently contained in the previous incarnation. Incoherence is a blessing and curse. We are broken, but our energies are released to be gathered together in a new transformation.

Having given this brief introduction to our three ways of life and the eight archetypal relationships, let us now proceed to consider in depth the eight relationships which are available to us by which to shape daily life. Within our discussion of the eight encounters we shall also return to the matter of choosing among our three ways of life.

What are the archetypal patterns of relationship which link us to ourselves and each other in society and to the sacred? From one moment to the next our theory sensitizes us to the realization that a concept, person, group, nation, or sources in the depths may be in the process of creation, nourishment, or destruction. Furthermore, the energies released in this perpetual process are given direction by the eight specific archetypal relationships, each with their own capacity to relate ourselves to self, sacred sources, others, and problems.

EIGHT ARCHETYPAL RELATIONSHIPS

For all encounters between self and other in all recorded human history and in all societies, there exist only eight different types of relationships which give people the capacity to deal simultaneously with continuity and change, collaboration and conflict, and the achieving of justice. That there are eight and only eight ways applies to all intrapersonal, interpersonal, and intergroup relations: In intergroup relations, it applies to any group, from a family or friendship group to a nation or to the human species as a whole. It also applies to the relationship of individuals and groups to concepts—any concepts of problems, ideas, values, norms, ideology and the rest. This hypothesis also applies to our connection to those energies which we may call transpersonal, whatever our particular name for them—whether we call them the unconscious, the sacred or God.[4]

Let us now proceed to an explanation of the eight forms of encounter and three ways of life. We will begin with the five relationshps in the paradigm of emanation that constitute what I call the Latino traditional model.

EMANATION

This is an encounter in which one treats the other solely as an extension of one's self. The other accepts the denial of his own separate identity because of the mysterious and overwhelming power of the source of this emanation—a yielding which is rewarded with total security. All of us began life as children without power adequate to meet the other. We therefore necessarily yielded our identity to the mysterious and overwhelming power of our mother until we freed ourselves to risk losing total security. However, some fathers or mothers seek to retain all members of their household as emanations of themselves. Others treat their property or their employees in this way. Many individuals remain eager to submerge themselves as emanations of another—of a political movement, a dogma or a lover.[5]

We may see emanation manifested in the Latina who sees herself as an extension of husband and family; the bureaucrat who acts solely as the expression of the supervisor's personality without any autonomous jurisdiction of his own. Also we see emanation manifested in the believer as the embodiment of the Catholic *carismaticos* or Protestant Pentecostals who often compete with each other to provide a more secure container for Latinos set adrift in our urban centers.

An intensely passive collaboration at the cost of repressing conflict, a willingness to purchase continuity by implicitly accepting or rejecting change solely at the behest of another, and hence granting mysterious and ovewhelming power to the one in exchange for total security to the other—these are the intrinsically connected manifestations of the relationship of emanation.[6]

SUBJECTION

Here both self and other are fully present, each with an identity of his own. The relationship is still asymmetrical; it still rests upon the experience of overwhelming power. But this power, which was mysterious in emanation, becomes naked in subjection—naked in its source, imposition, and resistance.[7]

It is the Anglos displacing the Californios from their land by lynching and beatings; the teacher demanding that Latino children speak English at all times; the U.S. Navy continuing to use Vieques for naval and aerial maneuvers involving the use of testing weaponry with live ammunition. Subjection, in our special use of this term, can also be exemplified by the use of instrumental rationality. Subjection exists whenever I control others as a means to my own end, whether I base this control on the naked power of the logic of deductive reasoning, on standards of efficiency or economy, or simply on the power of the gun.

In subjection, conflict is no longer repressed but suppressed. Latinos remain conscious of the loss of their right to step forward urgently and freely. Collaboration is based on explicit rules defined solely by the Anglo world. The dominant group, therefore, assures continuity and change in accordance with their power. Justice involves an exchange of the right of survival for the one for his acceptance of the supremacy of power of the other. We, as Latinos, survived by giving up our right to create conflict or change on our own.

BUFFERING

This encounter is managed by intermediaries. Such a position may be occupied by a mediator, a broker, or a concept. Buffering allows for change by permitting indirect, intermittent, or segmented forms of conflict and collaboration.[8] Among Latinos the use of mediators in the family, like a *padrino* or *madrina*, godparents, is common; so is the use of the parish priest, *el cura*, to arrange marriages and secure other advantages. Saints, and especially *La Virgen*, may be asked to intercede. Ritualistic language, such as *Ay Bendito!* (Oh, Good Lord), *Queriendo Dios* (God willing), *Ni lo mande Dios* (May God forbid), may be used to obstruct or ease moments of change. In all societies buffering is perhaps most often exemplified by mediating one's own experiences through a filter of habits and stereotypes. Justice in buffering is the attainment of self-determination circumscribed or enhanced by such indirect or limited exchanges, and therefore a self-determination similarly circumscribed or enhanced.

ISOLATION

Finally, isolation was available as an acceptable relationship by which to deal with the issues of daily life.

> In this relationship, individuals or groups agree upon one mode of collaboration—to refrain from demanding anything of each other. Both sides here collaborate in avoiding all conflict intended to lead to change in, with or by the other. Justice, in contrast to emanation and subjection, means self-determination—but at the price of not attempting to affect change in the others. Isolation in this use of the term cannot be achieved unilaterally. It demands collaboration. The attempt to isolate without an agreement to avoid conflict, change or new forms of justice produces incoherence, not isolation.[9]

Latino men could physically withdraw and do as they pleased, so that a wife felt herself unable to confront him to create conflict or change. As a matter of fact, the granting of such freedom to withdraw to men and not to women meant that isolation was used to enforce a woman's condition of submission and subjugation. But a woman could also practice isolation by being present but inaccessible to her husband, who at times might wonder what she might be thinking. A woman was allowed some inner psychic space and demonstrated this through

periods of moodiness, a sense of stoic forbearance, or just being dis-
creet in her movements and speech. This different use of isolation
by men and women underlines a structural inequality. Although men
could withdraw both physically and psychically, women for the most
part could practice only an internal isolation. But as we shall see
in chapter 3, women used their psychic isolation to help eventually
break the patriarchal container which justified their lack of a transformative kind of isolation.

DIRECT BARGAINING

In this form of encounter individuals and groups conflict and
collaborate with each other directly. Justice is not only the better
bargain that may accrue to one side or the other but above all the
reciprocal capacity to seek a different bargain as, from moment to
moment, the balance of power changes.[10] By means of gifts or favors
Latinos often create or maintàin a sense of indebtedness between self
and other. Or they do so in that form of rebellion which is in fact
a continuance of this encounter—that is, when one is entitled to remain angrily present while refusing to bargain in order to improve
one's bargaining position. A wife, for example, remains silent but
bangs dishes until her husband relents and buys her a new dress. In
this way anger is reduced to catharsis so that real change can be
avoided.

Whether the demand be for submission to the will of your father,
lover, or god, each Latino had five choices. He or she could entirely
give oneself up—to the best of one's power for yielding—to becoming an emanation or extension of the mysterious and overwhelming
power of father, lover, or the sacred. Or they could subject themselves
in deliberate response measured to the displayed power of the other.
Or he or she could bargain directly with the god of emanation, no
less than husband or father, saying in each case: "In return for my
submission I expect something for my good behavior or I will not
cease my aggravation without some kind of reward." Or if one possessed neither the power to bargain nor the will to submit or to give
themselves totally, they could resort to buffering—asking their
mother-in-law to mediate with her son or saying the rosary to intercede with *La Virgen*, using rose water with sugar to expel evil
spirits or using amulets to filter out "el mal ojo," the evil eye. Or
they could recede into a silent isolation. This was the repertory within
the way of life of emanation in which many Latinos were raised; these

were the linkages available to them in the traditional Latino world. What held the whole world together was the overarching sacred canopy of the paradigm of emanation that was made up of two similar cosmologies, the indigeno and Catholic/Christian hierarchies. In both worlds there was a clear chain of emanation that linked them to one common source, the divine. From that source emanated the authority that legitimized the link between ruled and ruler, husband and wife, child and parent.

THE WAY OF LIFE OF EMANATION

As mentioned above, our theory helps us to choose among three fundamentally different paradigms for enacting relationships. We shall express this deeper and larger context by speaking of a particular archetypal relationship, or polarity, being enacted *in the service of* an archetypal way of life or paradigm. One of these paradigms or archetypal ways of life is emanation.

> Politics in the service of emanation (for example, in the service of a fixed faith or tradition) holds us within containers in which all we can and need to do together is already codified and ritualized, and declared to be no longer a problem except for the skill and intensity with which we affirm, elaborate, deepen or refine what we are already performing together. The paradigm of emanation is a way of life in which a moment of truth has become frozen, distorted or corrupted. This paradigm of politics is everywhere in the world being questioned and undermined.[11]

Any attempt to transform means breaking with the inherited relationships in such a way that it will lead to a change of relationships for others. This is clearly heresy and dangerous to a cosmos blessed once and for all by the god of emanation. People were literally killed for such thought and behavior. It appears to the orthodox to be the demonic come to life. How many *brujas* were killed by the Inquisition because they advocated not magic but the heresy of contacting the sacred so as to participate in continual creation.

Latino traditional society was never dull or boring. Each Latino always differed in the specific ways in which they expressed these archetypal relations. From one moment to the next a person was bargaining for a better deal, seeking a friend to mediate with a mutual acquaintance, hoping to find security through attaching themselves to a more powerful saint or patron, withdrawing into moodiness, or simply surviving by standing in line for hours to get employment, better benefits, or to buy a necessary license. At times wives reversed the relations of emanation not only in the bedroom and kitchen but permanently in all areas of life such that their husbands lost their honor among macho males. Some wives also succeeded in physically dominating their husbands, so that he needed a mediator to protect him. These relationships were always acceptable because they were ultimately sanctioned by the god of emanation. The whole of the repertory was enacted in the way of life of emanation, a web of life blessed with divine sanction.

In the following chapters we shall be looking more closely at the traditional Latino's entire repertory to allow us to see his or her actual, daily behavior. We shall go beyond mere descriptions of the breaking of the concrete, inherited manifestations of these five archetypal relationships and the dying of the paradigm of emanation to consider how we might transform such incoherence. But as long as the traditional repertory in the service of the paradigm of emanation remained in effect, it gave Latinos, both in Latin America and in this country, the ability to cope with continuity and change, collaboration and conflict, with a justice of security. Many Latinos, for example, transferred their loyalty from the Catholic Church in their native country to that of the United States Catholic Church. For the time being the Catholic Church provided an important source of emanational fiber to help the continuity of their lives in the midst of great upheaval. But what the Church could not do was restore the original web of life with all of its meaning and security. Too often even the Church saw it as its duty to help Latinos to assimilate into the mainstream of United States society *without* having dealt with the incoherence of the people. The Church, like official bilingual programs, saw its role of helping Latinos as being assimilationist and remedial. Latinos were just another immigrant group to accommodate. This is why the Church has had such ambivalent feelings about Latino resistance to United States culture. This ambivalence also points out that the official United States Catholic Church is itself close to being in emanation to the American way of life. The Church has politically *assumed* the moral superiority of the United States government in foreign affairs and even in domestic matters. This is why the recent critique of the nuclear policy of the United States government by the Catholic bishops was welcome but unexpected.

This ambivalence of the Catholic Church disillusioned many Latinos. The Catholic hierarchy saw the racism against Latinos but did not condemn it as a part of United States society. Instead, the

Church sought to do charity; it tried to alleviate suffering through being a buffer without attacking the institutionalized racism of United States society. That is why, even for the Church, you made it by becoming more like the Anglos. In the final analysis the Church could not, due to her own emanational relationship to United States nationalism, help Latinos resist the violation of their culture and personal identity.

Eventually, in spite of the holding action of the Church, Latinos were overwhelmed by change and conflict with no goals to provide continuity and collaboration. There was no justice except that of survival in a hostile land. For these reasons barrios were a welcome island of relief from the daily onslaught. But they were islands of refuge, fragments of the dying way of life of emanation, that provided some security when all else was breaking. This is why *compadrazgo*, or creating a network of comothers and cofathers, godparents, for your children, was so important. Godparents, especially if they were better off financially, became new sources of emanation and buffering in a confusing world. The continuity of the old world in the midst of the new really meant an attempt to hang on to a way of life blessed by the god of emanation. The world outside the barrio, as little as a block away, or an alley way, was the realm of incoherence, of temptation and sin. This living between two worlds created a disconnected and fragmented way of life for most of us.

THE WAY OF LIFE OF INCOHERENCE

The way of life of incoherence turns the relationship of incoherence into a whole way of life.

Politics in the service of incoherence takes account of the fact that in the modern age, all our concrete inherited forms of relationships are breaking, but therefore builds fortresses in a desert it cannot overcome. The guardians who would contain us within these fragments insist upon removing much of what we can and need to do together from what they define as politics. They treat politics solely as an arena for contests of power. They seek to give their victories the appearance of final legitimacy (as if they were the true heirs of faith and tradition) in order to justify the exclusion from this arena of all fundamentally new issues and encounters which do not serve their already established power. Hence they compel most people to accept politics as the acknowledgement of dependency upon the powerful and to deny the value and importance of their own miseries and joys.[12]

Assimilation moves Latinos into the paradigm of incoherence. Latinos create themselves into upwardly mobile, aggressive individuals. Assimilated Latinos think like Anglos and become like them in such a way that they are cut off from their own selfhood, fellow Latinos, and sacred sources. "To make it" is the new heaven, the goal of this kind of transformation. Assimilated Latinos take a fragment of life, being a professional with power, and try to endow it with a new source of mystery that will give them identity. This fragment becomes the mysterious and overwhelming source of life. This loss of self with the accompanying rejection of others and our sacred sources is really a deformation. We have rejected the old god of emanation but have actually been repossessed by a new god, the god of incoherence. The system based on power became the new god, but it possessed us just as powerfully as the old god of emanation, only now without the same sense of security; the only certainty now is the insecurity of knowing that nothing is secure or lasting. Since there is no ultimate meaning or value or love, we have to get what we can while the going is good. This cynicism feeds our constant need to compete without ever being able to get out of the game unless we pay a price—to face incoherence and transform it.

Our parents lost much of their authority in this dual citizenship. Many parents, to cover their own sense of loss in the greater world, demanded a total loyalty at home. Resistance by a daughter or son was met by subjection or total exclusion. But unlike the *rancho*, there was another world literally beyond the door steps that provided a whole other repertory of relationships outside the concrete inherited forms of emanation, subjection, buffering, isolation, and direct bargaining. The Anglo world offered autonomy, both personally and socially in boundary management, the right to be left alone in isolation, as well as increased bargaining power through education, new buffers such as teachers and counselors, boyfriends, a new identity as an American, together with symbols of success portrayed daily in the media. With these options available it became increasingly difficult to re-create the vigor of the original repertory. Rebellion was merely a strategy to gain a better leverage within the family and therefore restore and strengthen the traditional repertory; rebellion was now far more serious, because the threat to exclude the child who did not obey or the pregnant daughter or the angry wife might end with them never returning. So instead of changes *within* the available repertory, there was now the threat of change *of* the repertory, of entering into a new way of living and relating that our parents, husband, or lover could not dominate. This brought about incoherence and the possibility of transformation.

Already in Latin America the cities were demanding a different repertory, or set of relationships. However, the new relationships were being used in the service of incoherence either by assimilating into a new way of life to seek a substitute security through pursuing power or by living in a fragmented world, caught between two cultures. In chapter eight I shall examine more closely the four models available to Latinos. Here we must, first of all, define the new relationships previously forbidden by the traditional repertory: boundary management, incoherence, and transformation.

THE FORBIDDEN REPERTORY OF RELATIONSHIPS AND WAY OF LIFE

All societies or the body politic shape our ego. Through socialization the community introduces us to the *acceptable* repertory of outward concrete forms of the eight archetypal relationships. That is to say that not all eight forms of our archetypal relationships are everywhere seen as positive options. Consequently, people are forbidden to exercise certain patterns of relating; often we are not even aware of the existence of alternatives. The same is true for the archetypal dramas and archetypal ways of life that are available to us. For example, in United States society the archetypal way of life in which we are all led to believe and accept as inevitable is that of incoherence, or the liberation of the pursuit of self-interest. Because of the brutality of the public realm where everybody sees each other as a competitor, in the private realm we are allowed the archetypal drama of romantic love. Liberalism enourages the fantasy of thoroughly private, intense love affairs that lead us to concede the brutality of the wider society. As long as we can return to a little corner of the world to be stroked and pampered, we cannot transform the public realm. In this way we are depoliticized. Latino parents could not name this paradigm, but in their bones they sensed its message of being either a rabbit or a wolf. As a result, many of our parents retreated and tried to make the old paradigm of emanation live again. What our parents and we have missed is an alternative to an absolute loyalty to either the way of life of emanation or the way of life of incoherence and power. As a result, both of our worlds, or ways of life, have not been able, or willing in some cases, to allow the way of life of transformation.

In the traditional way of life of emanation of Latinos the repertory of relationships that was excluded consisted of boundary management, incoherence, and transformation. As we have seen, incoherence as a way of life caused fear and withdrawal. Transformation as a way of life was seldom known or practiced. So let us now consider in depth the excluded relationships and way of life of transformation.

BOUNDARY MANAGEMENT

This is a process of encounter in which each self and other is entitled to claim an autonomous zone of jurisdiction based on some explicit principle of law, custom, status, value or competence that both share. As in isolation and buffering, individuals and groups must not try to affect each other's behavior directly. Continuity or change in the response of the other may be achieved only indirectly, through conflict under agreed rules designed to shift, or threatening to shift, the boundary of jurisdiction between the two poles. The individual or group whose zone of autonomy has been effectively reduced may as a consequence have to consider changing behavior. By contrast, emanation, subjection and direct bargaining allow one to perpetuate or change the behavior of the other directly. By contrast with isolation, there is no longer any frozen, forbidden zone separating the two claims; by contrast with buffering, polar occupants must now preserve or shift boundaries by themselves. Justice in boundary management is the reciprocal right of each to sustain or enlarge his autonomous zone of jurisdiction.

Boundary management is the form of encounter which allows us to be fellow-citizens, to separate yet keep in constant tension the three branches of government, to charter the limited liability corporation, to create autonomy yet collaboration among professions, scholarly disciplines, and bureaucracies. Boundary management allows large numbers of individuals and groups to collaborate on a sustained basis in connected roles, for each claim can rather easily be subdivided, or a principle found to add more connections in the chain.[13]

Boundary management demands aggressive, autonomous, calculating individuals who know how to advance their office by enlarging their area of jurisdiction or who know when to defend their zone of autonomy against another bureaucrat who seeks to redraw the area under his jurisdiction to include yours. Boundary management is the relationship enacted when the rights of Mexicans to work and live in the United States are involved. The whole question of undocumented aliens is a question of two autonomous jurisdictions, Mexico and the United States, stating those rights within their own borders. On the personal level it entails a skilled professional with competence relating to clients.

Traditional Latinos did not know boundary management and, therefore, have had great difficulties in working with strangers to achieve a common goal. The lack of this relationship helps to explain why Latinos were not being highly individualistic in their refusal to work together. If was really isolation that masked the fact of incoherence. Moreover, Anglos and even other Latinos who live outside the limits of their neighborhood are both considered strangers. Even today in the barrios of East Los Angeles many Chicanos do not trust Mexicans from Texas, and *Tejanos* do not trust undocumented Mexican migrants. A demand is being made on Latinos to transcend previous traditional patterns that blocked out people with whom they now must collaborate in order to change their lives. Puerto Ricans, Chicanos, Cubans, Colombians, and Peruvians, for example, are being asked to cooperate with each other even though they are previous strangers and even though they have never participated in large-scale, sustained, autonomous, and coordinated public institutions such as a labor union that works on explicit legal principles and that allows its members to protect themselves against large corporations. Labor unions may in fact be run from within by bosses who corrupt the original democratic nature of the union and run it on relationships of emanation, as a personal fiefdom through subjection. But unions do carry the potential to be used positively as organizations to achieve a just participation in the fruits of one's labor. Our lack of boundary management helps to explain why for so long Latinos were cheated when it came to contracts; they accepted vague promises based on the good character of the sales person. They were living and expecting the old repertory where honor and one's good word linked persons in a common emanational web of life. Latinos cannot count on the good intentions of the seller or landlord. Now they have to learn to demand explicit principles that guarantee their rights in a written contract. Many of us still feel embarrassed demanding these kinds of business relations because we would still like to believe that the other is honorable, that is, upholds the same values that we do. So to ask for it in writing is like a *falta de respeto*, or to treat salespersons disrespectfully. Many Anglos and Latinos who are *aprovechando*, or taking advantage of the situation, realize this hesitation and exploit it.

Why Organizers Fail is a study of a rent strike and the analysis of its failure.[14] The Chicanos involved found it difficult to confront Anglos with a sense of autonomy, and they also failed to organize different groups in the community for united action. The blacks did not trust the Chicanos because they thought that they were too weak, or, in our terms, did not have a sense of individual autonomy with which to confront Anglo bureaucrats. It is one thing to ask people to organize around common problems, but it is still another to ask them to let go of a way of life that they are desperately trying to make work.

INCOHERENCE

One of the decisive ways in which the paradigm of emanation became a container is that it prohibited incoherence and transformation. You could change and create conflict, but only *within* the limits of the orthodox repertory of archetypal relationships. Some Latinos were willing to face the change of being *sinverguenzas*, people without shame, by shattering the orthodox relationships.

> Incoherence in our theory is that form of encounter in which self and other face each other in the same place and at the same time but are unwilling or unable to agree upon how, simultaneously, to manage continuity and change, collaboration and conflict, and the achieving of justice between them. Incoherence is not a residual category for purposes of classification, but obviously an experiential alternative to the other forms of encounter. It is the experience of discontinuities rather than continuity; of change, yes, but unintended, uncontrolled change; of conflict without shared rules leading to injustice for both self and others.[15]

Now persons stand face-to-face and no longer know how to relate to each other. A few Latinos consciously broke the fixed embrace of their way of life. Initially one enters a time of personal terror. But there is also a new freedom. The old *verguenza*, or shame, is turned into a new kind of shame, the shame of not being a self connected to others and to one's sacred sources in a fundamentally new way. The veil is lifted, and all human experience becomes available for analysis, creation, and concrete experimentation.

Traditional Latino fathers, living in a repertory endowed with the blessing of the god of emanation, were now forced to exclude children who no longer respected them *because* they enacted new relationships. To introduce autonomy or incoherence to break with the traditional and fundamentally to change your life was incomprehensible. Unmarried Latina women who sought privacy and personal autonomy by moving to an apartment dishonored the family. The only *legitimate* way to leave home was to be handed over from one emanational container, the family, to another, the husband and marriage. Latino fathers prayed for the day when they could successfully hand over their precarious charge (meaning, an intact virgin) to an acceptable alternate. He was made acceptable by the buffering role of the priest who gave his blessing as a kind of divine matchmaker. To leave home without this ritualized process was truly incoherence. Some daughters used this as a way of increasing their bargaining power, so that when they did return home, more benefits would be granted. But many never came home again, in the sense of returning to the old repertory. All the psychic artillery of sin, shame, and guilt were used to attempt to restore a woman to her senses. The daughters, and sometimes the sons, insisted that they still loved their parents, but in a new way. The parents argued that if you love me, come home again, back to the way things used to be. The result is to speak past one another; persons now live in two different worlds and mean fundamentally different realities by the word love. What accounts for this is that they are now living in two different paradigms or ways of life. There are different gods and sacred dramas involved here.

TRANSFORMATION

The polarity of transformation is an encounter in which one's consciousness is no longer the mere embodiment of an external source of emanation but has become conscious of its consciousness. It has thus become free to use all four aspects of consciousness—sensation (what is), thinking (what it is), feeling (value it), and intuition (the hidden meaning and context of it.) To enact this polarity is to keep alive a consciousness aware of alternative patterns of relationship being created, nourished, petrified, destroyed or re-created; a creativity that empowers us to be acted upon as well as to act, and thus woo new combinations into being; a linking with others that is at once knowing and loving; a justice which is participation in becoming and being.[16]

Latinos who create a sense of self, new linkages to others, and achieve a new way of life by enacting new relationships previously forbidden to them have enacted the *polarity* of transformation. But even transformation can be distorted. The quality of the relationship of transformation is determined by the way of life in which it is enacted. For example, transformation in the service of emanation would mean that a person transforms their personality, but in order to be more loyal to their lover, hero, or mother. Transformation in the service of incoherence is exemplified by the Latino student who gets an excellent science education, graduates, and uses his or her transformation to build a better weapons system that makes life worse. Only transformation in the service of the way of life of transformation means the creation of fundamentally new and better relationships.

THE WAY OF LIFE OF TRANSFORMATION

Acting in the service of transformation means overcoming the fragmentation in our lives so that we might persist in creating and nourishing fundamentally new and better relationships. Perhaps the best way to explain the process we have been describing is to retell the story of the journey of transformation from the perspective of our theory. The archetypal journey of transformation in the service of the way of life of transformation is the vocation to which all of us are called. Intrinsic to each person's fulfillment is the threefold process of withdrawal from a way of life determined by others, initiation into a new way of life in the depths of our transpersonal self, and the return to the community so that we can transform it according to the vision we received during our period of initiation into the fundamentally new. This process is intrinsic in the same sense that the acorn carries within itself the potential of a magnificent oak tree. Anybody who prevents this journey for themselves or for others violates a sacred process. Only individuals together with other individuals who have made the same conscious choice to embark on the journey can create the fundamentally new and better.

The journey consists of a three-act drama that begins in act I with our still living in concrete, inherited relationships of emanation where we are merely an extension of others. The breaking of this relation of emanation, for example, with our parents, moves us into act II, into the polarity of incoherence. You do not have to turn the polarity of incoherence into a whole way of life. You do not have to get trapped in the paradigm of incoherence. The polarity of incoherence is different from the paradigm of incoherence in that the polarity is necessary to experience as a temporary period on the journey toward transformation. But act II has two scenes that we have to journey through in order to successfully reach our third act in which transformation is fulfilled. In scene I of act II we accept and suffer through incoherence, breaking connections with others, and resist going back to the fleshpots of Egypt, or the previous relationships, that promise us that forgiveness and security which only belief in a fixed and overwhelming power can bring. But at this point we are left very vulnerable. This vulnerability characterizes scene II of act II. We get even more depressed. In a sense things get worse. We realize that hope is only possible on the other side of conscious and creative suffering. At this point we have to go beyond getting rid of the concrete manifestation of the sacred source or archetype; in scene II, act II, we have to get rid of the gods who stood behind the inherited concrete manifestations; we must expel the old god or sacred source, or it will return again. To fail to do this means that our authoritarian father will return as an authoritarian husband or leader because we only got rid of the concrete manifestation and not the god involved. We must empty ourselves twice over: the concrete manifestation of the sacred source and the sacred source itself. We have to empty ourselves, suffer a real death in order to be born again. That is what our faith is all about, that on the other side of the dark night of the soul there is new life and hope.

At the end of scene II the sources renew us. All the mystical traditions agree on this one point: that when we suffer emptiness and death in the depths, we can count on being rescued. The Aztecs expressed this faith in a lovely image: "The bones of the dead shall flower again." When we are renewed, we are fulfilled by the sources and so enter into act III, the relationship of transformation in the paradigm of transformation. In act III what characterizes our consciousness at this point is an ability to differentiate between the sources which are creative and those which are destructive in relationship to the problem at hand.[17] In contrast to act I we no longer are in utter docility and obedience to the sources, nor, as in act II, are we blindly driven by or creatively struggling with sources that are sacred even though we have refused to or cannot acknowledge gods; thus, in act III we are no longer an emanation of mysterious sources, but we become a participatory self, so that we *and* the source creatively collaborate in giving shape to the new. The human and the divine can now continue to change in relationship to each other and also struggle and cooperate in order to bring about new forms of justice. We shall return to the role of the sacred in greater detail in chapter five.

Only when the relationship of transformation is enlisted in the service of the way of life of transformation does a fundamentally new relationship also become a fundamentally better relationship.

Why is this so? Only in the paradigm of transformation are the unconscious, consciousness, creativity, linking with others, and justice kept in lively tension with the changing realities of life, for in the paradigm of transformation, the concrete realization of the polarity of transformation is never experienced as a final solution. To enter into the polarity of transformation becomes the final moment of a particular turn on the spiral process of transformation. The next turn will inevitably reveal new suffering and threats and new joys and opportunities, moving us down or up on this spiral. To live in the paradigm of transformation is therefore persistently to experience an archetypal process of breaking relationships, moving into incoherence, and entering into the polarity of transformation. Through this same process, chains of emanations are turned into links of transformation.

To enter into the service of transformation is also to become free to put into play the fullest possible human capacity, i.e., to enact any or all eight polarities. To be sure, there is also protean man—people who have no compunction in using all eight polarities in the service of incoherence. But such people mistake their survival as chameleons on the run (careful never to run over a mirror) for the movement toward fundamentally new and better human relationships.[18]

To summarize, our theory of transformation speaks of eight archetypal relationships by which to shape simultaneously the five issues of daily life: continuity and change, collaboration and conflict, and justice. Moreover, we must be able to allow the five faces of capacity—new consciousness, creativity, new linkages to others, new kinds of shared justice, and our underlying sources—to define our openness for persistent transformation. Finally, all our relationships, the five issues of performance, and the five faces of capacity are given their meaning, quality, and direction by the three ultimate paradigms of emanation, incoherence, or transformation. Emanation is dying and has, in any case, shown its inability to hold back the night; incoherence prolongs our suffering through normless violence, repression, and insatiable striving; only transformation with its call to be ready to transform persistent incoherence into new possibilities is a realistic option.

Throughout the chapters that follow we shall give numerous examples from the experiences of Latinos that give this theory its validity. Any good theory must help us to see and understand what we have been living but what we have not fully understood. To re-vision our lives through a theory of transformation based on reflection and action exposes the threat of our present situation *and* also the promise if we choose to live what most of us have known in our depths.

2. The Search for Latino Identity

To keep people out of trouble, keep them out of themselves
—*J. J. Rousseau*

To be a self, and to have an identity rooted in the selfhood beyond the socialized self in the best of situations, is never a given, but a problem and a struggle to be resolved. A Latino identity is presently being forged out of the elements of our past with our present conditions serving as the catalyst. To choose to be a self and a Latino is a twofold political act; both are acts of resistance against a system based on the antiself and against a dominant society and culture that wants us all to be "white" or devoid of our color and consciousness. Finally we have to grow our own racial and ethnic identity, our own Latinohood.

GOING HOME

One of my earliest memories of being a Mexican, a Chicano, a Latino, was a profoundly sad and terrifying experience. Across the street and down the block a fight between a Mexican man and a white patron in a bar had spilled out into the street. The Mexican was bleeding; he staggered to the front of the tavern and began to shout "¡Viva Mexico! ¡Viva Mexico!" The only thread of hope that he could grasp was his native home, his fatherland and motherland, the focal point of his identity at the moment his personhood was being assaulted. Equally impressive was the fear that it created in me. I could not have been more than five years old, and yet I distinctly remember the paranoia I felt that others would identify me with him. I wanted him to stop shouting "¡Viva Mexico!" The whole scene is indelibly marked in my memory, especially when the siren of the police car at last broke the murmur of the crowd and increased the man's appeals to Mexico. When they took him away I was relieved.

I knew instinctively even then that Mexicans were supposed to disappear into the anonymity of the city. Anything that made us stand out in bold relief, such as a shouting Mexican, made us all uneasy. Nobody had given me, as a preschool child, talks about American society, the melting pot, or Anglo-Saxon values. They did not have to. I and others like me received the message in a thousand nonverbal ways: differences in food, clothing, speech; a sense of fear. I wanted to be like them and envied their clean homes and orderly lives.

Many years later in Mexico I learned that although I had become a professional person with standing in the United States, I was considered a "pocho," an Americanized Mexican born in the United States, a displaced person with no real culture or homeland. This experience is similar to that of Puerto Ricans from the mainland; they are often considered "Nuyorican" by their relatives on the island. There is a critical struggle going on over the identity of the Mexican that is rooted in basic ambivalence. In small museums in the states of Puebla and Queretaro there is evidence of a deep anti-European, anti-Catholic sentiment. Local artists depicted the Aztec and Mayan warriors as the romantic heroes of a pre-Columbian past. The Indian, in plumed headdress, lances the blue-eyed, blonde, bearded Spaniard, knocking him from his horse. In Mexico the year 1973 was officially designated as "El Año de Juarez," el Indio. Juarez was clearly of Indian descent: dark skin, dark eyes, black hair, stocky. In Peru and Bolivia, as well as in Mexico and Puerto Rico, local *curanderos* (healers) still resist the Catholic faith by performing their sacred rituals after 450 years of Catholic, European hegemony. And yet, the social, economic, and political reality of Mexico, as of all other Latin American nations, is just the opposite. It is the Europeanized, Catholic, white element that predominates. Throughout Latin America the advertisers use *rubios* and *rubias* (blonde men and women) for their models. The middle class there refers to the peasants as *inditos*, primitive and backward children. In Argentina the descendants of British, Italian, and German settlers do not identify themselves with the Spanish-speaking Indian strain of the population. In Brazil there is deep suspicion and confirmed reports that the government, through its Bureau of Indian Affairs, is following a policy of genocide against the Indians in the Amazon region.

It is their economic interests that have led the middle class to disassociate themselves from their own people. The economic penetration of all Latin America that began in earnest in the second half of the nineteenth century perpetuated a class structure that to this day has caused a great gap between rich and poor. The wealthy have no desire to be identified with an indigenous culture, so they create a culture based on consumption.

There was a strong element of racism in Latin America from its inception as the insistence on *limpieza de sangre* (purity of blood) by the Inquisition shows. Although this policy was aimed at Jews and *Moriscos* (Spanish Moors), it inevitably was extended to the Indian population of Latin America and still later to the African slaves. In some instances, as in Puerto Rico, the Indian population was completely decimated by a combination of disease, warfare, hunger, and slavery. The intermarriage that followed the conquest of Latin America was an unavoidable necessity. The Church insisted on blessing these unions, but it proved to be more of a forced wedding than a blending of cultures, religions, and peoples.

The "converted" Jews and *Moriscos* that found their way to the New World, in spite of the Inquisition, became an integral part of Latin American society. Some Jewish converts took the Christian name of "de la Cruz" (of the Cross) to emphasize the extent of their loyalty to the new faith. To this day, in places such as Santiago, Chile, important families with the name "de la Cruz" are the descendants of these converts. All Latinos in this country are a combination of various Indian groups, with Spanish, Portuguese, African, and Jewish strands. With all of these elements of blood and spirit combined in the crucible of his/her life, the Latino is instinctively a brooding person.

None of us knows who he or she is. The Spain of *Los Reyes Catolicos* (the Catholic kings) was itself an amalgam that was unified by blood and the cross. The Basques and Catalans still revive ancient nationalistic feuds that were never settled. In their campaign against the Jews and *Moriscos*, especially in Andalucia, Isabella and Ferdinand destroyed one of the oldest centers of cultural creativity. This was the land of the cabalistic Jews and of people such as I'bn Arabi. Many of these displaced peoples came to the New World to build new lives. They were among the soldiers, adventurers, and settlers who brought down the Inca, Mayan, and Aztec empires. Uprooted African blacks were brought to the Carribbean, the eastern areas of South and Central America. These people also intermarried and brought their gods and beliefs to the New World. All of these diverse elements were held together, at least on the surface, by European military might. The emergence of the coalition among peasants, intellectuals, and liberals during the wars of national liberation in the early part of the nineteenth century broke the European political tyranny. Unfortunately, it was quickly followed by European and American economic control. The old patterns of cultural behavior based on Mediterranean and Indian values of honor, respect, and deference to authority were devastating to a population faced with aggressive individualists committed to rationally organized economies and the logic of free enterprise. The native middle class became middle class precisely because it adapted to the European self-made man. It became the privileged buffer between their people and the international market economy. The industrialization that began in Latin America at the end of the nineteenth century further displaced indigenous cultural values. The behavioral patterns of the rural areas transferred to the cities spread exploitation. To survive one had to learn how to be aggressively independent, forthright, *listo*, an individual without the fetters of personal shame.

There is a brooding solitude at the core of the Latino's selfhood. As Octavio Paz has written, "We get drunk to confess what lurks in our depths, the white society drinks to forget itself."[1] No one should be fooled by the polite deference manifested in smiles, "Si, señor," and the stereotype of the Joses and Marias; these are but ritualized avoidances that hide unresolved feelings of anger and rage. A cultural habit of avoiding direct confrontation has led us to repress our angry feelings, chew them, swallow them, but they remain eating away at our insides.

As we look around we have to wonder how many of us are part of the problem: Have not all of us to some extent been maneuvered into being subtle supporters of a system of human relations that ultimately divides us and absorbs us? Hobbes told us over 300 years ago that our identities were being shaped, not by what we were inside, but by our class, power, prestige, possessions. In eighteenth-century France an *honnête homme* (honest man) was defined as being honest precisely because he knew his assigned place and kept it. Identity was exhausted by rank in society: a person was no less, but no more than that. Today deference remains, but it is edged by insecurity created by a competitive society.

When we look at the actual situation, we are amazed to see blacks and Chicanos telling other Latinos and blacks to go slow or that they were not chosen for the job because they have no previous experience. Unfortunately, affirmative action programs have often become positions of exploitation for blacks on the East coast and Chicanos on the West Coast. They have set up their own "old boy" system, but it is the same system. So we are caught in a web of roles and behavior that makes us do to others what is being done to us. To avoid being victims, we are forced to become the victimizers. We must not be naive about the power of systems to absorb us; none of us is so pure that power cannot corrupt us.

Latinos have somehow partially maintained their language, religion, and culture, although they are constantly reminded of how much they have actually lost. We are in a diaspora: we belong nowhere. We cannot go home or be content here, so we make a home within ourselves. And we see the real poison of racism: white people who forgot who they are forced others to forget who they are. We were made dull; we were not born dull. But we assist the process by playing the role, *jugando el papel que el otro requiere de nosotros*, that another assigns to us.

We have to break out of those roles, the patterns that bind us in a system of relationships that impoverish all of us. The real hope is an imaginative politics based on a people connected to their sources; otherwise we are simply doomed to perpetuate a system that is a permanent state of war. The means is a process of transformation that points us homeward, that is inward to our sources, *el tesoro de nuestra riqueza*, the treasure chest of our riches.

Through a variety of ways Latinos are becoming aware of a profound sense of alienation from others and ourselves. I had originally planned to speak out forcefully and eloquently on our present strengths and hopes for the future. But the possibility of our creating a new future is still problematic. I am not sure if we will choose to do it; that we have the capacity to create ourselves anew I have no doubt. What then is the basis for pessimism? Too often we try to blame the "Gachupines," the Spanish conquerors, or the new intruders, "the Yanquis," for our problems. No doubt there is some justice in this. But there is something else in us that tends to immobilize us, to isolate us from others and ourselves, so that the forging of a new people is aborted by individuals incapable of rising above their desire to be invisible and alone. The reason for this is both cultural and historical. We know that the Indians of our heritage charted time backward and not forward. The Mayas, for example, calculated 300,000 years into the past but calculated no further into the future than 20 years. Every two decades the world was doomed to end. Time was cyclical, and each person was connected to the cycles of death and rebirth. The arrival of the Spaniards and their conquest destroyed this cycle by imposing upon it linear time. There followed a series of political, economic, and social upheavals that postponed a radical analysis and response to the conquest. There was urbanization, the beginnings of industrialization, wars of national liberation, and the arrival of the international political economy, especially in the form of the American businessman. All of these events prevented us from resolving the issues of our own impotency until recent years.

We have survived in this country and in our own homelands. Yet this survival has often been miserable, and many have gone underground to work within the system to wait for a better day. Our isolation really masks a gnawing fear that we are powerless. We substitute for power a scathing rhetoric that attempts to prove our intellectual superiority. This type of detached superiority actually means that the system has won. While we outsmart the master in our minds, the real masters are reinforced in their belief about our inferiority because of our overt acts of docility. True, the master needs the slave for his services, but subtly the slave needs the master for his own identity. To show the bureaucrats of the system that we are real men and women, we engage in periodic paroxysms of violence. The system responds to these outbreaks by giving us consumer goods that will send us back to our solitude. By responding to the logic of the system we become mere rebels, since our response is directed by the consciousness of the system. In *One Hundred Years of Solitude* Gabriel Garcia Marquez writes an epic story of Latin America through the life of a family, the Buendias. There is plenty of activity: thirty-two revolutions, lovemaking, death, mass murder, birth, all of the elements of the drama of life and history. Yet nothing really changes for the characters; at the heart of the issue is a deadly solitude that permanently lames the individuals. All of the main characters die alone, incapable ultimately of sharing their life with others. The novel ends with the final obliteration of Macondo, the fictional city founded in the heart of the jungle. Just before Macondo is blown off the face of the earth by a biblical hurricane, the last survivor of the Buendia family is reading the Sanskrit manuscripts that contain the key to the future of the family. As he reads the parchment he is blown away and with him the memory of Macondo and all its inhabitants, all condemned to death because they never lived. The author concludes with this powerful statement: "Races condemned to one hundred years of solitude did not have a second opportunity on earth."[2] This is not simply death, but total and absolute annihilation with no possibility of new life to redeem it.

Creating the alternative is the most difficult task of our unfinished story. I would like to return to our most intuitive people: our intellectuals, artists, poets, and playwrights. This is a crucial strategy because so many of our social scientists, theologians, and philosophers who have suffered from the inferiority complex bred by years of being *nadie* (nobody) have always turned elsewhere for their theories and insights. The majority of Latin American intellectuals spend most of their time studying the works of Western European and North American theologians and social scientists. But nowhere do they refer to the gods and goddesses of Latin America, to the contribution or the role played by our myths in the universal symbols of nourishment, destruction, and creation. The alternative liberation that they seek is important, but it is equally important to build a new culture, taking into account the indigenous pre-Columbian resources of our people.

What I and others search for is a universalism that exists in the indigenous vision. We look again for the beginning of a new age that the Caribs, Mayas, Aztecs, and Incas saw in the landing of Columbus. Our Indian people shared with the rest of humanity a belief that the whole of creation participated in a cosmic process of creation, nourishment, and destruction so that the next generation might renew our lives and the earth. There lives in the consciousness of the Latino the impending sense of the new world that was promised by the gods. It arrived but brought with it a system of oppression for the majority of our people. Under the surface of disappointment is a response of solitude and invisibility that exacerbates our incoherence. But side by side with this docility there is emerging the hope of another apocalypse that we hope will end not in violence but in the creation of a new humanity: "It is as though the guilt of the victor stands on the threshold of a creative breakthrough in the darkening consciousness of the victim as prelude to the birth pangs of a new cosmos."[3]

The purpose of our writers, theologians, philosophers, and professors must be not to "civilize" us in the present system but to politicize us. Two Latin American novelists, Alejo Carpentier in *The Lost Steps* and Luis Asturias in *The Green Pope,* lead us in their works on an imaginative journey into the subconscious that they see as the beginning of our search for reunification and spiritual renewal. Their concerns with the past "demand a kind of cyclic computation where one is aware of moving into the future as much as one is aware of recreating the past." They urge us not to repeat the past or fall under the spell of its romance, but to *recreate* it: by choosing and discerning those elements that will lead us now and in the future out of a dead end. For these writers the peasants are not mere natives but are the roots of our past, of our cultural continuity. Their culture is in our bones. By acknowledging it we cause the darkness of the apocalypse to recede, and Garcia Marquez's novel of destruction takes on new meaning. There is a collective breakdown in Macondo. The author is reminding us of the indigenous myths, and in these myths we find a fuller expression of universal archetypes: the re-creation of the individual person and of the world that follows destruction. The appeal to these myths has both a psychological base and a value as a social protest:

> Asturias is therefore taking up the stream of writing which had been established by the Indians centuries before him. Always it expresses the need to transcend the condition of entrapment by use of the universal myth. Therefore, in Asturias's portrait of the President as the archetype of the Terrible Mother (in *El Señor Presidente*), there is at once social protest in its own right against the dictatorship of Estrada Cabrera, and also the continuity of the Indian literature of myth. The novel, on these levels, describes a condition of social and psychological entrapment which is also universally applicable to all races and cultures of the world that have developed an indigenous myth of suffering.[4]

By wrestling with our heritage we can go beyond the despair of entrapment that ends in political passivity. It is important to know that our ancestors knew about and *participated* in a universal drama of creation, nourishment, and destruction. This is the process that we choose to reenact with the necessary adaptation to our own historical period.

Politics is a threefold dialectic: the creation of a new environment, the nourishment of our systems, and the freedom and ability to put those systems out of business when they no longer serve our needs. But the *spiral* continues as we choose to create again. It is a spiral because we move beyond the cyclic repetition of the past in order to re-create the past toward an open future. Systems take on a life of their own only when we lapse into solitude, invisibility, docility. For example, NASA got so involved with an efficient system based on hierarchy that they made it impossible to hear the engineers who were closer to the concrete reality of the safety of the astronauts. In such a case the system was more dedicated to its own authority to the point where it could not see or hear the problem. In a similar vein, the hierarchy of the Catholic Church considered itself as the Church and thus seldom heard the views of people outside the ordained hierarchy. This is why Vatican II was such a revolutionary event, since it affirmed the Church as a community, as *all* of its members prior to and more essential than its hierarchial structure. The world and the networks that shape it constitute a persistent cocreation of persons rooted in their sources and giving expression to the truth by naming themselves and the world simultaneously. Thus no system has the right to become an object over and against us; its objectivity is never perfect or finished, because we as personal creators are not finished. We are always more than our creations.

I return to where I began: it is precisely because we cannot be who we are in our deepest selves that we have to reject this current system. We do not reject a system because it is called capitalism, socialism, or materialism, white or racist. We ultimately reject a system because the realities it fosters are symptoms of a deeper demonic cause; we share complicity in our own alienation. When we are strong enough to confront the system, what will we bring to it if not our authentic selves to pass judgment on it? Do we need jobs, housing, employment? Yes. Yet we want more than that; we want the right to all of these human necessities *and* the right to be ourselves. This means confronting racist institutions, but with a purpose: to use the means of the old system to create an alternative. This does not mean that we will reject our sisters and brothers of other cultures and races. Far from it. We owe it to them not to continue to give the impression that making it in this system is what life is all about. If we love ourselves, our God, and our fellow human beings, we owe it to ourselves to create conflict. The conflict is capable of breaking the spell of the deep sleep into which we have been cast through hearing that we live in the best of all possible worlds.

Let us consider why we are not at home in our present system by examining an attempt to lull us back to sleep. Bilingual education for Latinos may be a subtle form of co-option and assimilation. It is clearly intended to be transitory; it is a tool to give people new opportunities. The ultimate goal is still assimilation, bilingual assimilation. But the issue for the Latino is also the question of biculturalism. Clearly language has much to do with culture, but many of the advantages of bilingualism are considered economic: bilingual secretaries, businessmen, lawyers, and so forth have greater opportunities. This reduction of our native language to status pursuits divorces it from its cultural matrix. To emphasize the bicultural means that there is a struggle going on within us; the bicultural never allows us to be truly at home here. We live in an economic system that wants us all to be "nonbody" producers working to have a better future. Once again it is our artists, Luis Asturias and Octavio Paz, who warn us that we are a people of festival, of the celebration of the body, and of the eternal return contained in the present. The cultural implications of this must not be lost. The Anglo-Saxon inheritance castigates the Latino for an attitude of *mañana* because it is nonproductive. The English ancestors of this nation sought purity from the world and the body through hard work. As Weber and Tawney have taught us, it was this kind of religious ideology based on purification that contributed so much to the rise of the capitalist economy. But the religious views that helped make the Anglo-Saxon superior in banking and industry made him uncomprehending of those who are not Calvinists or Horatio Algers. The Indian was considered to be a lazy and soulless heathen, never a person.

As a result, as Octavio Paz has written, the United States has no Indian past, no dialectical opposite, no shadow, no specifically American roots that can fulfill, balance, complete, or transform the European ones.[5] The United States did not merge with the Indian but extinguished him. This cruelty had another result: the strain of domination and segregation in the culture exalted behavioral patterns traditionally called virile: aggressiveness, individualism, and competitiveness.

In comparison the Spaniards, who were also cruel, at least did not deny the humanity of the Indian: they at least granted him a soul. Therefore, the approach in Latin America, thanks largely to people like Bartolome de las Casas, the first bishop of Mexico, was to assimilate and convert, to include the Indian, which resulted in the mestizo reality of the region. Initially the Indians yielded themselves to the Spaniards and resisted too late. What remained after the conquest was a people of superimposed pasts that every Latino carried in his or her bones: the continuity of several thousand years of history. It is this facing between two pasts, between two civilizations, that provides the Latino with an internal dialectical force that lies fallow. Octavio Paz powerfully demonstrates the emergence and confluence of the Indian and the Spanish traditions in the frenzy of the festival.[6] Paz states that festival is what makes the Latino *political*. It is a sign and time of resistance. Earlier Paz had written:

> . . . modern time, linear time, the homologue of the idea of progress and history, ever propelled into the future, the time of the sign non-body, of the fierce will to dominate nature and tame instincts, the time of publication, aggression and self-mutilation—is coming to an end.[7]

The myth of the eternal return frees us; it is the return of the revolution as festival. Festival celebrates the other, communion; *la fiesta* is Dionysiac, frenzy, voluptuousness, color. It is a communion that is participation not separation, joining not breaking away, a great coming together, a bathing in the waters of the eternal return, in the primordial waters of beginning. It is baptism, renewal, transformation, a fundamentally different existence beyond the Anglo-Saxon purity and impurity, the deferral of pleasure and repression that separates us from our bodies, one another, and the world. But above all festival, fiesta time, is the victory of the love of the body, renewed, re-created, redeemed. The spirit of the eternal return rejects the linear one-dimensional search for a future and roots us firmly in the present, here and now. But the here and now is past, present, and future fulfilled in a new incarnation of who we are. Thus if a society is essentially defined by its concept of time, there can be no more glaring difference between the Latino and the Anglo-Saxon. The Anglo-Saxon, as Philip Slater has written, lives for the future, saving money for the sake of money, deferring pleasure and relationships, and seeing pleasure and festival as a waste because it is a loss of money and power.[8]

It is because of our rootedness in an incarnate spirit that knows itself in festival and erotic connections that we, as Latinos, must not allow ourselves to turn against the body as Anglo-Saxon society would have us do. We have to act as a countercommunity, a countersign to the stunted life based on the war of all against all. To begin with ourselves, with our bodies, is a point of departure leading beyond the body to the other. We have an opportunity to stand as a symbol of what every person is capable of: a new creation. According to Octavio Paz this is the age of *el quinto sol* (the fifth sun), the era of motion, of earthquakes, of the collapse of the pyramid of established power; this parallels the historical situation in which the whole world is living. We will be saved not by power and stability but by the capacity for change.[9] We can be a people characterized by resistance, a subversive people, through whom a different spirit speaks. We can manifest humanity's hope of renewal. We cannot afford to be absorbed, fused, or bought off. To preserve our Indian-Spanish past is to reaffirm festival, the body, death and rebirth, the erotic, the present here and now, the love of the other, and the resources within our creative selves.

There are universal resources to be rediscovered in our Indian and European heritage that speak of hope, creation, love, and community. It will be our task to educate ourselves to these sources of transformation, both those within our Indian-European roots and those that are to be discovered here in our new land. To bring together countertraditions from both cultures is to affirm that our sources speak in all times and places. We are the crucibles of the new incarnation of the sources. If we lack a home in the system, we have ourselves and each other once again; it is all that we have, and it is more than enough.

Politics is more than a constitution and its implementation through laws and governing parties. It has to do with participation in the building of human community. The institutions that are created are the result of the linkages or patterns by which people have chosen to bind themselves in a social union. Therefore, politics of its very origin and nature presupposes a human-made network of human relationships that can be put out of business to form new institutions. In this sense we are all (and must be) political. And now we are ready, finally, to redefine, to transform, our solitude. The quality of this solitude is fundamentally different from that of docile solitude; the retreat that we speak of here is temporary, not permanent. It is a withdrawal into ourselves to seek the strength and creativity to return to our people to make concrete and act out the vision that was revealed to us in our solitude. This is a solitude with a transformative purpose. Our time has come not because we are on the cover of *Time* but because our period of gestation is over. Again we are called upon to be the fathers and mothers of the divine by giving birth to the divine child—our new selves—so that we shall be as gods, cocreators made in the image and likeness of God:

> The hibernation is over. I must shake off the old skin and come up for breath. There's a stench in the air, which, from this distance underground, might be the smell either of death or of spring—I hope of spring. But don't let me trick you, there *is* a death in the smell of spring and in the smell of thee as in the smell of me. . . . And I suppose it's damn well time. . . . Even hibernations can be overdone, come to think of it. Perhaps that's my greatest social crime, I've overstayed my hibernation, since there's a possibility that even an invisible man has a socially responsible role to play.[10]

This is the essence of alienation: we repress our feelings, lose control of our actions to set roles. To politicize people is to put back into the hands of the people themselves their own relationships as the means to build human community. This is what it means to participate in the creation, nourishment, and destruction of human relationships. When the human institutions by which we structure life become destructive, it is our right and duty to put them out of business. We destroy not human beings but the linkages between us. Nevertheless, the deliberate and conscious breaking of relationships is violence; it is at least a psychic violence. But certainly the depression that an absentee landlord feels because he can no longer make exorbitant profits due to withholding heat and hot water is preferable to the violence that destroys both the body and spirit of the tenants. For tenants to organize a rent strike is to destroy the linkage that allowed him to use them as a means to his own end; the intent is to break patterns, not the landlord's body or his livelihood. New patterns will have to guarantee the rights and duties of *both* owner and tenant. To create conflict and change, to initiate the breaking and the creating of alternative patterns, is to care enough to develop an opportunity for both sides to experience themselves afresh. This is the essence of nonviolence.[11]

The concrete inherited patterns into which we were socialized in the way of life of emanation can now be used in the new way of life of transformation as created patterns. For example, the inherited isolation that was so debilitating can now freely be chosen to create something fundamentally new. But for isolation to be creative it must be a temporary strategy. In the final analysis the most revolutionary people in a time of breakdown will be those persons who can create new relationships among strangers. Whoever shares with Puerto Ricans, Chicanos, or Cubans a consciousness of wanting to build a society in the service of others—these people too will belong to *La Raza, Boricua,* and *el Pueblo.* In this way the original meaning of such phrases will have been transformed. Once a sense of identity has been achieved, it is necessary to move beyond the initial exclusivity of the original meaning. By redefining the concept to include people who share common joys and sorrows is to demonstrate that ethnic identities belong to humankind. *Boricua* and *La Raza,* therefore, are no longer statements of color, language, or race as much as they are concepts indicating a consciousness—a consciousness of creating linkages with others in justice.

GROWING ONE'S OWN RACIAL AND ETHNIC IDENTITY

Studies done on ethnic groups have usually told us that ethnicity is based on shared culture, religion, geography, and language. These linkages normally lead to a sense of kinship, loyalty, and, in times of stress, mutual help, especially if directed toward threatening external groups. Discussions of race, on the other hand, distinguish between the Caucasoid, Mongoloid, and Negroid as the three primary groups of humankind.[12] Furthermore, scholars speak of inherited racial characteristics, the effect of geographical position, historical factors, and so forth.

"Race and ethnicity" are conceptual terms, intended to encompass observation of facts, experiences, and human activity in general. In other words, concepts should be viewed as in a fluid state precisely because they are abstractions that seek to express the flux of human experience.[13] The point is that social scientists have failed in general not only to point out the flux inherent in "Arab," "Chicano," or "white" but also to speak of the qualitatively different ways by which people can relate to their own Latinoness or Arabness. Ethnic groups are constantly being born, destroyed, or transcended by larger ties. For example, Arabs are not sure in what practical terms they are connected as Arabs. Nasser's greatest problem was to build a common Arab identity for people who shared the following proverb: "I against my brother; my brother and I against my cousin and I against the tribe; my tribe against the world." To become an Arab is to reduce one's loyalty to family, tribe, and religion. Thus it is not easy to create Arabs, Israelis, Latinos, or blacks. The sense of race or ethnicity cannot be taken for granted; it waxes and wanes.

Whether scholarly monographs seek to be either neutral toward or strident advocates of a given race or ethnic group, they end with the same result: they create a false consciousness about race or ethnicity since they merely report what is there without helping us to distinguish the specific ways or quality by which people are choosing or not choosing to link themselves together as individuals in their respective groups. Simply telling "what is" perpetuates racism or romantic claims of ethnic greatness since the conventional wisdom is to equate reality with the persistence of existing relationships. But there is a further step involved, and that is for us to consider how relationships to such ethnic and racial groups can be consciously analyzed, broken if necessary, and new linkages created. In other words, we are not limited to inherited relationships; one of the greatest gifts of human beings is to *in-form* the world, that is, refashion it according to new perceptions of possibilities.[14] Other theorists believe that racism or ethnic discrimination will end if there is a redistribution of wealth. But this often results in co-opting the previously powerless group, and the price is usually paid by other, more unfortunate groups. The issue is not the redistribution of wealth, as Marx so clearly saw, but to create a new wealth, a new society by first of all creating a new consciousness.[15]

In places such as Liberia, the United States, and South Africa a legitimized violence has been employed to maintain the powerless fragmentation of Gios, Chicanos and Puerto Ricans, and Bantus.[16] As the subjection broke down, whites and members of the ruling ethnic group faced the loss of a way of life based in great part on the subordination of other groups. Such endangered groups responded to their incoherence by conjuring up a mystifying group consciousness, usually based on their white ethnic heritage. Such aggressive and defensive exclusion of others on grounds of racial or ethnic differences is what we call racism. But notice that racism is an attempt on the part of a group to hold together a chaotic world for its members. In order to block out the collapse of their world they create a fragment—skin color—as the sole meaning of their new life. This refusal to see others as complete human beings is to create white into a whole way of life, a pseudoemanation as a way of life, a false mystification that deepens the way of life of incoherence leading to deformation, since it destroys both whites and people of color. Members of such exclusive groups see themselves solely as extensions of their own ethnic or racial group. Individuals in such a group thus give up the right critically to evaluate or create options. Blood becomes fate and destiny; people are presented with race and ethnicity as permanent facts of life. Such a sense of blood enhances the ability of groups to have internal cooperation and continuity in the limitless security of the mass. But the price is high: there is no individual self present to deal with conflict or change. In the face of other groups, suspicion and confrontation end by turning both into bloodless stereotypes.

Modern consciousness gives us hope that people can become aware that racist and ethnocentric ideologies with their resulting relationships are human made; that such patterns are breaking down; and that we can create alternative ways to relate to ourselves as members of a particular race or ethnic group in order to relate to other groups.

Until recently minorities in the United States lacked the strength to preserve their identity or to win political and economic rights because they remained unconnected to one another. Other groups developed their own power because of the disconnection of groups such as Mexicans, Puerto Ricans, and blacks. Thus, power groups developed a vested interest in assimilating Latinos and other minorities into American society. Puerto Ricans, Mexicans, and other Latinos who entered white society did so at the price of agreeing to avoid conflict or demands for change. Integration estranged them from their own communities: their own people often became an embarrassment.

Different societies create linkages between people by which they organize daily life. Such links constitute institutions. The bonds of a particular society can be analyzed as the relationships that count, what C.W. Mills called the sociological imagination or the patterns behind the flux. In official United States society the dominant relationship is boundary management, an autonomous zone within which one can establish a power relationship with others. Unions and General Motors would be examples on the group level; on the personal level it can be seen in student-teacher relations or between man and wife. Another important relationship is direct bargaining, that is, the ability to win a better arrangement by negotiations with other individuals or groups. For example, every three years the steel unions reopen contract talks to redistribute benefits. Both sides bargain with the hope of enhancing their own boundaries.

In American society groups or individuals who are isolated from one another and who are subjected by other organized groups will not be able to enter into official American society. To survive in the United States society, direct bargaining power and boundary management are essential. Co-option is easily practiced in such a situation by allowing individual blacks, women, or Puerto Ricans into power positions. The logic of individualism, "I've got mine," has worked too well. Some Mexican Americans have counseled others to go slow and let the system work. Dispossessed groups such as the Chicanos, blacks, and Filipinos in California chose to end their isolation and subjection and to organize themselves as the United Farm Workers to gain autonomy and to bargain with the farm owners. The Teamsters, who went through a similar struggle in the 1930s, closed ranks with the growers to sign sweetheart contracts. This latter coalition of autonomous jurisdictions, or boundary management, was used to preserve power and prevent change. This is an example of boundary management as institutionalized violence, or boundary management used in the service of incoherence because it perpetuates the economic and political fragmentation of a whole group of people based on race and class. In their own ways marginal ethnic and racial groups understand these dynamics. But there is a danger that they will exploit the system and thus end by being controlled by the present consciousness of United States society; in other words, when they achieve their own autonomy they will close out the group that has not yet learned to survive in America. But there is another way by which to re-create American institutions as autonomous jurisdictions in the way of life of transformation. This will be developed later in the chapter.

The sixties saw the awakening of racial and ethnic pride led by the black power movement. "Good" and "quiet" Mexicans became Chicanos and began to create conflict and to agitate for change. But the achievement of a power base by a whole group does not guarantee winning the revolution against exploitation. David Gordon has documented the refusal of Moslem men to allow true liberation for women in Algeria.[17] Thus we must look within an ethnic group at the quality of relationships of members to one another. The liberation of a group cannot be authentic unless the individuals in that group are free.

As has already been stated, there are qualitatively different ways by which people may relate themselves to that emerging minority group known as Latinos, and including La Raza, Boricua, or Chicano. Many Latinos have been disillusioned by their attempt to enter into the embrace of the American way of life. They had to sacrifice too many aspects of their heritage: their color, ancestors, language and culture, and even themselves in order to belong. More recently some Mexican Americans, for example, have sought a newfound security in another total embrace, an embeddedness in a particular group, Chicanos or brown-power people. In other words, some people fall in love with being Chicano and not with people, who may or may not have accepted what others mean by Chicano. To lose oneself in any group is to give up any fresh insight into oneself and to repress change and conflict for the sake of security. Such is to treat oneself solely as an embodiment of an ethnic group because of the seemingly mysterious and overwhelming source of power of the group.

Other Latinos, separated from the American stream of life and pressured by fellow Latinos, feel compelled to grab hold of this new identity so as to be able to survive in a time of ethnic "in-ness." There are Latinos who will gladly accept being ethnic because it is a marketable commodity. Some choose to isolate themselves from the problem of ethnic identity and seek to be left alone. Being a member of an ethnic group provides other people with a filter by which to interpret reality for themselves. Thus only Latino is valid; white, black, yellow are excluded from the area of mysterious power. Color, language, and ethnic identity help to provide horizons within which people feel secure, superior, and autonomous. Too often they overreact to their suppression of identity and claim that everything Latino is good. But there are many who do not want to be uncritically in love with being Third World or Latino. They refuse to be pushed into accepting a definition of who they are and do not wish to isolate themselves from other people who are not brown; they believe that they can see the world through other perspectives. These Latinos refuse to become an ethnic commodity and refuse to use their heritage, language, and culture to erect limits to exclude others. Such Latinos are persistently in the process of critically evaluating what it means to be a member of an ethnic group. They are growing their own racial and ethnic identity.

It is our thesis that concepts such as La Raza are not so much a statement of color, language, or race as it is a matter of consciously continuing to create links with fellow Latinos and others in justice. Therefore, people who are white, yellow, red, black, or brown who help Latinos to realize themselves as persons are their friends, their guides. After all, the role of the friend or the guide is to lead one back to the mystery of the self. On the other hand, those who seek to oppress, of whatever color or racial background, are not brothers and sisters.

But before Latinos can form coalitions with others, they must first be able to accept those aspects of their lives which constitute their own heritage.[18] The tragedy of the melting pot was that immigrants, at least by the second generation, began to ignore, or were forced to ignore, their national and cultural past in their rush to be Americans. People now have to go back and reconnect to themselves as Chicanos, Cubans, Poles, Swedes, Chinese, or Puerto Ricans before they can form a new American identity. A people cannot forge meaningful connections with others until they have connected themselves to themselves. Mexican Americans, for example, connected to one another can then begin consciously to re-create what it means to be a Chicano. After all, it can be legitimately asked, What do we mean by Mexican American, Chicano, or member of La Raza? Chicanos are a group who do not always look upon other Mexican Americans as "true" Chicanos, even though they share a common land of origin, language, and customs. Thus, ethnic groups are constantly in process and evolving because their members are continually redefining who they are. For this reason it is crucial that not only ethnic groups but the individuals within that group be liberated as well. Only freely connected individuals can pose new questions as their consciousness of who they are grows.

Once Latinos accept who they are, they can creatively set about forging new connections within their community and to others. It makes no sense to create a militant rhetoric which compels people to reject others before they experience them as persons.[19] To do so is to fall prey to a false vivification, that is, we endow concepts with life and thereby turn our lives into the tools of ideologies.

The transformation of ethnic and racial groups will mean the conscious and creative breaking of destructive linkages and the refashioning of new relationships. The principal creative force will emerge from the reversal of emanation instead of being unconsciously embedded in the mysterious power of the group. Rather than remaining immersed in the group, the individual is set free to analyze and experience patterns of encounter within the self and with others. Rather than being the extension of another individual or a group in the relationship of an inherited emanation, either in the ways of life of emanation or incoherence, the individual is transformed into the embodiment of himself/herself in the way of life of transformation. New relationships can now be created, consciously selected, and maintained, but only as long as they give capacity to generate and absorb a constantly changing world. Since a person is armed with a new consciousness of self and other and with a willingness to create new relationships, a new kind of wealth is now possible.

An awareness of concrete linkages that preserve racism and destructive ethnicity along with a consciousness of alternative relationships frees one from attacking abstract "systems," a strategy that is tantamount to beating the air. Ethnic and racial groups that have become conscious of their strength can now use their power to develop strategies of change within their own community and with other groups.[20] Legal subjection can be used to enforce civil-rights laws; groups can freely withdraw temporarily for each member to experience oneself and the others within the group afresh in order to discover how to relate to American society; new possibilities can be opened by supportive whites and other ethnic groups; political brokerage leading to political coalitions can be used to bargain for economic, social, and political rights; coalitions of Latino and other professionals can be created to provide services and opportunities for powerless minorities to organize a new, larger, more coordinated and competent base from which to turn to the transformation of their own groups and the larger society. Finally, Latino guides using a new and created form of emanation in the way of life of transformation can inspire new identities, produce pride, and give rise to solidarity.[21]

> The politics of transformation or if you prefer, permanent revolution, is always taking the next concrete step in the creation, nourishment or destruction of the next encounter. It is a process whereby the Latino worker for the first time opens up construction unions to his membership, comes to recognize what kind of housing he is not helping to build, recognizes through his work and its immediate rewards new aspects of his own being, struggles to alter the leadership of his union, etc., etc. Transformation is not salvation but sanctification of human relations; never perfection but ever renewed movement toward networks of wholeness.[22]

Thus, instead of using one's boundary management to suppress change and consolidate one's power, the base won by an ethnic group is an essential container for nurturing more creative ways by which to give themselves and others new directions. Such a use of boundary management is not working "within the system"; it is the process by which to build alternative institutions open to all groups. In this way boundary management is itself transformed; rather than being used for the sake of incoherence, boundary management is now re-created in the paradigm of transformation. This is the true meaning of subversion—people turn systems around from below by creatively using institutions, not to prevent change but as a stepping stone for further development.

Finally, the irony of all this is that my search for ethnic and religious identity as a Chicano and Roman Catholic was greatly helped by a Jewish friend of German descent and an Italian with an Irish name. What they did was give me confidence in myself, so that I could accept myself; together with the Latino community and especially my Latino students, they acted as the guides in my life who helped to return myself to myself. In the midst of such concrete personal experiences I could never accept definitions of racial or ethnic identity that would exclude my friends. If we know the joy of experiencing who we are, we must share this with blacks, Poles, Jews, Slovaks, Italians, and Irish. I believe with Gandhi and Cesar Chavez that humankind can only know a part of that truth. To discover the full truth, ethnic and racial groups must cooperate in the task of rebuilding American Society.

> The victory of any group will remain a success only if it also helps all human beings to link themselves or to change such linkages in order to overcome the common and persisting incoherence of the human species in the modern age.[23]

3. The Politics of the Latino Family

"A child is a guest in the home to be loved and respected, not to be possessed because he or she belongs to God." J. D. Salinger. The family is perhaps the most important institution for Latinos. We have heard and read much about the collapse of authority in the family due to changes in the relationship between male and female, parent and child, and husband and wife. This crisis is seen as a great danger by many Latinos. Yet it is not the family and authority relations per se that are breaking but a particular kind of family and authority. Latinos must hold onto the family but grow a new kind of family with male/female relationships, authority patterns, and a cariño, affection, that prepares each of us for selfhood. In this way the family will not help to socialize us into the dominant structures but prepare each of us to be participants in shaping our barrios.

INTRODUCTION

In an excellent monograph David C. Gordon wrote about the status of women in prerevolutionary and postrevolutionary Algeria.[1] A similar study done by Gregory Massell in Soviet Central Asia described the attempt of the new government to transform male-female relations in a traditional society.[2] These two readings were brought to mind in a recent conversation with friends in Mexico regarding the changing role of women in Cuba since Castro. There was a remarkable coincidence in all three cases. Three revolutions had gone on record ideologically as well as legally to alter definitively the traditional relationships between men and women which had permanently structured women as inferior. In the case of Algeria it is quite clear that the women at a crucial point took a lead in the revolution. This revolutionary experience served to change the consciousness of the women in respect to their own self-image and the roles that had created such a subservient attitude. Yet curiously enough, in spite of the new laws, the rhetoric, the countless confrontations, and the establishment of the new society, too often male-female relationships slipped back into the old world. Any revolution that does not radically alter the human linkages constitutive of institutions is not a transformation of society but a coup d'etat, a mere seizure of power that leaves the structure of that society largely untouched. Male-female roles in a society and especially in the family can be a good indicator as to the radical thrust of a movement. Thus, when in Soviet Central Asia avowed communist youths began to sexually abuse women who had removed the *purdah,* the traditional veil worn by Moslem women, the revolution was clearly not won. When Algerian men expected the women to return to old authority patterns based upon male dominance, the revolution was left lacking. Similarly in Cuba old customs of male dominance refused to die.

Surely in these three cases as well as elsewhere there is no lack of good will, ideology, conviction, or revolutionary ardor. The problem is that all of the above were at best a sincere effort to confront age-old customs and at their worst a naive intellectual conversion. But in the final analysis it was not revolutionary enough. People generally have not taken into account the trauma, indeed the death, of the old ego-identity that has to be sacrificed before the new can be created. Carl Gustave Jung has taught us that we are not merely the product of our own personal life span. We all carry within us a history that is our glory and our burden. The real revolution consequently will have to be fought out in terms of a deep personal transformation or conversion process. There is no attempt here to reduce transformation to an individualized private realm. Rather, the issue is to recognize that liberated groups of people must be composed of liberated individuals who together link themselves in such a way as to move freely and consciously to solve problems. The lively tension between the individual and the group must be preserved not for the sake of competition but for mutual fulfillment. Similarly, personal and political transformation, especially in the modern age, are two sides of the same process. When a young person raises his or her voice and says "Enough!" this is not only a private, psychological liberation, but it moves beyond this to pass judgment on the social and political roles that have structured her/his reality. Yet all the revolutionary rhetoric will not free us from the demons within that have to be wrestled with until they bless us. It is this level of the transformation of our underlying sources that has too often been overlooked by the advocates of social change and revolution.

THE FAMILY AS CONTAINER

Institutions and social structures such as the family are made up of patterns of human relationships. The family is a pivotal unit in all societies. Although its structure may vary, it has and will continue to play a vital role in the nurturing of persons. It is certainly the key vehicle for handing down or altering traditions. The issue to which we shall address ourselves is the quality of the relationships that exist within the family. The family like any other social relationship must be judged on its capacity to free the individual member of the group. There are two gods at odds here, that of the collectivity and that of the individual. Both have their legitimate demands that must be met. The key issue is to transform the collective unit of the family from a completely sealed container into a dialectical process of nurturing and liberating its members simultaneously in such a way that the family is preserved yet changed within an atmosphere of affectionate conflict. The family has often been seen and used as the unit of stability that prepares the new generation to repress what is within them and to live a life of virtue, that is, to preserve the status quo.[3] The very term "husband" betrays a prejudice toward cultivating and securing a safe haven for loved ones. Fixed sexual roles in the family have made the family dependent upon the economic potential of the father, thus removing men from significant political protest. Indeed, for many years insurance companies have made it a practice to favor married men with children in their premium coverage.[4] Seldom in the literature on the family, until recently, was there any attention given to the changing *consciousness* of the partners or of people growing their own marriage or sex roles. Nor was there discussed the necessity of men and women confronting each other with their dreams and fantasies. For according to many psychologists, especially Jung, it is in dream and fantasy that our innermost person, our unconscious self, is revealed to us. Dreams compensate for the issues not consciously faced in everyday life. They constitute manifestations of the unconscious elements that seek to be integrated into our personality. The symbols and images carry a message from within.[5] But we need new language, new mythologies, to appeal to, or else we shall remain confused trying to justify these kinds of confrontation in a culture dedicated to patriarchal rationality. It is precisely our theory which allows us to ask new questions and to break out of the common-sense, culture-bound knowledge. Theory is in its initial inspiration a kind of ecstasy that allows us to step out of the old consensus and to participate afresh in the shaping of the self and society. We can go beyond merely reporting dysfunctions to pointing out clearly the relationships that constitute social institutions, how they are inadequate, and, if necessary, to advocate breaking those linkages for the sake of forging new institutions. This is what the politics of the family is all about—participation in relationships in motion.

But where, it may be asked, will people find the strength or capacity to deal with such a process of destroying-creating-nourishing? The source of that strength lies within the context of the human person as a spark of the divine. It is the basis of human transcendence, of creating again, of hope that alternatives are possible. In this realm we enter into the company of the mystics of different ages and of all faiths who sought their sacred sources and the new self *simultaneously*.[6] Nor should the introduction of religious language alarm us. It provides us with a universal language, an archetypal language that allows us to speak of how people can be as gods creating the world afresh.

THE LATINO FAMILY: CONTINUITY AND CHANGE

The Latino family has been all but ignored in the literature.[7] Oscar Lewis has written some fascinating studies, but they did little to help us move beyond a sensitive awareness of what *is*.[8] Often all families of whatever racial or ethnic background were grouped together in studies and discussed under headings that betrayed a white middle-class orientation. We now move to study the patterns of the Latino family, to evaluate those linkages and to speak of breaking old patterns for the sake of new ones. Much of what follows will allow people other than Latinos to recognize themselves. Traditional families the world over have remarkably similar patterns of interaction.[9] Our hope is to present a theoretical framework which is not culture bound.

The Latino family has provided a strong container for the security of its members, but the cost to those same individuals seeking to grow within and beyond the group has been prohibitive. There is a poverty of relationships available to the members of the Latino family. The father is the source of the mystery (and in some cases a strong mother, grandmother, or aunt), the eldest son replaces the father in his absence, and the women exist to serve the needs of the men and the household. The father can coerce, cajole, mediate, and bargain, but he will not allow female members of the family to physically isolate themselves or to develop an area of autonomous jurisdiction such as a life style that allows them their own jobs, paychecks, and schedules. But not even the father is free, since he is an extension of the father's role in the Latino family that he inherited. The mother often becomes an institutionalized mediator who is dedicated to softening the conflict between members of the family. It is her role to reconcile the children who have attempted rebellion. Outsiders who appear on the scene are dangerous insofar as they do not accept the repertory of relationships within the family. That is, if a friend was *malcriado*, "poorly raised," he might contaminate the sons or daughters by introducing bad ideas or attitudes into the self-contained unit of the family. What this means is that they might inject possible new ways of relating that threaten the sovereignty of the father. For this reason Latino immigrants were alarmed by the culture in the United States that stressed autonomy for children. A veil of sin, shame, and guilt quickly surrounded any attempt to question the authority of the father. This sense of guilt is a fragment of the old paradigm of emanation which is dying. Sons were given freedoms denied to daughters. As an extension of the father, the son was expected to repeat the manly exploits of the father. But for many Latino families "A daughter is the jewel of the family, one cannot be too careful with them."[10] In other words, a daughter carries the honor of the family, and she can be made pregnant, thus dishonoring the family.

LATINA WOMEN AND PATTERNS OF DEPENDENCE

Women from the Latino culture have for centuries belonged to men—whether a father, husband, brother, bishop, or other male guardian (emanation). Their ability to create conflict or change was minimal. Their lives were limited to cooperating with and seeking to continue the strength of the male who gave them security. Women were unable to create alternatives and exercised only those strategies acceptable to the culture (subjection). Women were allowed to withdraw only into a psychic state of moodiness (isolation). An aunt or other mediator could intercede on their behalf and win for them some concessions (buffering). If the stress and strain went beyond all reason, a woman could become bold enough to confront the dominant male in her life and ask for a better life (direct bargaining). If she succeeded or failed, she was still left with the only option of returning to normal, that is, seeing herself only as an extension of others and therefore limited to what they would permit. This was their life space: possession and domination softened by a limited isolation, a brooding silence, mediators, and bargaining. Women were devoid of the right to be physically left alone, the right to go away to renew themselves (isolation), denied any autonomy (boundary management), and, ironically, forbidden even to descend into depression (incoherence) lest it cast a shadow on the family image of contentment. People forbidden to feel their own deep discontent cannot generate the conflict and the energy necessary to break the old and transform their lives (transformation). In an interview a Peruvian woman stated that if she hurt her husband, "she would feel dirty, cheap, and useless." It is these internalized feelings fostered by linkages of dependence that allowed the tradition of male-female roles to be repeated generation after generation.

For centuries Spaniards possessed their wives. Indian males, having lost connection to their indigenous culture, which at the very least recognized the complementarity of the masculine and feminine, began to ape the Spaniard as male role model. Sadly, they tried to regain their dignity by emphasizing their power over women. In many conversations with relatives and friends some outline of the demonic possessiveness operative in the Latino family began to emerge. Men and women have done terrible things to one another in the name of stability and *cariño*, affection. Adjustment, balance, and harmony in the Latino family meant accepting one's inherited role. Thus, a woman accepted as her fate a male who would do what he wanted. Often this male freedom expressed itself in a sexual manner. A Latina woman has known and knows that she will never be able to control her husband's affection. Many felt free to go out with other women and do as they please. But she too would have her revenge. To compensate for this loss a wife turned to the son, who became the object of her frustrated affection. The son was made to feel loyal to the mother against the defiler, the father. In cases of abandonment this protective filial role was intensified. When the young man married, he could not so readily shake this first loyalty; he ended by accepting the oft-repeated warning of his mother, "Your mother comes before anybody, even your wife." The cycle is put in motion again: the rejected wife will now do to her son (this may be one reason why sons are preferred over daughters) what her mother-in-law did to her husband. Herein is a constant process of violence whereby a mother who has been violated prevents a son from developing his own selfhood. He becomes an eternal son so that she might remain an eternal mother and thus fulfill her empty life.[11] In a similar vein young women in the Latino culture are also felt to be disloyal, even on a sexual level, to their fathers when they prefer another *macho* to their father.

Tragically, both Latino men and women realize at a later time that they have really married their own mothers and fathers. Too often in looking for freedom from a dominant parent by marrying, they were not conscious that they had internalized the whole way of life of the parent. To break externally with the mother or father was not enough since the internalized need of belonging to others or possessing others has not been exorcised. Similarly, as we shall see in more detail in chapter five, the god of emanation who legitimizes their cultural patterns of dependence has also not been confronted. Thus we repeat the same old dramas and relationships with new persons. It is these cycles and feelings of loyalty that are now being broken and questioned by Latina women. Women who merely find sources of mystery within their sons or families still fail to find it within themselves. Many Latinas use a relationship of emanation to avoid facing the failure and unhappiness of life. It is therefore emanation in the service of incoherence. The relationship of incoherence following the loss of one's original security is not transformed but deepened by escaping to find total security in one's children. What makes it painfully incoherent is that they are conscious of what they are doing but cannot or will not create a new life. This constitutes an attempt to replace the broken container of the way of life of emanation with a new one that merely hides and perpetuates the incoherence, thereby turning the relationship of incoherence into a whole way of life.

Men have always been aware of a certain mysterious power in women which they sought to control. Taboos arose regarding the menstrual cycle, veiling women, and purifying women after childbirth. Women were identified with the moon, dark forces, the demonic, and the irrational.[12] Women in traditional societies have learned to cope with male jealousy and dominance through a process of covert manipulation or subversion. Women were allowed to work their mystery, or the relationship of emanation, only in the home. Here the dominance of the male was reversed. The male could afford to be seduced, to show dependence, and to allow himself to be magnanimous. For a short period he is an extension of her feminine prowess and mystique. This helps to explain why women have always gained concessions or better bargains from men through their cooking and sexual prowess. However, the threat that this domesticated power might become a source of public competition is a haunting, irrational threat to many men. In some cases women even gained power in the family. Yet there was still no transformation since any change strengthened the system, that is, the existing relationships. The changes only allowed a woman to exercise her mystery over a man because he failed. They are the same linkages based on power and domination. Consequently the person in power has changed, but men and women are still trapped in the same relationships: one is the extension of the other; the other is controlled by the mate; one or the other can withdraw into themselves; mediators are sought; and bargaining is set in motion to gain a better deal. These five relationships enacted within the way of life of emanation are not adequate, and it is the breaking of these linkages and way of life that constitutes the current revolution in the Latino family and in male-female relations.

There is something new happening within people. Women are breaking the old connections, in some cases with the support of their husbands. Such a revolution is threatening the role, identity, sexual status, socialization process, and hierarchical structure of the family. The container of the paradigm of emanation is broken, and those lingering fragments of the traditional culture create more and more incoherence.

The response of the Latino male to the breakdown of his traditional role is often one of a refusal to deal with the problem. In some cases a male drinks himself out of a job and into oblivion. The wife takes over as the possessor and wielder of power. But this frees no one; the same relationships are maintained in which the self cannot be released, only possessed. There is a mutual castration: neither men nor women can assert their own consciousness; they are powerless but to repeat. Latino males who are facing opposition from their wives see this frustration as the result of not being able to find a woman who will love them as their mothers loved their fathers. They consider the failure to achieve total security in total possession as the core of their problem. The issue is to be able to love a woman as an *equal* and not as a projected mother or challenge to the mother. When a *macho* looks at a woman he sees not a person but an image in his mind that he projects. Thus, he really sees his own image, seeks to embrace that image, and ends in a narcissistic nightmare. Such relations reveal with a vengance the poverty of power. Males have power to control but are reduced to whimpering children when it comes to the capacity to transform their lives and their relationships to women. The end result of these kinds of sexist relationships cripples *both* men and women. Men cannot grow and become full persons unless they can love women as equals and accept those aspects of themselves which are feminine. The breaking of the traditional patterns of dependence of women on men creates the relationship of incoherence: they stand in the presence of each other and admit that they do not know how to relate to each other. To try to reestablish the old patterns or to refuse to create new and better patterns is to enact all relationships in the paradigm of incoherence, that is, a man now resorts to power and domination and refuses to accept the changes in the other or himself. Thus he builds a fortress in a desert, and all have to suppress their new consciousness. But there are alternative ways by which Latino men and women can relate to each other.

MYTHS AND SYMBOLS OF TRANSFORMATION

Countless fairy tales and myths from around the world speak of the journey of the hero in search of a fulfillment which is achieved through integrating the feminine into his personality. There are many versions, but the following account contains the main elements. A young man leaves his ancestral home, often after confrontation with representatives of the tradition, usually his parents. He overcomes their appeal to love and guilt and sets out. On the road he confronts obstacles such as dragons, robbers, or a forest. He succeeds after great struggles and resists the desire to return home. Finally he comes to the last gate or passage. On the other side is the princess or fair maiden whom he rescues from witches or ugly suitors. The hero is now fulfilled: he has found his feminine counterpart without which he was doomed to be an incomplete, disconnected self. Although these are not sexist stories intended to justify the dependence of women on men, yet there is no denying that given the historical condition of women, these stories were given a male bias.

Our own cultural heritage has much to offer us regarding the complementarity of opposites. In the ancient cosmic mythology of the Nahuas and Mayas (in precolonial Central America) there was the god beyond all gods, the Lord of the ring, known as Ometeotl. This god represented the opposites of the universe: negative and positive, living and dead, light and shadow, male and female. Furthermore, Ometeotl was said to be at the center of the cosmos. To reach such a center of fulfillment, it was required to traverse through passages and rites of initiation involving thirteen heavens and nine hells, all representing a progression to higher levels of existence.[13] The important aspects for our purposes is the awareness that our ancestors had of the integrity of existence—the coming together of opposites, especially the masculine and feminine, for the purpose of wholeness or totality. Furthermore, there is ample evidence of a transforming process which is necessary to achieve selfhood, symbolized almost universally by the birth, journey, death, and rebirth of a hero-guide.

In another story the gods descended into a cave in which a prince was lying with the goddess called Precious Flower. From their union was born a godlike child called the Well Beloved, who immediately died and was buried. Out of the ground, from his body, there sprang many of the plants that were to supply humanity's basic needs.[14] These stories contain apsects of the archetype of the journey that the ego embarks upon to find the source of life within the self. As a tender and emerging reality, the ego breaks from the feminine, maternal hold to assert masculine individuality. But as the myth continues, it is the feminine that is clearly missing in the personality of the hero. When Siddhartha kissed Kamala, and Cinderella was kissed by the prince, there is a magical awakening symbolizing the coming together of opposing principles, masculine and feminine, in a new way that overcomes the old antagonism and leads to the wholeness of the self. Thus, constantly to project the issue of the feminine onto women is to seek liberation by possession of the woman, not by struggling with the feminine within the masculine psyche. Similarly, women also seek to be possessed in order to find security. The mystery is placed in the male, but not in their own selves as women confronting the masculine mystery within. Thus the following dilemma:

> The reward for what his masculinity has become is power. The reward for what her femininity has become is only the security which his power can bestow upon her . . . How do you call off the game?[15]

As we know women are now telling their own stories, forging their own journeys and thereby revolutionizing our understanding of self, male and female, the family, marriage, culture, and the sacred.[16] Ann Belford Ulanov has beautifully and brilliantly written about the search of Dorothy in the *Wizard of Oz*[17] for her masculine counterparts *within* her own psyche which will lead her down the yellow brick road to the center of her own mystery, the self within. Dorothy's quest constitutes the journey of the heroine in search of a fulfillment which is achieved through integrating the opposite masculine into her personality. But traditional male-female patterns do not allow this kind of liberation. Instead, people cling to one another. The male seeks a Don Juan liberation by going from one woman to another, never achieving liberation but simply striking out at the mother-feminine-women-sex demons that he cannot confront. It is difficult to find and identify the enemy.

> The idea of restricting a relationship with a woman to a purely animal-like sensuality, excluding all feelings, is often enticing . . . In such a union he can keep his feelings split off and thus can remain "true" to his mother in an ultimate sense. Thus, in spite of everything, the taboos set by the mother against every other woman remain inflexibly effective in the psyche of the son.[18]

THE AUTOBIOGRAPHICAL: THE JOURNEY WITHIN THE SELF

In autobiography, at least for the moment, a writer knows in his/her depths that he or she is exactly as his or her vision suggests, that for the moment one speaks for humanity as a whole. For now I wish to speak autobiographically. As a male from a Mexican heritage, I feel that so much of what I have experienced and am confronting with my wife and family has a wider significance that I believe will speak to the lives of other Chicanos and Latinos and well beyond our own groups.

> The task of the philosopher (person) is to search himself and to find his own Einsteinian equation against chaos, his own Socratic theory to prevent blindness of the soul.[19]

As a person, as a male, as a Chicano, as a Catholic Christian, I am confronting all of the issues mentioned above. I have found myself for the last several years trying to identify the enemy. I was surprised to see myself and not my father or brother, the representative males in my background, as the problem. I discovered that what I had acquired from them and from the culture was really the drama of possessive love and the god of emanation that gives us permission to possess each other. During the last several years I have had a series of recurring dreams that give some direction to the struggle. Recently my wife and I have exchanged dreams and fantasies. There was nowhere else to go but within, because we had *intellectually* exhausted ourselves trying to find out why we were disconnected. Each crisis ended in a catharsis—a purging of the emotions but with no real change. Everything reverted to the way it had been before.

We cautiously, almost by accident, began one day to move to a different realm. Casual comments about dreams led to an extended conversation. In our exchange of dreams the following motifs emerged. One dream found me in Toronto, where I had attended a university and where I significantly failed to face my own sexuality. Zapata (one of my heroes) and I were in a mazelike trap. We escaped together, and as we were leaving the sports stadium, a man asked for my gun, saying that I would not need it. I gave up the gun, and Zapata and I proceeded to leave. I became aware of the presence of another powerful force. Zapata slipped away. As I walked, I saw Celia, my wife, walking in the opposite direction. I felt guilty that she was not the one who was pulling me—I feigned trying to call to her and kept going. In the distance I saw the attraction: a young woman from my past. I was filled with the sense of urgency to reach her. I quickly awoke. The young woman in the dream was pivotal in my adolescence. I was sexually afraid of her and saw her as a threat to my neatly packaged image of asexual innocence.

In a related dream I remember being in the basement with the same young woman with my mother in the shadows. Recently another dream revealed something further. A young woman whom I had chosen to protect me from sexual chaos because of her strict Catholic moral code appeared in a dream. As I approached her, I saw that she was wearing a black bra; but it was different—it was a nursing bra. Soon I found myself walking down a corridor and saw myself as a young man. I saw the same young woman with her mother, but I was very happy when the mother left. I now felt free to approach the young woman in an erotic manner. She had her back turned to me and was undoing her blouse. I was about to approach her when I awoke.

The dreams point out that I was not able to relate to my wife or to other women as an equal. I either dominated them or, as in this case, allowed them to dominate me when they fulfilled the archetypal mother role.[20] Also the presence of the two young women from my past I recognize as aspects of my own personal needs. What is clear is that Zapata, or myself as a conquering hero, is powerless to win the revolution by forceful domination. There is something new taking place within me. It is important to recognize that the issue in the dreams is not to go and find the woman in the dream. To project onto women what has to be dealt with *within* the personality of the male would be to perpetuate the problem.

My wife has had similar dreams. She has dreamt of living by the sea alone. In other dreams she has been with an old friend. I was threatened by these dreams and wanted to make them cease by dedicating myself more to my wife. In a recent dream I became interchangeable with her father, and she awoke confused. This indicates that there is a father-daughter relationship which is similar to that of the son-mother linkage. Both sets of relationships in too many instances have led to arrested personalities, since they cannot see the opposite sex as a *mutually* fulfilling person.

What Latino men (and it is safe to say that most men) find almost impossible to accept is that their wives could have meaningful and honest friendships with another man. Like Tolstoi's Karenin, to recognize this is to accept that his wife has an emotional life of her own that he thought could not exist apart from him. She has a life of her own, hidden, perhaps, but nevertheless a life of her own.

> But now, though his conviction that jealousy was a shameful feeling and that he ought to have confidence was as strong as ever, he could not help feeling that he was confronted with something illogical and absurd, and that he did not know what to do. Karenin was face to face with life; he was confronted with the possibility that she might be in love with some other person besides himself, and that seemed quite absurd and incomprehensible to him because it was life itself. . . . For the first time the possibility of his wife's falling in love with someone else occurred to him and he was horrified at it.[21]

Latino males have always accepted friendships with women as a possibility for themselves, yet they denied the opportunity to their wives. This is a failure to realize that meaningful friendships with others, for husband and wife, allow them to grow individually and to bring something *qualitatively* new to the marriage.

CREATING THE ALTERNATIVE: THE FAMILY AS RELATIONSHIPS IN MOTION

The family remains a necessary and merciful container for all of us. It provides us with the necessary security, affection, and continuity to begin the process of individuation. But we fail to realize that patterns of relationship emphasizing security and protection are only temporary. In the hostile area in which most Latinos grew up it was essential to have a close-knit protective family. Yet this has led too many Latinos in this country to romanticize and to pass over the abuses in the Latino family. As Latinos we must be careful that in our resistance against the assault on our culture we do not glibly state that *everything* Latino is good. Revolutions have to remain consciously critical of self and other and not allow a tribal fusion to hide the fragmentation. We require courage based on a new consciousness to form our own marriages and families which are neither Anglo-Saxon nor blindly Latino. There is no desire here to consider love, affection, emotion, or close relationships as outmoded. A family that as a group is dedicated to the liberation of its individual members will never be out of date. We need the family but in a qualitatively different way. Too often love is oppressive. What we need is love that frees us to become what nobody can give us—the decision to shape our own selfhood. This is the inner force that begins to demand that the family give us space both internal and external. Thus, to perpetuate relationships beyond the time that they are necessary and to fail to transform our linkages is to create neurotic personalities.

The danger for Latino couples as they attempt to act out new and better relationships in the service of the way of life of transformation is to drift into their own worlds and to create autonomous zones of life. For example, a Latina woman who becomes economically independent can have her own car, schedule, career, friends, and money. The emanation has ended, along with the other relationships used to control her in the paradigm of emanation. She and her husband have become autonomous. The affection given to a possessed wife has grown cold since she made the break. Too often we use sex in retaliation to repossess and renew the mystery. Yet now that the mystique is broken, there is no place for sexual dominance. Slowly there forms what Ulanov calls the rational marriage.[22] Both have busy lives, and there is no transformation. To avoid the real price of incoherence, Latinos might do what middle-class Anglo-Saxon couples do: pull yourself up individually by your bootstraps and develop separate but equal lives. This constitutes a refusal to deal with the deeper issues of mutual love, feelings, emotions, risk, and sorrow. It is a strategy to *avoid* one another. It looks like liberation, but it is not. This is a form of rebellion that ends by allowing our traditional love, affection, and emotions to die rather than be transformed. The "enemy" has won again. The enemy here is the use of contractual relationships, or boundary management and direct bargaining, in the way of life of incoherence. Both partners agree to stay together, knowing that the contract means mutually suppressing passion, spontaneity, and love. This is to participate in mutual fragmentation.

Before a new marriage and family can be built, the old ones must die. Transformation is always preceded by the relationship of incoherence, the breaking of the inadequate relationships that were in-herited or those used to avoid a new and better relationship. The task will not be to set up new permanent roles that result in separating men and women into power positions. We have to create another quality of security, love, affection, and tenderness *without* the price of one's own identity—the family will be free and loving only because its members are free and loving. To create one's own womanhood and manhood is to create one's own marriage and family. Such a task of transformation will demand not set actors but persons growing their own lives with mutual love and respect. Some have succeeded in breaking the old container of the inherited Latino family. These inherited concrete manifestations of our eight relationships proved to be crippling, so they have begun a process filled with risk. Rather than remaining the embodiment of one another or of the inherited image of what the family should be, each of them feel the need to become an embodiment of their own individual self. Now they are free to create a new relationship with one another. They can con-sciously select and maintain linkages, but only as long as they give them the capacity to generate and absorb a constantly changing rela-tionship. They are engaged in the process of growing their own mar-riage and family.

A husband and a wife, a father and a mother, having broken with the inherited concrete manifestations of the eight archetypal relation-ships, are now free to create new forms of the eight in the service of transformation. Previously they were limited to five patterns: emana-tion, subjection, isolation, buffering, and direct bargaining. The posses-sion and jealousy inherent to the relationship of emanation in the service of either the ways of life of emanation or incoherence is based on the need to love and be loved and so can be consciously trans-formed into an affection and love that mutually liberates and fulfills both men and women. Subjection also has its place, such as when a husband or wife, for example, demands that their partner not go to work when they are ill. Such exercise of authority is now clearly for the *benefit* of the other and not to control. Unlike the inherited or created patterns in the way of life of incoherence or emanation, relationships are now exercised for the sake of persistent transforma-tion and are therefore temporary. Thus, after nursing one's partner with care and affection, refusing to allow them to endanger their health, and mediating or buffering between them and their sickness, the time comes for the husband or wife to return to their rightful autonomy as a person with her or his own duties and plans to be carried out. In such a different world of created relationships in the way of life of transformation, a woman can go physically and psychically away to renew herself, advance her own personal skills that will increase her autonomy, bargain with her husband and children for less housework, love her family deeply without possessing them, use subjection for children reluctant to study, admit when she has lost her way, and, finally, be ready to descend into her transpersonal depths again and again and to experience herself as a person open to new ways of being a woman, a lover, a mother, and other roles that now belong to her.

There is no orthodoxy to which to return. Men and women have the same rights to create, nourish, and destroy the inadequate so as to create again. Both are now wealthy with new relationships available to them. Thus, in addition to affection, dominance, mediating, and bargaining there is autonomy, the right to be alone, the right to be confused, to doubt, and to come out of the doubt with a radically transformed life. Nor are there only these eight relationships by which to relate to self, others, problems, and the sacred; we have an infinite number of each one of these archetypal patterns which we can dissolve, shape, and maintain time and again. Men and women relating in such freedom can now see conflict and change as positive, as necessary counterparts to continuity and stability. Their newly won justice is *mutual* growth. Neither women nor men need sacrifice their new ideas and consciousness; they can seek ways to creatively act out their new insights. Men and women are now able to create new linkages to others as persons with skills to share so as to protect and nourish the emergence of others; their justice is one of creating shared benefits for all who come into contact with them; the source of this renewal has been the sacred sources within which were previously blocked by relationships that placed mystery outside of the self. Our own sacred sources are constantly renewed by the same journey that led us beyond the power and possessiveness of the ego to the other within us—the transpersonal self.

Dorothy, like a woman's ego, discovers a central truth, that otherness is

> located both far inside herself and far outside herself. We are once again confronted with the mystery of the two sexes, both far apart from each other and contained within each other, and the mystery of the divine and the human, both far apart from each other and contained within each other.[23]

In a similar manner parents can transform their relationships to their children. Legitimate authority means to lead a person to herself or himself: to lead their children to the center of their own lives so that they can participate in the process of planting the new, not only nourishing and increasing but also learning to uproot the inadequate so as to begin again. This is not a case of liberal permissiveness. If a parent knows that her life is sacred, then she knows that together with her husband they have been given a temporary task to bring other persons to fruition. Thus, all the strategies of transforming used by a woman and man to fulfill each other are also available in relating to their children. For example, one child who has been slow to develop physically must be buffered and given closer attention than another child who seeks less affection and more respect for his or her own growing autonomy. Still, the most independent must also have affection to protect and nourish that autonomy. Parents must be ready to exercise subjection to protect an impulsive or headstrong child against herself or himself. But always a parent must ask, Do I exercise this authority to keep them dependent (in the service of the container of emanation), to hide problems (the paradigm of incoherence), or to allow them to be able to discover their own personhood (the service of transformation). True authority leads each child toward selfhood. The role of the parent is to be a guide, and an authentic guide can only lead a person if they too are on the journey. This is what socializing children is all about—not lectures but concrete, everyday nitty-gritty relationships in motion.

A wife, husband, and each child have as their goal to be at the center of their own mandala, where they can be free to create whatever relationships are necessary wherever they find themselves in relationship to any particular person or problem. To be restricted to enacting only a certain group of relationships at home, to another set at work, and to still another combination with friends is to be fragmented. Freedom means to have available all eight possible relationships and an infinite variation of these. We must avoid having autonomy in the office and returning to inherited patterns of dependency at home. Our fuller freedom heals the split between the private and public, the personal and political, realms of our life. Each of us has the right to be fully who we are whether in the private or public realms of our lives. In enacting any of the eight archetypal relationships we also have the freedom which is both moral and political to enact our relationships in the way of life of transformation and consciously to reject the ways of life of emanation and incoherence.[24]

CONCLUSION

This is what constitutes a true politics of the family: consciously, mutually, lovingly choosing how to relate to one another, ending inadequate relationships and creating afresh in the service of the way of life of transformation. What better way is there to prepare children to grow their own personhood? How better to relativize the power of institutions and to demonstrate that our marriages, our families, our schools, churches, culture, and society consist of our relationships to one another. Institutions are human ways of relating and therefore belong to us to be uprooted when inadequate so that new ones may take root and grow.

Latinos have to be about the business of growing their own peoplehood. As I understand this process, it means the refusal to be assimilated and socially adjusted into an official white, middle-class culture. Boricua, Latino, La Raza, and Chicano are words that represent a political decision to create an autonomous and self-determining life for Latinos. If this is so, then we must resist adopting a married and family lifestyle that represses our spontaneity, our affection and warmth. As marriage partners, people can have their autonomy and self-development *without* sacrificing the best that is within their heritage. Let me give an example. Two mothers kiss their child tenderly and with great affection. However, one woman kisses the child to possess her, while the other gives love to prepare the child for the day when she must leave. The exact same exterior act is involved, but it is radically transformed in the one case by the conscious intent of the mother, by the quality of the relationship involved. The former uses affection to cripple, in our theoretical language, as the relationship of emanation is used in the service of incoherence, whereas the latter mother enacts emanation in the service of transformation. Unless we take the risk of breaking the inadequate and often violent relationships which we now maintain, we will not be free to transform ourselves or our society. The revolution must take place first of all in our depths. Mary Lou Espinosa, a young Latina in Milwaukee, Wisconsin, put it this way in her poem "La Madre de Aztlan":

> Creative solution to social change comes with people who have creative life within themselves, a free woman can creatively contribute with radical solutions because she knows life from within.[25]

William Blake, the great English poet, said the same thing when he wrote that creative union between people was possible only when we have achieved creative unity within ourselves.[26]

Finally, let me comment on our Indian-Christian heritage. We urgently need to rediscover symbols of transformation which have been buried under the debris of fetishism. We have to search out our ancient myths which carry within them the seeds of a sacred process.[27] Let us consider one example from the Christian, Catholic history of Mexico, La Virgen de Guadalupe. The power of her symbolism has been co-opted by a clerical attitude intent upon perpetuating the mother from whom we seek help, making us dependent upon the official Church. But La Virgen can legitimately be interpreted in a different way. Like the White Buffalo Woman who appeared to Black Elk,[28] La Virgen appeared to a poor Indian. She was dark and Indian, *La Virgen Morena*, and she spoke *Nahuatl*, the Indian dialect. She appeared on the very hill where for generations the Indians had worshipped Tonantzin, the Mother goddess. This tired Mother goddess, Tonantzin, was now re-created in a new *mestizaje*, or coming together of the old and new world, the Spanish and Indian, the Christian and Indian religions. The new virgin affirmed the concreteness of the Indian reality while transforming it, something that the official priests and elites failed to do. She came representing the feminine principle of liberation that can only begin the process by first of all bringing chaos. La Virgen can be interpreted as the feminine goddess, the counterpart of the masculine god within the sacred, who does not preserve the status quo but dissolves violent structures in order to build afresh. Furthermore, Mary's virginity was meant to emphasize never the biological but a person who was *at-one-with-oneself*. Thus virginity symbolized a psychological transformation, a new wholeness in both men and women. La Virgen brought about the mixture of the human and the divine that gave birth to the pilgrim warrior, Jesus Christ,[29] the beginning of a renewed humanity. To be like Mary, the Mother, earth goddess, is to be pregnant with our own inner mysteries: the marriage of the human and the divine within each of us can result in the birth of other pilgrim warriors, new manifestations of the god of transformation, other selves, new daughters and sons of the sacred. Such persons will be free to create families and cultures so as to grow new lives for old.

4. The Politics of Transformation in the Latino Community

The Latino community in the barrios has been hampered by internal isolation as well as by economic exploitation in the wider society. Strategies for being political are necessary so that the relationships that impoverish us both economically and politically can be broken and new ones created in their place. To be political is to move beyond transforming our life in the private realm, the family, to reach out to transform the wider family, the community, that is, the public realm.

INTRODUCTION

A culture is said to be a total way of life encompassing such priorities as the values, feelings, beliefs, and traditions of a people. Different cultures, therefore, structure life in a variety of ways. A people patterns, shapes, or institutionalizes its energy according to such priorities. These priorities are in turn shaped by geography, historical necessities, religious myths, and age-old traditions. United States society, or official United States culture, socializes its young from a variety of ethnic and racial backgrounds into patterns largely constituted by Anglo-Saxon and Western-European patterns. In order to compare any two cultures, it is crucial to name these patterns, to identify them, and to spell out their logic. Familiarity with these patterns gives a person the ability to survive in a particular society. They are linkages providing a person with the capacity to deal simultaneously with the five issues of everyday life: how do I live in such a way as to *continue* my relationships with people, yet *change*; how do I *collaborate* with my parents and society's priorities yet *conflict* with

81

them in such a manner that there is mutual benefit and thus *justice* promoted in society? By the same token, the lack of such patterns by which to relate to self, others, and problems constitutes the deprived status of a person or group. Such also constitutes a unique kind of poverty, a poverty of relationships or patterns. Thus some patterns or relationships emphasize continuity and collaboration at the expense of change and conflict. This means that stability is often purchased at the cost of repressing one's own intelligence and experience.[1]

NAMING THE LATINO PATTERNS

Why are Latinos said to be passive, easygoing, quick to show deference? Certainly these are stereotypes, but there are patterns of relating that Latinos share that lend credence to the perceptions of others. Every group socializes its young into patterns, usually four, of which one is a dominant relationship with two or three subdominant patterns of encounter. Latinos have experienced emanation as a dominant relationship, a powerful sense of belonging to a mystery outside themselves, usually focused in the father or mother. Out of respect the children create little, if any, conflict or change. They learn to cooperate and to have a continuous security in the overwhelming strength of the family. Subjection is employed to enforce the stability of the container. Buffering is a relationship through which a third-party mediator, such as an uncle or *padrino*, godfather, can bring about change or conflict on behalf of others. Experience can also be filtered through a web of cliches by which to rationalize life as it is, for example, the phrases ¡Ay Bendito! Good Lord! or ¡Primero Dios! God Willing! When persons in such containers undergo great stress, they can direct bargain with the source of their mystery so as to gain a more tolerable situation. Finally, Latino culture also allowed persons to withdraw into a moody isolation. Men had the right to isolate both physically and emotionally, but due to the burden of carrying the honor of the family, women were not allowed to physically withdraw. When young people marry and grow into adults, they socialize their children by relating to them in these same patterns. The difference is that the son now becomes the father and the new source of the mystery for his family. This is how traditional patterns are repeated, generation after generation in the way of life of emanation.[2]

Others outside the family call forth different relationships, with direct bargaining as the dominant one, such as a father bargaining with a landowner or *patron*, the boss, to exchange labor for crops as

in sharecropping. Middle-class families in Latino countries are precisely middle-class because they have learned other relationships, that
is, the relationships of the international business community. It is
this new way of relating that gives them their status, power, and
prestige, especially when competing with their fellow Latinos.

For quite some time an abundant literature written by such
authors as Oscar Lewis has provided a descriptive analysis of the
Latino family and culture.[3] But this description was inadequate
because what it did was analyze in detail what many of us already
knew: that the Latino family is certainly different from the Anglo-
Saxon model that is presented to us for emulation. Educators have
told us that the Latino child does not look into the eyes of the authority figure out of respect and that they find it hard to compete. These
points we have heard time and again. But what has been missing are
three key ingredients: first, naming and identifying those patterns by
which Latino culture shapes everyday life, second, the alternatives
open to Latinos as creative persons by which to create a new cultural
matrix and, finally, the way of life in which these patterns are being
enacted. Too many writers have merely reported the world. Our task
is to search out a process by which Latinos can go beyond their im-
passe to participate in a process of creating, nourishing, and destroying patterns, relationships, or institutions in order to create again.
This is the open-ended process by which all of us shape our lives and
environment.

UNITED STATES OR WESTERN EUROPEAN PATTERNS

Boundary management is the dominant relationship in the
United States, Western Europe, and increasingly in Japan and other
countries seeking to industrialize. Boundary management is a pattern or way of relating in which persons occupy zones of autonomy,
or areas of jurisidiction, on the basis of custom, competence, or a ra-
tionalized legal system. It stresses the ability of a person to put himself
or herself forward as a competent, aggressive, mobile individual who
is tough. It is a training for future bureaucrats who are concerned
about enlarging their personal boundaries (upward mobility) by fulfilling the expectations of the corporate world. There are three subdominant relationships that usually accompany boundary management:
direct bargaining, subjection, and isolation. Direct bargaining power,
or leverage by which to gain autonomy, is achieved through isolating
oneself and deferring pleasure, by subjecting oneself in order to gain

goals. But as we shall see later in this book, there are other ways to enact these archetypal patterns other than in this socially acceptable manner.

When the Latino and the Anglo-Saxon patterns vie in the United States, there is no doubt as to which will win. This unequal competition begins in the schools. The majority of those who arrive from Latin America have been brought up with relationships stressing respect and deference that cannot compete with the children who have learned aggressive behavior in the relationships of boundary management and direct bargaining in their home environment. This also holds true among Latinos and helps us to recognize the conflict between, for example, middle-class Cubans and migrant workers from Mexico or Puerto Rico. The majority of Cubans, especially those who fled Castro's Cuba in the period 1959-1965, arrived with the key relationship of boundary management, having learned this pattern of behavior and corresponding skills before coming to this country. Thus, although they share a common language and religion, the learned relationships put them in a different socioeconomic class.

Alongside the language barrier is the painful awareness on the part of Latinos that they are being outmaneuvered, outfought without knowing why. This leads to a growing sense of fear, outrage, apathy, or cynicism. In any case, it creates incoherence, a breaking of connections with one's own culture and tradition which is now identified by many Latinos, especially the young, with powerlessness and defeat. The incoherence increases with the inability to relate to one's past in Puerto Rico, Mexico, Peru, or Santo Domingo. They perceive United States society as baffling and rejecting them. The result literally is a group of people *sin raices*, without roots, in either country or culture. At this point some Latinos rebel against their past, reject it, and learn the Anglo-Saxon mores and patterns with a vengeance. Still others choose to remain aloof from the official culture and see any attempt at accommodation as selling out. Too many Latinos end in a kind of schizophrenia: wanting to make it here but rebelling against the heavy cost of repudiating their own cultural roots. Since it is a rebellion, their life now becomes dominated by that against which they rebel, but in an unconscious way. They swallow their past without being able to confront it and to transform it.[4] As one Puerto Rican student related recently, he saw his own culture as weak, nonprogressive, and inadequate. He became so serious that he could not play or enjoy anything lest he lose the initiative in showing this white society that he could beat them at their own game. He did. But at a very heavy cost—his own identity.

Yet we cannot romanticize the Latino culture and condemn the Anglo-Saxon as a monster. Certainly freedom must mean in this context the right to create relationships that include the full range of human patterns. As we have seen, the politics of freedom involves the participation in the creating, nourishment, and destruction of patterns that serve our needs as human persons in the way of life of transformation. Nor is it simply a question of mixing together several patterns. The quality of our lives will depend upon the quality of our relating to ourselves, one another, our sacred sources, and the problems. In the modern age we have come to recognize that all patterns are human made, that they are breaking, and that we now have the option to create new ones. Anglo-Saxon patterns are in trouble because they do not return people to themselves as creators but to an ever-widening search for power and possessions in the way of life of incoherence that locks us all into an insatiable competition. The irony of Anglo-Saxon culture and institutions is that with all their power they end by being powerless to create afresh.[5] On the other hand, for Latinos inherited emanation as a fragment of the dying way of life of emanation cannot provide security in the mysterious other nor sustain us in a time of personal awakening and emergence.

STRUCTURAL VIOLENCE AGAINST THE LATINO COMMUNITY

Latinos have been assimilated into white society on a selective and individual basis. They were not promoted, hired, or selected as members of a group but as exceptions who could be made tokens. Often minority members are isolated from their own communities as a result of their upward mobility and begin to identity with their new colleagues and status. A tacit agreement is made to avoid conflict or demands for change because one's interests are now vested in a respectable position. There is a basic assumption, naive or cynical, that everybody will eventually make it. Advancement is considered automatic as long as people work hard, go to school, or follow the system.

But structural violence cannot be so easily covered up. Some have a vested interest in maintaining their boundaries at the expense of others. Thus when a dispossessed group such as A.T.A. (Associacion de Trabajadores Agricolares), the Puerto Rican migrant organization, attempted to enter the mainstream of American political and economic participation, they were denied. Puerto Ricans and Chicanos are two groups that in relationship to the greater society were isolated and subjected. By organizing they sought to end these debilitating linkages and to create a direct-bargaining relationship that would lead to the formation of an alternative autonomy, a brand-new form of capacity, linked creativity, that cannot be carved out of existing zones of autonomy. In New Jersey A.T.A. has faced an array of hostile law-enforcement officials, a powerful farm lobby, and an indifferent public. Buffers who have sought to intervene on behalf of those who were voiceless have been physically and emotionally abused, such as Representative Byron Baer of Bergen County. This kind of maneuvering constitutes structural violence, since it exemplifies the desire of people to preserve power by excluding others from the very opportunity to gain human standards of living. In this case law and order become a mask for violence in the way of life of incoherence. The above example is an excellent way of seeing how persons enacting boundary management in the way of life of incoherence fundamentally differ from those creating new forms of boundary management in the way of life of transformation.

Let us consider some other examples of "invisible violence" presented to us by our "best and brightest" boundary managers: it is invisible violence because it has become part of the fabric of our everyday life.[6] In 1972, when negotiations were being carried out by the State Department and North Vietnam, the Pentagon continued to bomb because those bureaucrats had their mandate to expend their ordinance (bombs and rockets) so that they would be able to justify a larger share of the budget. The A.M.A. has consistently stifled legislation in favor of national health-care insurance so as to maintain a scarce medical delivery system, thereby assuring the medical profession's inflated salaries. We have all heard of the old-age-home operators, the mental-health personnel who have a vested interest in creating dependence, the direct opposite for which they were established; like the Pentagon some law enforcement officials develop a vested interest in promoting false crises to justify bigger budgets, power, and prestige. These are acts of structural violence against all of us. Like Big Nurse in *One Flew Over the Cuckoo's Nest*,[7] the power of so many people in our society rests upon keeping other people crippled. Within her boundaries she creates a turf, with no limits, through a deliberate mystification of her authority and person. At this point bureaucrats cease to be efficient, rational managers and become obsessed with their area of jurisdiction such that it becomes a personal fiefdom. It is no longer boundary management but emanation; the office is now an extension of one person's views and whims. This is one reason why so many hardened bureaucrats fight change: it is viewed no longer as an attempt to change an office procedure but rather as a personal attack. The irony is that they become irrational through having created a small fragment of life into a life-and-death issue. As a result it becomes emanation in the service of incoherence.

And finally, let me give an account of an example in which I was personally involved. Three years ago an Anglo student who was in charge of a several-thousand-dollar budget for student entertainment approached a Puerto Rican and asked him what he would consider appropriate to fit the cultural needs of Latino students. The Puerto Rican student was offended and suspicious. The Anglo student was hurt at this reaction. This is a perfect example of incoherence: two people stand in the presence of one another and do not know how to cooperate or continue, for everything is conflict, and they do not know how to change so as to relate meaningfully. Both feel there is an injustice. Now who is the enemy here? Certainly it is not initially either of the two students; it is the hidden agenda of U.S. society. That hidden agenda consists in the following: those with positions of power believe that they have achieved it legitimately and that they have every right to wield that power. Those who have no power will have to get it like everybody else—by hard work and other legitimate means. But the Latino student knows when he confronts an Anglo student with power that it is not merely one Anglo that he confronts face-to-face but that this established student has all manner of benefits at his disposal: he has a strong fraternity as a base; he has the keys to the Xerox machine; his father, a lawyer, knows the dean on a first-name basis; he himself knows the ins and outs of setting up a complex concert and carnival; he is usually a full-time, resident student; in short, the Anglo student at that point *is* U.S. society. The Anglo student saw a "deprived" minority student and genuinely wanted to reach out. But he extended himself as one with power to dole out some privileges. The word "privilege" here is most significant; too many whites do not consider minorities to have a right to good health, employment, adequate education, and decent housing. For Latinos, blacks, and Asians these are privileges, benefits which may be distributed by whites, but which whites feel they have an inherent right to, since their ancestors earned them for them. Ultimately the term privilege is a racist term. The privilege here is to be white, and since all the tricks in the world will not make people of color white, too many Anglos see minorities as their burden living on the edges of white beneficence and power. In other words, power of its very nature is power because it is scarce: you find out how much power you have by comparing yourself to those who have no or less power. Power in this logic can never be shared. The incoherence here is the good intentions of the Anglo student in a cultural context dominated by competition, power, and an institutional racism that reduced those good intentions to condescension and humiliation. In the final analysis what the Puerto Rican and other Latinos want is the capacity to affirm themselves, and therefore zones of autonomy become important *because* they protect the task of creating alternatives. As long as power is in the hands and at the whims of others who hand it out, it perpetuates a relationship of dependence, which is made more tolerable by occasional flashes of paternalism. The confrontation between these two students described here has its carbon copy in the whole welfare mentality. Welfare payments do not change the relationships of isolation and subjection. Welfare often deepens the despair by hiding or buffering the real issues. In Alan Paton's superb novel of South Africa, *Too Late the Phalarope*, Japie, the social worker, is a buffoon.[8] He prevents and puts off the confrontation with the real causes of crime, unemployment, and bad housing. He tinkers with the fringes of the system when the real cause is racism. But his duty is not to expose but to preserve the illusion that people are poor, ill-fed and badly housed because of their own fault. This public relations facade hides the real ironic cancer of such a society: when one group of human beings systematically deprives another group, they brutalize themselves in the process. There are no victors, only victims. This is the real meaning of the powerlessness of power.

The logic of gaining strength by uniting and negotiating for autonomy is a dangerous one. The same old, tired politics in the way of life of incoherence have been reproduced in the various social service agencies in Washington to the effect that as a minority group learns official United States patterns—boundary management and direct bargaining—it then dominates the minority groups arriving later on the scene. A hierarchy has developed among minority groups. Blacks promote blacks; Chicanos, Chicanos; and the Puerto Ricans who are the last to arrive are in their turn at the bottom of the pecking order. This is the logic of individualism on the societal level. The system has had its revenge. Those who sought to beat the system and to tell others what they wanted to hear end by themselves being controlled by the present consciousness of United States society; in other words, when previously dispossessed groups achieved their own power, they closed out the group that has not yet learned to survive in America.

THE POLITICS OF TRANSFORMATION

We need a politics of transformation. To be political is to participate on a plane of equality with others in shaping our daily lives and environment; politics is what we can and need to do together. Nobody gives us permission to be political; it is part and parcel of being human. By transformation is meant the conscious breaking of inadequate patterns, the movement through confusion, and the creation of fundamentally new and better patterns that capacitate people to experience themselves, one another, their sacred sources, and problems afresh. There is a growing awareness that mystery lies not in the mystique of the powerful other or in the efficiency of systems that end by reducing us all to victims. The mystery exists in individual persons who discover that their own personhood is the source of creativity. People can take patterns and relationships into their own hands and transform them. Now when a Latino *chooses* to use boundary management or direct bargaining, it is a temporary choice that fills limited needs in the fuller human process. Boundary management and buffering used in the matrix of transformation produces men and women with professional skills who protect human dignity in liberated zones. A lawyer can now use legal skills to protect rather than exploit. The liberal agenda of living with incoherence allows an entrepreneurship that exploits the needs of others for personal gain. Boundary management in the way of life of transformation demands on the personal and group level selves acting autonomously but for the common good. Emanation is also transformed so as not to contain and possess but to be a temporary relationship to nourish until emergence results, so that there is a mutual realization of each one's own mystery. Parent and child are now free to become friends. Persons thus awakened can bring to bear on problems a new consciousness, creativity, new relationships, and a mutual justice—all made possible because these persons are in touch with their deepest selves or sources of transformation.

To be political in our communities consists in empowering ourselves to use all eight of our human relationships in the way of life of transformation rather than the three or four which most societies employ in order to relate to self, others, and problems. We have only eight archetypal patterns but an infinite number of different ways of enacting these relationships. How better to relativize the power of institutions and to demonstrate that our political organizations, our schools, churches, economies, and neighborhoods, the *barrios*, consist of our relationships to one another. What changes in every use of the patterns is the intention, the quality, the ultimate way of life in which we enact them.

EMPOWERMENT IN THE LATINO COMMUNITY: THE HELPING PROFESSIONALS

The modern age comes to a society when there is a breakdown of the linkages by which a people have dealt simultaneously with continuity and change, cooperation and conflict, and justice. This is the experience of incoherence. We live now during such a period characterized by separation and the inability to communicate with or understand each other. We are all in trouble. Both the Latino and Anglo-Saxon cultures are inadequate. Latino and Anglo alike are now truly equal in their mutual need and vulnerability.

Latinos in need of services approach agencies with a sense of their subjection and isolation. Social welfare agencies constitute large boundary managements which were established to buffer on behalf of those who could not create change in their lives. Too often the roles created by these patterns establish a power relationship. Bureaucrats usually take on the consciousness of defending the system. Some genuinely desire to help but find themselves frustrated and eventually embittered by the red tape. The bureaucrat and the citizen are both victims. To insist on standard operating procedures in a situation demanding alternatives is to demonstrate that bureaucracy is based on repression. The bureaucrats who wish that they could reach out and who have genuine compassion must repress such sentiments because they would wreck the system. The system, or ways by which people are trapped in relating to each other, stands convicted because it takes on a life of its own and turns the service personnel and the clients into things. And yet what is this system, this thing, this ogre but our own relationships, our own institutions that have run away with us. This is incoherence. But many seek to press on, thereby avoiding the truth of how they feel. They continue to work "as if" there was nothing wrong. "Lifers" are found in all agencies who believe that if you keep the rules, the rules will keep you. This loyalty to a system, or fixed way of organizing life, is an example of emanation in the service of incoherence. To give one's self to a system in order to block out the pain is the denial of self and other.

Yet there are those who can now set about creating new relationships in order to confront the problems of daily living: Latinos who have shattered the inherited container which demanded submergence in the mystery of another and Anglo or Latino helping professionals, such as public health nurses, teachers, social workers, welfare workers, and other community aides, who have liberated themselves from an inherited reliance on bureaucratic methods by which to process people. Our political and sociological imagination does not allow us to stereotype. Two women walking into a government agency may look like two hardened bureaucrats with the same job description, but one might be prepared to use her personal skills to create structural change. We need allies everywhere.

Some helping professionals are "wounded healers."[9] This phrase means that only those who realize their own pain and wounds can reach out and help heal others. It must be a mutual therapy. This attitude removes the power relationship and introduces a different kind of nurse, teacher, or social worker. This type of helping professional does not give people anything nor reach down in condescension: he or she is always ready to seize the opportunity to put themselves out of business in the lives of others so that new relationships of mutual healing might be wooed into being. They realize that poverty is more than financial difficulty; poverty is also the absence of vital connections. There is an awareness that what constitutes a real problem is that the incoherence caused by the lack of crucial linkages destroys our wholeness as persons. Consequently, they ask what relationships are missing and what linkages are essential to provide us with the necessary kind of capacity and performance to remedy our lives. These sensitive and caring people can be appropriately called political innovators.

An example of such transforming people are those who planned and carried out a marvelous conference in New York City on mugging and the senior citizen.[10] At first sight it seemed like the typical approach: protect your purse, carry a whistle, and so forth. But the conference listed seven muggers, and heading the list of perpetrators was the Social Security system itself. Last on the list was the youth who was himself considered a victim of high unemployment and poor educational opportunities. This was a remarkable program that allowed the seniors to identify clearly the enemy: a culture and ways of relating that logically led to a society attempting to buy itself out of their lives by sending them a check once a month. Senior citizens also came to see that their own personal situation was caught up in a broader systemic context. This helped them to see the causes and not the symptoms. In this example social workers did not function as buffers to prevent conflict and confrontation but enhanced the need for reflection and action.

Let us analyze what took place here. Social workers aware of the processes of transforming relationships used their professional position in a structure, or their boundary management, in a subversive manner. They used their official status to buffer or mediate on behalf of senior citizens not to perpetuate but to end their isolation and subjection. Senior citizens met one another, discussed their common problems, and established linkages that now allowed them to have their own boundary managements, senior citizens' organizations, which empowered them to bargain with politicians, state agencies, universities, and others. This is a transforming boundary management that was shared in a context of community that allowed caring relationships. Here the nuclear family was extended to include a larger family of people sharing the same concerns and vision. This kind of strategy has freed many senior citizens from self-pity on the intrapersonal level, liberated them from a dependency on their mobile children, and brought them to a keen political and social awareness of American culture and society. In this way senior citizens who were victimized as isolated individuals were now politicized. They shaped an environment that took into account their needs. Thus, their poverty had consisted in more than lack of money and services; they had also suffered from a lack of relationships to each other. This is why it is so important to know which relationships are present, what relationships need to be broken, and what relationships to create in order to enable ourselves and others to confront problems. This is the kind of creative imagination with which we wish to challenge the whole of the caring profession. There are no blueprints or formulas but only human beings with their emerging consciousness and creativity who know that institutions as human linkages belong to all of us. This drama of create–nourish–destroy–re-create demands social workers who go beyond job descriptions and who are still creating what it means to be a helping professional, that is, they are in the process of nurturing their own relationships to real people.

The condition of Latino senior citizens is one of being trapped in the same debilitating relationships of isolation and subjection. Their isolation is often increased by their lack of knowledge of English. Fear of being mugged or robbed and of arson leads to increased isolation because senior citizens are afraid to leave their homes and apartments. Thus the incoherence is deepened. The strategy described above is an excellent example of what can be done in all of our *barrios* to end the relationships of solitude and mere survival and to set in motion a whole chain of events. And this is exactly the strategy used by Chicano/Latino organizations such as Communities Organized for Public Service (COPS) and United Neighborhood Organization (UNO) in the Southwest, especially Texas, and in California. COPS is probably the largest neighborhood organization in the United States. In fact, COPS has had a lot to do with transforming the valley of Texas and even the rest of the state from an Anglo political reserve to one where Chicanos are now a force both politically and economically. Organizations like COPS, UNO, La Raza Unida, the G. I. Forum, the League of United Latin American Citizens, and Valley Interfaith have given voice, hope, and a feeling of accomplishment to Latinos who were ignored for so long.[11]

In all of these examples we see empowering relationships being created in a new context of transformation. People were now able to change and create conflict with others, whereas before they were limited to continue cooperating in their own loneliness. To confront politicians and bureaucrats as a group and to realize successful intervention on at least one issue led to a different and new kind of consciousness of what they could do together. They creatively set about establishing new institutionalized forms of power, in organizations, that did not exist before. This institutionalization of power assures that they will not be sent back to their solitude by being a one-issue, overnight phenomenon or a one-act drama of transformation. To be successful, they had learned to share their ideas, apartments, resources, and lives. This is a new kind of justice that allows everybody to participate in the cost and the fruits of a common struggle. The process was initiated by activist organizers or helping professionals acting as guides. However, it was the people themselves who discovered the ability to risk, to begin life anew by drawing the strength from their own personal depths. Furthermore, these are examples of people enacting new concrete forms of the eight relationships and especially creating for the first time in their lives new relationships like boundary management, the most important relationship in United States society. But this is not assimilation, since the people enacting this relationship were not pursuing *individual* power and self-interest according to the way of life of incoherence; this is the liberal Anglo agenda. They enacted boundary management on both a personal and group level in order to connect themselves to each other in a particular alliance to achieve *common* goals. The people created a fundamentally new and better relationship of boundary management in the way of life of transformation.

Let us now turn to consider another area of extreme importance to the Latino community's empowerment—education, specifically the role of bilingual/bicultural education.

*CREATING NEW CONNECTIONS: BILINGUAL/BICULTURAL
EDUCATION*

Our phrase bilingual/bicultural must be taken seriously. It already implies and demands a synthesis, a coming together of opposite cultures and languages out of which emerges a third enriched reality that was not there before. To lose either one of these cultural expressions as a result of racism, colonialism, or other forms of subspeciation is to impoverish us all. We who are both members and representatives of the various Latino communities in the United States must take care not to allow the permanent wounding of our people. It is estimated that prior to 1940 only 1 percent of Chicano children growing up in the Southwest were enrolled in school.[12] This helps to explain why we have so few persons from that generation who were prepared to protect the community with legal, educational, and medical skills. They were consciously crippled by an Anglo attitude of superiority and an economic policy that sought to create a permanent illiterate and unorganized work force. Even now the dropout rate among Latinos in our schools, due in part to a lack of bilingual resources, is alarmingly high. In New York City 31 percent of all Dominican adults speak no English. It is no wonder that, given the lack of English skills, together with other factors, the median income for Dominican families in New York City is $9,681.[13] In order to prepare our youth for these patterns that are necessary to survive in U.S. society, we must provide them with the tool of language. Recently a young man from the Brookings Institute who represented a Latin American nation in its dealings with a multinational corporation spoke of how he could have cried in reviewing past contracts that put Latinos at a disadvantage. It was a twofold language problem: the Latinos did not know English nor did they know the legal language of contracts. English allows our people to participate in recognizing how established power manipulates them. The ideal is to educate simultaneously in English and Spanish. Our desire is to maintain Latino language, culture, and history, while acquiring new cultural traits and English. But wherever bilingual programs exist, we must be equally serious about the bicultural dimension, that is, Latino history and culture. However, we must not forget that bilingual/bicultural programs carry the philosophy of the funding agency, the Department of Education. As a bureaucracy, the Department of Education is not committed to the transformation of our society. Federal programs are primarily intended to alleviate the social and political pressure brought to bear by groups who are essentially excluded from American society.

Too often government buffering hides, or buys time in order to avoid, the real issues of dependency and powerlessness. In fact, federal programs strengthen the system; they are not intended to transform it. Thus, this really is an example of buffering in the paradigm of incoherence, because it allows most of United States society to pursue power as individuals while fending off the poor to save the system. This is the liberal agenda. The guidelines for establishing federal poverty programs give us an insight into their ultimate direction. Those guidelines stipulate that professionals, or, in our language, boundary managers, are to initiate, organize, and implement the programs. Thus a stronger middle class too often emerges at the expense of people who remain in hopeless impoverishment. It thus becomes a class issue that splits our community because some people increase their status, power, and prestige, while members of the same ethnic community remain behind. We have to remain critical of these programs lest they lull us into a false sense of security.

Our basic hope lies in essential linkages being formed between the bilingual/bicultural programs and the community. It is necessary to subvert the intentions of bureaucrats whose conscious or unconscious aim is merely to extend the doctrine of individualism to our people. By "subvert" is meant to do the direct opposite of what was intended: rather than allow bilingual/bicultural programs to assimilate us into the mobile, competitive mold of living with incoherence, we have to prepare our youth to survive here by teaching them English, but simultaneously to assist them in finding the sources of creativity in their own cultural background and above all within their own selfhood.

Bilingual/bicultural programs can truly politicize our people. First we must remain critical of programs run by our own and other professionals by asking questions: Do we have the resources to teach English and Spanish simultaneously? If not, then which language should get priority, and why? What is necessary for our people to survive here? Second, our people must have the right to critique *both* cultures, not just the Anglo-Saxon. And finally, through a return to their own personhood, as a source of creativity, they can now set about truly being political: participating in the shaping of their daily lives and environment. Perhaps the greatest danger to avoid is the permanent isolation of our people from the rest of society. It is possible to argue that the French in Quebec helped to structure their own political and economic subordination in a predominantly English-speaking nation. Their official language and cultural policies to an extent helped create the recent political climate of separation. Feelings of powerlessness were aggravated by not knowing the English language, which is the vehicle to more economic, political, and social participation. Too many French responded with a permanent posture of going it alone over and against a hostile, English-speaking Canada. The blacks in the United States did not make the same mistake when some tried to romanticize and teach black English in the schools. Blacks saw this as a subtle form of racism, because it would prevent them from communicating with the world of power. In a very real sense blacks are bilingual. They have their black colloquial forms of communicating, as all groups do, but they also knew the necessity of knowing the language of the market economy. However, it is essential to know the complexities of the market economy in another sense so as to be able to transcend it, that is, not to allow the mentality of competition to dominate our consciousness. Thus, persons well schooled in the tricks of the market can also establish viable cooperatives that economically and politically allow people to participate in their own advancement.

Nevertheless, given all of these objections and warnings, bilingual/bicultural education has become a rallying point for Latinos throughout the United States for several reasons. First of all, the large influx of recent Latino migrants into a society and economy that is increasingly becoming more dependent on high technology makes the learning of English essential. When my father arrived in Detroit from Mexico to work at Ford Motor Company, he did not need English to get and hold a job. He made a relatively good wage and never learned to read or write English; he understood English but spoke it only when necessary. But these kinds of jobs are no longer available to Latinos. The millions of jobs created in the last three years are primarily in the service area, which are generally low paying and nonunionized with little chance of advancement. The new generation of Latino children need bilingual/bicultural programs to avoid becoming a permanent economic underclass, or what Mario Barrera has called "a colonial labor force," with ranks filled by Latinos whose needs are made subordinate to the greater society.[14]

Another reason for Latino insistence on bilingual/bicultural education is to remedy the wounds of the past. We have few professionals today because past generations of our children were, and still are, labeled as "disadvantaged," "culturally deficient," or "linguistically deprived" and are often placed in E.M.R. classes (Educable Mentally Retarded), remedial classes, low-ability groups, and vocational tracks. I.Q. testing was always done in English and so resulted in lower scores. Transfer students from Puerto Rico are inevitably placed in lower grades. These policies based on an attitude of racism caused many Latino students to drop out or fail. Latinos are the youngest population in the nation, with at least 44 percent under the age of 25. Therefore, what happens in the schools is of fundamental concern to the Latino community. Some cities already have a very high percentage of Latino students. In New York City, as of 1979, Latinos comprised 30 percent of the school population; in Los Angeles, 45 percent; in San Antonio, 52 percent; in Miami, 32 percent; in Denver, 31 percent; in Hartford, 35 percent.[15] Many of the children speak only Spanish or are not proficient in either language. Language problems together with discriminatory attitudes have devastated Latino students as is evidenced by the following facts based on the 1980 U.S. Census: A mere 24 percent of all Latinos in the United States have completed high school; 3 percent have graduated from college (usually, junior college) as compared to the total U.S. population of 19 percent. The dropout rate in many urban centers reaches as high as 85 percent. The dropout rate in Newark, New Jersey, for a Puerto Rican student is four times that of the state's average and twice as high as that of black students. In 1975-76 Latinos received only 2.8 percent of the B.A. degrees awarded; 2 percent of the M.A.'s; 2.6 percent of the law degrees; 2.3 percent of the medical degrees; and 1.2 percent of all doctorates.[16] These educational statistics largely explain why fully 38 percent of Latino families have a yearly income of under $10,000. These figures clearly highlight the correlation between educational achievement and socioeconomic well being. For these reasons Latinos are adamant that this educational terror shall not continue.

To address this crippling of Latino children, the community became politicized on the local and national levels. For the first time on the national level Latinos were politically successful. The passage of the first Bilingual Education Act in 1968 was largely due to Latino political pressure. This law and the Lau vs. Nichols decision, primarily involving non-English speaking Chinese, made the retention and advancement of language and culture a political right.

The creation of bilingual/bicultural education provided access to Latinos in many areas of the country to city, state, and federal jobs. It opened up a whole new area for Latinos in teaching, administration, grant-proposal writing, consultant work, publishing, and law. For the first time Latino parents were elected or appointed to school boards. Federal monies funded bilingual fellowship programs and bilingual teacher training grants; many states opened offices for Hispanic Affairs as a direct response to the influx of federal grants and political pressure. The result was a gradual closure of the gap between the demand for bilingual/bicultural programs and the availability of personnel to provide the services. Much needs to be done, but a solid beginning has had its effect.

There are the inevitable arguments over whether bilingual/bicultural education is or should be compensatory, transitional, and ultimately assimilationist. Some Latinos demand complete bilingualism on all grade levels; others are not sure if this is desirable. Such a policy should be decided by the local Latino population, who know their own needs and the resources available to fulfill them. The bottom line is that some form of bilingual/bicultural education is a nonnegotiable right to help Latino children acquire the educational development necessary to survive in the United States. Bilingual/bicultural education is not separation but *mestizaje*, the blending and enrichment of two ways of life and linguistic expression. The other goal of bilingual/bicultural programs is to provide enrichment for a monolingual and culturally impoverished society. Therefore, a foreign language should be universally made available in grade school, especially Spanish. By the year 2000 three out of every five persons in the Western hemisphere will be Spanish-speaking. Finally, bilingual language opportunities give to all minorities who need the assistance the right to become participants in the nation's economic, political, and social life without abandoning their language and culture.

For all of the above reasons bilingual/bicultural education has become a symbol of both the gains made by Latinos in this country and their hopes for the future. For the foreseeable future Latinos will continue to come in large numbers to the United States, regardless of pending legislation like the Simpson/Mazzoli Bill. Bilingual/bicultural education is here to stay, not only to ease the transition from Latin America to the United States but also for the continuing enrichment of all Latinos and their fellow citizens.

The real creative task remains: How shall we continue what is best in the Latino culture while accepting Anglo-Saxon patterns of behavior essential to survive? In other words, is it possible to be authentically bicultural. It is conceivable that our youth will simply assimilate as some have done. Perhaps this is a hopeless task. But I believe that these issues can be addressed from within our heritage. It is precisely our cultural resources that have largely been forgotten, within which we can rediscover age-old symbols and myths of transformation.

LATINO SYMBOLS AND MYTHS OF TRANSFORMATION:
A PEOPLE OF THE SUN

> Whereas the first half of the night, when the westering sun
> descends into the belly of the whale, is dark and devouring, the
> second half is bright and bountiful, for out of it the sun-hero
> climbs to the eastward, re-born. Midnight decides whether the
> sun will be born again as the hero, to shed new light on a world
> renewed, or whether he will be castrated and devoured by the
> Terrible Mother, who kills him by destroying the heavenly part
> that makes him a hero. He then remains in the darkness, a cap-
> tive. Not only does he find himself grown fast to the rocks of
> the underworld like Theseus, or chained to the crag like Pro-
> metheus, or nailed to the cross like Jesus, but the world remains
> without a hero, and there is born, as Ernst Barlach says in his
> drama, a "dead day."[17]

A symbol or myth of transformation can be said to be a bridge
of concrete and colorful images that puts us in contact with the
timeless and unseen rhythm of the universe. The nature of this contact is such that we are reminded that we are the living carriers of
such a rhythm. We participate in the rhythm of creating, preserving,
and destroying so that we might create afresh. We are sparks of the
divine who, when we create in the way of life of transformation, show
forth the face of the Source of Sources in the world in a new way.
If we do not participate in this process, we impoverish ourselves, our
sacred sources, and the world. This is the poverty of the god of emanation, the *status quo*, the orthodox and repetitious. Our symbols then
have the power to elicit and reawaken in us our divine spark, our
selfhood, which is rooted in the transpersonal. The best of our *curanderos* (healers), shamans, *espiritualistas* (those who could divine evil
or benevolent spirits), and *brujas* (women with mysterious powers)
of Latin America were aware of this mystery of the human and divine
intercourse in the depths of the self. Our many gods and goddesses
are a religious realization that the sacred is expressed in an infinite
number of ways. Our lives become the vessels within which the
sources will come and brew their new transformations. But we must
wrestle with these forces to make sure that they are manifestations
of the god of transformation.

> "After all," he said, "we are a people who live on the roof of
> the world; we are the sons of the Father Sun, and with our re-
> ligion we daily help our father to go across the sky. We do this

not only for ourselves, but for the whole world. If we were to cease practicing our religion, in ten years the sun would no longer rise. Then it would be night forever."

I then realized on what the "dignity," the tranquil composure of the individual Indian, was founded. It springs from his being a son of the sun; his life is cosmologically meaningful, for he helps the father and preserver of all life in his daily rise and descent. . . . Knowledge does not enrich us; it removes us more and more from the mythic world in which we were once at home by right of birth.[18]

Taino, Aztec, Maya, Aymara, Inca, Tlahuica, Puebla, Moor, African, Basque, we are all people of the sun.* From time immemorial our people have watched the heavens and daily participated in the death and resurrection of the sun. Our rituals, lifestyle, religion, survival, culture has largely revolved about the sun-god-hero. The sun brought warmth, hope, growth, and life itself. For our ancestors it meant the essence of existence. Marvelous associations grew up centered around the sun. What a magnificent scene it is in "The Blood of the Condor" when Ignacio, the Quechua Indian leader, goes to the top of the mountain to "fill himself with the light." For to be enlightened was not to be able to see the externals but to perceive the *internal* threat to their way of life by the presence of the Peace Corps. Ignacio was filled with a new consciousness as a result of placing his own source in touch with the Source of all life. This renewal led to a political participation to alter his environment.

Let us look at two specific examples of the role of the sun in our heritage. First of all, let us consider the myth of our participation in divinity and creation. A Pueblo Indian tale, *Arrow to the Sun*, as adapted by Gerald McDermott,[19] is extraordinary in its beauty and

---

* Latinos are certainly also people of the moon. Among the Indians of Mexico and Central America gold was considered to be the sweat of the sun-god, whereas silver was said to be the tears of the moon goddess. If we are to maintain our understanding of reality as dialectical, that is, that transformation emerges out of dialectical opposites, then certainly the moon must also be reinstated to its central position. After all, the poverty of the Christian God was that there was no struggle, no competing opposites, only a repetitive god that knew all things. The Indians of our heritage realized that every god had his counterpart goddess. The masculine alone was not human, but totality of selfhood was feminine and masculine. Thus the pyramid to the sun-god at Teotihuacan in Mexico is dialectically related to the pyramid of the moon. The dark side of the moon was the unknown or dark side of the sacred, whereas the sun represents the magnificence of the divinity in all *known* splendor. But it is the undifferentiated source that haunts us as we struggle to bring the dark into the light.

simplicity. According to this tale we are sparks of the divine, offspring of the sunfather who seeks and needs our cooperation in the building of the world. It is essentially a creation myth that tells us of our divine origin.

Long ago the Lord of the Sun sent the spark of life to earth. As in the biblical tale of Jesus' miraculous conception, the hero is born of a virgin with the Sun as the father. All heroes are god-begotten. But when the boy grew up, he was unhappy in the world of mortals. He was anxious within himself to know his father and his true origins. To prepare himself for the struggle of life, he sought his source. He traveled about, asking for help until a wise man, the Arrowmaker, realized his divinity and reshaped the boy into an arrow. The Arrowmaker as guide fitted the boy-arrow to his bow and flung the boy to his father-sun. When the boy landed, he cried out with great joy, "Father, it is I, your son." But the Sun would not accept him without testing him. The boy was given a fourfold test: he must pass through the four Kivas of lions, serpents, bees, and lightning. By passing through this second birth the hero is twice born. When the boy came forth from this last stage, the Kiva of Lightning, he died but was transformed with a new life. Anyone who has suffered the double birth must be regarded as a hero, a child of God. Consequently, the father and son rejoiced. By having entered into the devouring jaws of death, the hero now won the right to be called the Son of God. The Sun-God now flung the son back to earth in the form of an arrow to bring the spirit of the sun, or participation in divinity, to the people. When the son appeared, the people celebrated his return with the Dance of Life. As Jesus on the Mount, the boy was transfigured and showed forth his father in the radiance of his face. Like the Buddha and Jesus, our Pueblo Indian hero lives among the people to bring them the message of all heroes, that you must find the spark of divinity, your own hero and heroine, within yourself. This mythological tale of the hero portrays the fate of all conscious development, and the four Kivas, or rituals, represented here symbolize the development and journey of every child. The boy has put himself, and we through him, in touch with a participatory self, so that *together* with our sacred sources and others we build the world.

> Now I know what it was, and knew even more; that man is indispensable for the completion of creation; that, in fact, he himself is the second creator of the world, who alone has given to the world its objective existence—without which, unheard, unseen, silently eating, giving birth, dying, heads nodding through

hundreds of millions of years, it would have gone on in the profoundest night of non-being down to its unknown end. Human consciousness created objective existence and meaning, and man found his indispensable place in the great process of being.[20]

THE SUN DANCE

The sun dance religion of the Shoshones and Utes of the Central Rocky Mountains and Great Basin of North America was born of misery and oppression, in the early reservation period (circa 1890-1900). It persisted in a context of misery and oppression, and in the late 1960's it flourished as the major religious movement on the Wind River Shoshone reservation in Wyoming, the Fort Hall Shoshone-Bannock reservation in Idaho.[21]

In his book on the sun dance Joseph G. Jorgensen points out that the dance was rediscovered as a result of the incoherence in which the Indians were caught. They knew that the days of freedom on the Plains were gone forever, yet they did not know how to proceed beyond the abyss. The dance was in many ways a response to the depths, a profound desire to return to transpersonal sources for the necessary courage to transform their lives. However, there are times when the author misses the importance of the sun as a symbol of transformation. Jorgensen saw the sun dance as a sign of rebellion in the face of the white world that forbade such rituals. But it is more than rebellion; rebels are dominated by the consciousness of those that they attack. The danger is that the old gods might reappear in new clothing and simply try to restore a dying world through rituals or warfare. The sun dance represented the emergence of the sacred, that is, the numinous experience that there was a sacred process that was being reborn in the Indian. The brave dancers knew that they were suffering not only for themselves as individuals but for their people, for the whole of creation. The dancer was tied to the center of four poles and understood that the four directions met in his body, so that he himself represented the center.[22] It was essentially a dance of faith that allowed the individual to be vulnerable to the rays of the transpersonal that would destroy the old sloth and renew the face of the earth. Often the new vision that was given was unacceptable precisely because it did not attempt to return to the old world and tired gods. The Source of Sources was entering into a new participation with individual persons who would then carry the message to the people.

Each was asked to participate in the new rituals that linked the individual to the sacred in a new conversion.

Perhaps one of the most remarkable aspects of the sun dance is its ability to symbolize and reenact the synthesis of opposites. This is a very important point because it makes us aware that inherent in the Indian culture was the attempt to reconcile opposites. We have spoken of creating a new synthesis between the individual in United States society and the demands of the sacred and of the community on our love and loyalty. United States society has chosen the individual and the way of life of incoherence to the exclusion of communal well-being in the way of life of transformation. This highlights the importance of the Latino culture rediscovering the sources of transformation. The sun dance was not a means to achieve power but a capacity, or linked power; it was a ritual that affirmed the transpersonal, the individual, and the community *simultaneously*. Individual power is an Anglo-Saxon trait that is based exclusively on conflict and competition. Capacity, or linked power, is fundamentally and qualitatively different because it asserts the fulfillment of all through mutual commitment.

> The attainment of power through individual and collective effort, through individual and joint suffering, should not be minimized. Each living thing sacrifices its power—the trees, the bushes, the earth, the flames of the fire, the singers, the dancers, the committeemen, the spectators—so that others may live. The synthesis of death with life, the passing of power from one form (dying) to an opposite form (the living), is made complete in the sun dance.[23]

THE SUN AS MANDALA

Our forebearers performed all their dances and rituals, built their lodges, passed the sacred pipe, and constructed their villages in the form of a sphere, circle, or mandala. Their most important symbols, the sun and the moon, were spheres radiating their blessings in the six directions: north, south, east, west, upward, and downward. The center was simultaneously the center of the individual, the tribe, the universe, and the sacred. To be at the center of the mandala was to be in touch with "the" Source and one's own sources.

> Among the mythological representations of the Self, one finds much emphasis on the four corners of the world, and in many

pictures the Great Man (self) is represented in the center of a circle divided into four. Jung used the Hindu word *mandala* (magic circle) to designate . . . the "nuclear atom" of the human psyche . . . The Navajo Indians try, by means of mandala-structured sand paintings, to bring a sick person back into harmony with himself and with the cosmos and thereby to restore his health.[24]

The mandala is a symbol of totality and eternal procession. What occurs in the inner cosmic psyche of the human spirit has its counterpart in the cosmos without. An ancient alchemical text entitled *Amor Proximi* tells us that:

> Ye see that the earth turns to the sun but the reason ye know not . . . so this turning around shows us that the world was once renewed, and in its beginning, as sun is punctum, it desires to return, and its rest will be alone in that; therefore the soul of men is also similarly gone out of the eternally divine sun, towards which it also yearns.[25]

In this creation myth the deluge signals the beginning of the work of rebirth. Similarly, the Indians of Borinquen, the Tainos, believed that following the destruction of the evil spirit of wind and flood, Huracan, the transformative god of fire, Yocahu, or the sun, who had his throne in the high mountain, would appear to renew the souls of the people and the land.[26] The mandala as magic circle, sun wheel, sphere, symbolized the totality and wholeness of human beings and the cosmos. Each day the rising sun encompassed the awakening world in its sunburst.

There is a danger that symbols and myths of transformation, which are too often excessively masculine in their imagery, will be subverted and be used to co-opt our inheritance. Some people would use these symbols of renewal to lull us into a world of the golden past that is no more than tinsel. Our culture resides within us, and our symbolic treasure has the power to elicit from us again the creativity that has lain fallow. In the final analysis I have not presented these images of color and beauty to develop a mystique of passive reflection. The culture belongs to us as men *and* women who have the right to re-create it. Here I return to the theory with which we began. The symbol for our theory is a sunburst, a mandala that returns us to the realization that as sparks of the divine we must participate together in the building of a new culture and world.

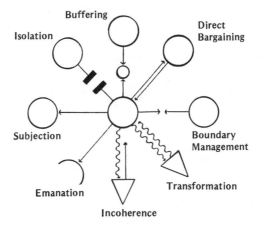

This means that we must be political and sacred people who are capacitated by their source to break the hold of demonic forces (the Huracan) and to be reborn (the Yocahu). As centers of creation we refuse to be links in a long chain of tradition that merely repeats the past. Rather than living on the fringes of the mandalas of others as satellites, we must become links in a chain of transformation. To do so we have the ability to participate in creating the fundamentally new. Thus Mexicans, for example, are not trapped in an Aztec heritage that involved sacrificing human hearts to the god of death, Huitzilopochtli. Our sacrifice shall consist precisely in devising new ways by which to enhance the sacredness of our lives. We must not allow the gods and goddesses of our past to rule us. As sacred persons, our tradition is to struggle until we win a new blessing from the Source of all Sources.

5. Latinos and the Sacred

To be a self and to be political is to be nourished and renewed by one's own sources that in turn are grounded in the realm of the sacred, the Source of Sources. Latinos have always been a deeply religious people, but at times our religious fervor went astray and we accepted the false gods of possessiveness, power, or assimilation. The god of orthodoxy always legitimizes a status quo *that denies the struggle between the human and the divine which is necessary so that the* we *and our source can be* mutually *transformed.*

LATINOS AND THE SACRED

The sacred is discussed throughout the pages of this book; this is as it should be, because the sacred permeates our lives. The sacred has always been with us. Every civilization and culture has created rituals and religions, literally links to the sacred. Gods and goddesses were given human or animal characteristics so that humans could contact a quality or virtue with which they could identify. Symbols and symbolic tales or myths also pointed us beyond the concrete, tangible world to the unseen sources of our lives. People have always had visions, heard voices, received messages in dreams, or have fallen into trances. People who had such special gifts were considered blessed by the community because they communed with the sources of the spirit. These gifted individuals were set aside by the people and called shamans, witch doctors, *curanderos* (healers), *espiritualistas* (spiritual mediums), rabbis, priests, or ministers. They were honored because they could put the community in contact with the sacred. So they became mediators between the human and the divine.

Gods waxed and waned; they came and they went depending on the needs of the people and their own maturity. Tired gods were retired, and often new gods came with conquering armies. Competition among gods also took place. Greek and Roman gods became angry, fell in love, became irrational, and fought each other. The gods were often playful. The Aztecs, Mayas, Tainos, and Aymaras had gods for the sun, death, water, fertility, hurricanes, rebirth, and transformation. The German god Odin ruled the primeval forests. Quetzalcoatl got drunk and was expelled; he took a trip to recover his powers and promised to return. The alchemists attributed divine power to their alchemical experiments; they spoke of and practiced a process of transformation whereby sacred elements like quicksilver and sulphur acted as gods in transforming base metals into gold. They participated with the gods in the ancient alchemical process of transformation: *coagula et solve*, that is, creating and nourishing and dissolving in order to recoagulate or give new form to the underlying realities.

The people of the Middle East had temple virgins who served jealous gods. At times the priests took the virgin in the name of their gods in order to fill the virgin with the power of the sacred. Often this divine-human intercourse became a mere cover for lust and passion. The Jews were always on their guard against false gods of the surrounding tribes because Yahweh was a jealous god. Christians spoke of the one, true God in a triune mystery of Father, Son, and Spirit. Yet Mary and the saints were often gods and goddesses who represented regional deities, that is, local gods were baptized by being given a Christian name.

Tolerance among religions and gods was the usual state of affairs. Often gods with different names were adopted gods and so were actually the same god. The Muslims were especially tolerant of other people's gods as long as they were considered to be lesser gods before Allah. Intolerance sometimes led to murder and slavery in the name of the sacred. A move toward strict monotheism in Christianity, especially medieval Catholicism, led to an emphasis on the only true religion. Inquisitions were established to determine doctrinal purity, and God became an avenging god: people were killed. The Spaniards brought the Catholic religion to Latin America and declared the religion of the *indigenos* as idolatry. The codices of the Aztecs were burned because they were considered demonic.

The Bible is a story of the relationship between the sacred and the human that clearly points out the desire of the sacred to interpenetrate the human and the desire of the human to become divine. The Old and New Testaments are the stories, the tales, the myths of the human, divine struggle. To wrestle with sacred sources was to wrestle with the meaning of life. Freud's contention that people turned to a god/father out of fear is partially true, but the sacred was not there as an alien, imagined, or external god; the Source of Sources was in the depths of our being represented by a whole pantheon of gods. Some gods did what Marx and Freud criticized: they left us childishly dependent and passive in the building of the world. But not all the gods demanded the same docility. The Book of Genesis, in fact, tells us that we are made in the image and likeness of God. That image is not a physical description but a symbolic one, of a God busy creating. If we are of the same image, it must be as co-creators of the world, together with the sacred.

The gods express themselves through archetypal forces or underlying patterns that shape our daily lives. Archetype is the name of a power doing something to us: it is a relationship with the sources.

> I call archetypes "necessary" forms because if we are to enact any relationship concretely, we can do so only by expressing our energy and matter in accordance with underlying forms hammered out with our participation by the force of the sources.[1]

But if human beings were not to be merely the playthings of the gods, subject to their every whim, how could we participate in the shaping of new and better lives? Moreover, what really is the significance of the human/divine struggle, what is the purpose of it all? What we have already seen in earlier chapters is that we are moved within our depths by three ultimate paradigms. These three ways of life are fundamentally different ways by which we interact with the sacred to shape the emanations that emerge from our depths. Moreover, it is only by struggling with these sacred sources that we can give expression to fundamentally new and better relationships.

The sacred is present to all humanity and has been expressed in an infinite number of different ways. All the gods referred to above come from the same undifferentiated source, or Source of Sources. It is up to us to distinguish between the forces that emerge from this transpersonal source.

> Ever since we left the realm of the concrete we have been talking about a realm of living forces which is not ours to command but which can command us. They are forces that come through us, and may well run counter to external or internalized conditioning and preferences. If our ego is not strong enough to contend with them, we will become possessed by them; at times we can even become psychotic. If our ego is strong enough to

repress these forces, but therefore also not strong enough to deal with them freely, we are likely to turn neurotic. In order to prevent our being inhibited or undone by these living forces, our knowing participation with them is crucial. And participate we can, if we prove to be at once receptive and struggling in helping to give concrete shape to these forces.[2]

Our theory of transformation allows us to ask new kinds of questions that more adequately address themselves to the religious situation of Latinos. It is time to renew the religious quest again. Max Weber, Emile Durkheim, and Karl Marx all did the necessary analysis for their time through showing the dialectical relationship of religion and society.[3] These men took religion and its impact seriously; it was a fact of human life whether they agreed with its influence or not. Lately too much of our study of religion has been just that, the study of *religion*, that is, the residue of the religious factor. Weber and Durkheim perhaps more than Marx saw this dynamic aspect of the religious and traced its hardening in specific cultures. It was this residue that Marx and Freud primarily[4] referred to in their critiques of religion. Ernest Troeltsch, in his classic work on church and sect, also saw the human tendency to canonize, legalize, and routinize original religious insight and creativity once the fervor of the original experience cooled.[5] In this work we shall agree with Wilfred Cantwell Smith's distinction between religion as object or thing, as residue to be analyzed, and the religious as adjective—as a quality of human life that has an autonomy of its own within the context of human life.[6]

Our alternative theory by which to study Latinos and the sacred holds the following hypotheses: that it is only through a symbolic analysis of what it means to be human that we can hope to reach the religious source of persons. Our theory holds that the sacred is a fact of human experience, and this religious dimension can best be approached by the incarnations found in human religious symbols and myth. It points to the quality of our relationship to the sacred. These patterns or relationships of encounter are dialectical, that is, they involve a mutual interpenetration of self-other-world-sacred sources. In terms of method this means that there can be no such thing as a value-free, detached analysis, resulting in quantitative studies, nor can we have participant observation as semidetachment. Our method is based on the foundation of the religious, that is, transformation, and that takes place only in persons.[7] The religious is not to be ignored or passed over to other disciplines. Our problem is not with social science but with an inadequate social-science paradigm.

What we need, then, is a theory that will allow us to analyze the religious experience of persons without doing violence to human inquiry or to the experience of the sacred.[8]

Traditional social scientists merely report the residual categories of religion in an empirical, positivistic, behavioral manner. With questionnaires and statistical correlations they turn our vibrant struggle with the sacred into an abstraction. They never tell us anything about the revolutions in our depths. Consequently, they miss the revolutions and see the new only in terms of the old. Our theoretical perspective can point out the inadequate linkages that inhibit the growth of the religious and even enter into a participation that will lead to the breaking of religious ties for the sake of creating alternative ones. This is a theoretical approach that enables us to develop a political and sociological theory that parallels the theological, religious, and personal witness that all reality is subject to the three acts of the drama of transformation: emanation, incoherence, and transformation. From time immemorial we have religious myths and symbols that tell us that the rhythm of the micro- and macrocosmic is symbolized by a three-headed god-goddess: Brahma, the Creator; Vishnu, the Preserver; and Shiva, the Destroyer.[9] The alchemists also realized that base metals could be dissolved (solve) in order to be recreated (coagula) into gold.[10] Similarly, the heart of the Christian Kerygma was the birth, death, and resurrection of Jesus. The moon waxes and wanes, all of the cosmos follows this rhythm.[11] According to this perspective, reality is of a piece but with an infinite number of different expressions. The American Indian was aware of this same cosmic unity. The Oglala Sioux, for example, believed that wherever they pitched their tepee, there was to be found the center of their own being, the center of the tribe, the universe, and God simultaneously.[12] In other words, this was a felt and experienced philosophy and epistemology of being. Being is synonymous with reality.[13] God, the religious, the sacred, the source of all being, the undifferentiated source, the holy was always considered an integral part of life. But due to reductionist and positivist trends, especially since the eighteenth century, myth, symbol, the religious, and mystery became cause for embarrassment. The traditional social scientists, eager to quantify like their colleagues in the natural sciences, cut us off from our sources. Thus, when social scientists say that they know something, they know only a truncated reality. They know, for example, how many go to church but not the quality of their relationship to the sacred.

Subjectivity and intersubjectivity are the touchstones of reality to which there is now a fruitful return. How do persons experience being/reality? By experiencing oneself first of all and encouraging others to experience themselves, persons participate in reality. In the Muslim, Jewish, and Christian mystical tradition there is a beautiful proverb: To know yourself is to know *your* god, not God or *the* god, but *your* god.

Symbol and myth are central to understanding and interpreting all religious experiences. The source, or the dark side of our consciousness, was twofold: our personal unconscious and the transpersonal unconscious, or God. Both of these were for C. G. Jung the source of our mystery. It reveals itself to us through the images inherent to myth, symbol, and ritual. Symbols and myths are thus our bridge to the source which sustain us. The quality of our lives in every regard—psychologically, sociologically, religiously, politically—can be determined by the quality of the connection that we have to our source. We externalize, incarnate, or concretize the sacred source as one of the three gods to which we are related. If we simply repeat the incarnation for generations as in the service of emanation or incoherence, then we break the dialectical relationship and allow the source to possess us, thus robbing us of the ability to create change or conflict. Thus, routinization, or symbols turned to fetishes, lose their authority simply because they no longer connect us to our source in a transformative manner. For example, the eucharist becomes a legalistic banquet detailing the disposition of every crumb lest Jesus be lost on the altar or communion plate. This is to reduce Jesus as a god of emanation. This linkage must be destroyed in order to reaffirm the force of Jesus as a transforming god who seeks a new incarnation through us by which to express the Source of all. For this reason, even in the midst of the most inquisitorial conditions there arose the countertradition, that is, the recognition and implementation of the fact that human beings could reexperience themselves, the universe, and the sacred by participating in gnosis, or knowledge of the process of transformation. Orthodoxy in the service of the god of emanation knows only to preserve the tradition and can never allow us to reexperience because it would mean the death of the tradition which was part and parcel of the legitimation of social, political, and religious structures.

We do ourselves a grave injustice and create distortions by refusing to take our sacred sources as part and parcel of our daily lives. Heisenberg has taught us that even the scientific community returned to philosophical and religious issues when the prevalent scientific view was in its death throes. Niels Bohr underwent what was in fact a religious experience that provided him with the courage and renewed creativity to plumb the depths of the atomic mystery. He first of all had to reexperience the reality of mystery in himself[14] and beyond his own personal depths to a more profound transpersonal mystery. There is a further distortion and loss that affects the scientist, the doer of inquiry. If a scientist merely mirrors the world, he can never participate in his own or the world's transformation. He is caught in a one-dimensional world. We have ample evidence that scientists have discovered parallel phenomena in nature by creatively playing, that is, imagining and seeing new possibilities.[15] The implications of this are crucial for human participation and creativity. It gives a significance to the scientist which is of ultimate importance. She does not repeat nature or other phenomena; she actually creates, together with underlying sources, herself and the way we see the world in a new manner. The scientist participates in giving direction to forces within and outside herself.

> What really landed him in trouble was that he saw the concrete archetypically. He saw the motions he saw as necessary relationships. The Pope objected that Galileo was necessitating god, so that god ceased to be all-powerful. . . . God himself thus becomes subject to the laws of creativity through which he expresses creativity. The science which grows out of this position . . . is an inquiry which liberates, energizes and gives significance to the scientist.[16]

Our purpose is to use mythical, religious, and symbolic language to free ourselves and others from the paradigm of fixed faith. Fixed faith, in whatever area of human knowledge, ends with a sterile orthodoxy that does not permit a renewal through a personal experience of our own sources.

ARCHETYPAL ANALYSIS

> We know the fix of stereotypes, not the movement of archetypes.[17] Everything has two faces, its own face and the face of God.[18]

Some forty years ago Arthur O. Lovejoy delivered his famous lectures on *The Great Chain of Being*.[19] Lovejoy's study correctly criticizes the Catholic Church that sanctified a frozen, permanent, fixed chain of being. Everything flowered from on high and was incarnated once for all. The course of human history was fixed and irrevocable. The eternal ideas manifested themselves as a continuity of an already finished scenario in the ultimate paradigm of emanation. In the paradigm of emanation human beings merely receive the world and final truth. Lovejoy's mistake was that he himself never understood that the *Aurea Catena* was a dogmatic reinterpretation of a continual transforming process. In contrast to the paradigms of emanation and incoherence, the paradigm of transformation demands our participation in the completion of the self, the undifferentiated source, and the world. Our dialectical process tells us that there are three stages to being or reality: destruction, re-creation, and nourishment. To incarnate once and for all is to deny that anything fundamentally new can emerge. Myths and symbols of transformation, if they have not been reduced to impotent fetishisms, allow us to bridge the movement back to the experience out of which we created our gods and religions in the realm of the sacred. Through the image and emotion elicited by myth and symbol we contact the other side of the established institutions of a society, the transpersonal sources.

Now archetypes are the necessary forms in which concrete relationships manifest themselves; we contact the archetype through symbols in dreams, visions, and fantasies on the personal level and in myths and religion on the societal level. Although the archetype is universal, it is imperative that we, as individuals, constellate archetypes in a personal concrete manner.[20] We are constantly enacting sacred dramas. Archetypes have their origin from the undifferentiated source, or the god beyond god. They represent the collective inheritance of humanity rooted in the Source of Sources. The source of all, therefore, manifests itself through archetypes. Every concrete expression, creation, or incarnation in the world is thus the manifestation of the transpersonal archetype that is an expession of the nameless source. We have thus a trinity: the source from which we all derive, our connection to the source, and the concrete. When a person or persons incarnate themselves as history, culture, and society, they differentiate and express the sacred in their midst. But which god is being incarnated? If we *and* the Source of Sources cooperate in creating, nourishing, and destroying in order to build again, this is only possible with the god of transformation. When a political ideology, a scientific paradigm, a marriage, a religion, or a theory stresses stability, normalcy, continuity, equilibrium, growth indices, or puzzle solving, it breaks the dialectical process between the human and the divine and seeks to establish and nourish an orthodox face of the holy once for all.

The exclusive choice of one religious expression cuts us off from our source and allows us to be possessed by that one god of emanation or incoherence. Any form of possession is demonic. This is the essence of idolatry. There are three gods in our personal, political, and historical drama. In order to create and reexperience self, other, and history, we must first break the security through enchantment. To simply repeat self, other, and history is to stereotype the world as a particular god's final revelation. This is a disservice to all involved, especially to God. We have rejected the orthodox chain of fixed creation in the paradigm of emanation primarily because it posits a preestablished plan for all time. Human freedom is of ultimate significance for the following reason: if God is indeed the undifferentiated souce, there is no concreteness in the source. Furthermore, the undifferentiated necessary existent possesses no differentiated consciousness. Human beings, because of their consciousness, are necessary to the source to continue the pouring forth of the divine creation into the world.[21] Therefore, it can be said that if humankind needs the source, then the source is in its turn dependent upon human persons for the completion of God. This gives us a more relational and dynamic insight into revelation. Revelation has been defined as God's entry into man's making of man.[22] But our theoretical perspective allows us to restore the full implication of a theory of transformation, that is, that revelation is mutual in that it is also humankind's entry into God's making of God. Whenever this archetypal process of transformation is reexperienced, it constitutes a rejection of the god of emanation, an acknowledgement that we no longer know what we thought was permanent, but also involves refusing to serve the god of incoherence, to pursue power and self-interest so that we can participate in the formation of the new energies together with the transforming god emerging from the undifferentiated source. This is the essence of personal therapy, political and social change, and religious conversion.

The implications of this understanding of revelation is that neither humankind nor the undifferentiated source is complete. Galileo and all the members of the countertradition speak of necessary forms in which any concrete relationship must express itself. Thus, it follows that in their understanding the Source of Sources is not all-powerful but is himself subject to the laws which are laws of relationship in motion. God also, therefore, ceases to be fixed and is still flowing forth with creativity.[23]

Human beings become creative gods in the realm of the concrete through an act of participation in the ultimately significant relationship with the sacred. This perception of the human role in building the world, in incarnating the divine, further underlines the complete bankruptcy of detached, value-free, quantifying science carried on by many social scientists. Our theory allows us to be dialectically related or connected to our source and to the concrete world. We can *scientifically* ask whether the *quality* of this connection to the sacred allows us to change yet continue, to cooperate with one another yet free us to disagree, so that we can go on creating new forms of justice. Are we free to allow new consciousness to emerge from our transpersonal source into the process, create new kinds of linkages to ourselves and others in such a way that our development is not at the expense of others but ends by opening up new possibilities for everybody? Let us repeat: *our* choice is crucial, so that the above questions are posed in relation to self (intrapersonal), others (interpersonal), groups (intergroup), and nations (international) and our sacred sources. Our freedom is rooted in the following:

> We are free to choose which archetypal drama will best serve the purposes of transforming.
> —Our freedom of choice is based on the realization that there are many and competing archetypes or gods from which to choose.
> —Our choice is archetypal otherwise we would not be able to move beyond our own concreteness; this is the basis of our transcendence rooted in our own godhead or selfhood.
> —All archetypes are not finally established; if they were, our freedom to participate in transforming would be an illusion. Thus, if the human being is to be freely creative, God must be imperfect, i.e., unfinished.
> —Finally, we must be able to participate in the creation of new archetypes, which posits ourselves and the source as mutually vulnerable.[24]

Our paradigm based on a theory of human relationships sees the encounter between self, other, and the sacred as the most fundamental dialectic in human life. According to this view, connection between individuals, groups, ideas, and the source from which everything comes and the quality of those connections are what gives us capacity to simultaneously change yet continue, to conflict yet cooperate and achieve justice.

REDISCOVERING TRUTH IN THE PERSONAL ENCOUNTER: THE LATINO CATHOLIC SITUATION

Happily the archetypal human being is attracted to our participation both by necessity and by affinity. The story of creation speaks of a drama which moves teleologically, but not by the power of a single-minded will, either god's or ours, but through a dialectical struggle whose very nature was set in motion by the source of sources. Our kind of consciousness and work is needed in this struggle because it exists nowhere else in the links of transformation. Since the source of sources did not create anything *ex nihilo* but out of himself, he lives in us as we live in him. Therefore, our participation is the vocation of our being and a sharing in being.[25]

Most Latino Catholics[26] were reared to believe that in religious matters they were never to follow their own interpretations. They always had to speak "the mind of the Church." Dreams, visions, speaking in tongues,and other religious experiences were denied validity. Heresy was always around the bend. The Roman Catholic faith was a powerful container that nourished and answered definitively all of the perennial questions: life, death, meaning, hope, love, God, the world, and the whole of reality. This was fixed faith in the way of life of emanation.

The crisis of this nurturing stage came quickly and furiously following Vatican II. The challenges to authority are familiar to us all: the birth control controversy, celibacy, collegiality, liberation theology, the demand for married and women priests, and so on. Many of us were caught off guard by this upheaval. But the breaking of the secure container ended once and for all the monolith of the Roman Catholic Church. For this reason we shall include no statistics of Latino Catholics in the United States, diocese by diocese, and no graphs attempting to demonstrate the rise or fall of contributions in relation to liberal reforms. The question to ask now is: What is the quality of the connection that those of us who call themselves Roman Catholics and/or Christians have to their own tradition? Are we, as Latinos, in the process of nourishing, destroying, or re-creating our tradition? And we cannot make this determination once for all, since from one moment to the next a Latino who has been secure in a religious tradition might find himself driven out of it by the exigencies of responding to concrete problems. Also such people can reject their own pain and choose to submerge themselves deeper in the inherited past in order to escape the incoherence. We only know that we cannot stereotype or label Latino Catholics, Pentecostals, or any other group; nor do questionnaires and statistical studies offer us much help. We need to study the flow of life for all groups and ask not only what choices are available to them but also will they be willing to pay the cost of such choices? But how can our incoherence be transformed? The polarity of incoherence is a necessary experience of the journey on the way to act III that all of us must take: it is not necessary for us to become trapped in the paradigm or way of life dominated by incoherence. The encounter of incoherence means that we stand in the presence of others and of ourselves, and we no longer know how to relate. We only know that we cannot go back to the old ways of relating. It is part of a process of breaking out and relinking. Let us turn now to an analysis of our task through the perspective of the archetypal journey that successfully continues only when we walk with the god of transformation.

THE ARCHETYPE OF THE JOURNEY

We can perhaps best speak of the religious quest as a journey. It is a journey that takes place both within the depths and without in the everyday world. In prehistoric times people consciously enacted rituals which involved traveling to almost inaccessible caves which they transformed into sacred spaces by adorning the walls of the caves with representations of animals upon which they were dependent for life. The journey was a hard and dangerous one. Christ enacted this same archetype in his *via crucis* (way of the cross). Through this way comes redemption. "I am the way, the truth, and the life" was a conscious utterance on the part of Jesus which transformed the archetype and shaped the attitudes of all the ensuing generations of Christians that have tried to reenact this road of conversion and salvation. Christianity, Buddhism, Confucianism, and Islam all represent conscious religious formulations of the archetype of the journey whose pattern determines the behavior of persons moving toward a sacred goal.[27]

The journey consists of an archetypal drama with three acts: the stage of the container, the shattering of the container with the experience of loss and dread, and the creation of a newfound wholeness. These three stages also correspond to our three ultimate paradigms of emanation, incoherence, and transformation. Erich Neumann traced this movement from embeddedness in others to the emergence of the individual by speaking of the gradual separation of consciousness out of the unconscious.[28] This process of differentiation was necessary so that human beings could shape an ego consciousness in relationship to its personal and transpersonal unconscious sources, that is, the sacred realms. But first the ego had to assert itself against the nurturing instinct symbolized by nature as silent, dark, and unconscious. The unconscious was from earliest times symbolized by nature. The rejection of nature in its role as overpowering source initiates the stage of the hero who was born in rebellion, protest, and fear. Polarized in this way, the danger was that the assertive ego would soon tire of its rebellion and be devoured by the dragon of emotional exhaustion due to sin, shame, and guilt, to return as a prodigal child to the eternal truths of the parents. However, by responding to the voice of the spirit, or higher principle within, the ego could successfully face and slay the dragon. But this is not yet maturity but only adolescence. The hero still lives by his wits and seeks to overcome others through strength and domination. To pursue power and self-interest as a way of life is to enter into the paradigm of incoherence. The ensuing sense of suspicion fragments him from others; yet he seeks wholeness. So the final act or stage of the archetypal drama is to rediscover the transpersonal realm of the sacred sources no longer as devouring but as the source that is now also dependent upon human participation in order to come out of the depths. This is symbolized by the integration and rediscovery of the underlying sources as a necessary aspect of the pilgrim warrior as a participatory self that together with the sacred sources bring about the wholeness of the human person. Human and divine activity as opposites are now coinciding opposites that cooperate to bring about a new reality.

Manfred Halpern has re-visioned this journey of breaking, polarizing, and relinking in more explicit religious terms.[29] He speaks of *ein-sof*, the god beyond god, the undifferentiated source, as being connected to three archetypal gods: the god of emanation, the god of incoherence, and the transforming god. Each god has its own kingdom that corresponds to what we have described earlier as our three ultimate ways of life. Moreover, all lesser gods are in the service of one of these three major gods. Opposite are some sketches that symbolize the activity of the three deities and the journey toward mutual participation with the Source of Sources.[30]

The source of sources in act I emanates or creates first ego, which corresponds also to the stage of nourishment. The child, or first ego, is not yet fully conscious of its own innate abilities but it is conscious of being fulfilled by others. In a sense the person here is really in a pre-ego stage because he or she is not aware of alternatives; they can only live within the givens of their world. If our first ego remains in this stage because of fear, a sense of sin, shame, or guilt, then the god that presides over persons is the god of emanation. The connecting link with the Source of Sources actually freezes the endless flow of relatedness in a one-way divine monologue that becomes an arrested flow. Furthermore, it is like Jacob forever needing God's protection and remaining Jacob rather than becoming the man who resists security and thereby is renamed Israel, he who struggles with God. To stay in the container is like Dorothy of *The Wizard of Oz* returning to Kansas and acting as if nothing new had happened to her; there is no new consciousness. The god of emanation is a jealous god who legitimizes and gives rise to a whole socioeconomic order based on possessing the body and souls of others: jealous husbands, the possessive ruler, the person accepting their niche in a given reality. This stage is also characterized by repression, an unconscious psychic control of one's own desires. In chapter three on the family we spoke of the patterns of dependence that were used to rear women in the Latino culture. These linkages were not just man's will: it was a scheme of life blessed by god, but not just any god but a tribal god, the god of emanation. So the god of emanation links us to the Source of Sources in such a way that the Source is not challenged, revealed, or resisted but only repeated. This constitutes an arrested manifestation of the Source of Sources. An example of this god of emanation as a tribal god was the Aztec god Huitzilopochtli, who gave the Aztecs permission to sacrifice nonbelievers.

Act II is initiated by an original sin against the orthodoxy of the fathers. In a sin committed against the parents, the god of emanation is also slighted and so sends anxiety attacks in the form of guilt. The Spanish for guilt is a very powerful and image-provoking term:

THE ARCHETYPAL DRAMA OF TRANSFORMATION

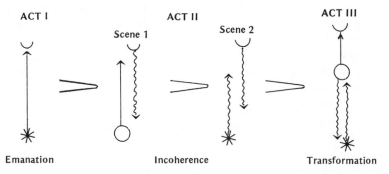

remordimiento is derived from the verb *morder,* to bite. So guilt is intended not only to bite but to *re,* continue to punish you. All of the energy locked up in the repressed self is now released. The energy initially takes the form of anger, *coraje,* in order to make us bold enough to make the break and to let the god of emanation die in our hearts. Once we cancel the guilt, the old web of meaning falls apart. But this is a dangerous period. We are now polarized, with the old god of emanation dead or dying. What now will hold us together in common cause with others? Now the original shattering of the container of emanation and the demise of its god is act II, scene I. Scene II of act II begins with a sense of loss and depression. We descend deeper into the depths and are there open to transformation as well as to deformation: a new god of emanation returning with an old face or the god of incoherence that organizes the chaos and so makes it possible for us to live with incoherence. Notice how the symbol for this stage shows a disconnectedness from the transpersonal and yet includes an attempt to reach out and assert human independence. It is a flowing forth and forming but still a stage of fragmentation. In scene II, act II, we are really emptying ourselves so that we do not return to the gods behind the old concrete relationships. The gods take on new forms such that we believe that they are dead when they are still there. The gods are always present, but the more we ignore their presence, the more they will possess us. So even "secular" men and women pursing power are serving a god, the god of incoherence. The god of incoherence impoverishes the Source of Sources since this god links us to the Source in a way that cuts us off from any creativity intended to transform our fragmentation. In deformation the lord of nothing captures us *and* the Source of Sources and binds us both in the depths.

> We are in touch with *ein-sof* as the depth of our transpersonal unconscious only when we are gods of transformation. When any other god becomes our source of being, then that god stands as a barrier to our further access to *ein-sof*—to our deepest source . . . and so also as a barrier to transformation. The other gods present themselves to us as if life started with them and not with *ein-sof.*[31]

In act III there is, for the first time, a mutual interpenetration of the human and the divine. The Endless is free to reveal itself as the Source of Sources because we have now chosen to participate and become a transforming self due to the inspiration of the god of transformation. Our symbol for act III shows a mutual activity that involves a new qualitative link to the sacred; the god of transformation links us to the Source of Sources, so that we now have a chain of transforming links in which the sacred and the participatory self is essential. We can now place something new *concretely* in the world that was not there before.

> The god of transformation is never omniscient or omnipotent. The god of transformation is perfect only when we are prepared to participate in order to create. . . . Our task is to help god into wholeness ever more often and covering an ever larger network of life. . . . The Source of Sources has incomparably more power than anyone else but the Source of Sources has complete capacity only when it connects to the god of transformation and also manifests itself thus in human beings.[32]

We ourselves constitute and are the god of transformation in the sense that each of us can be one of the manifestations of the Source without exhausting the Source. And yet we are always more than merely a concrete manifestation of the Source, since our personal identity is always rooted in sacred sources.

This image of the journey allows us to make important distinctions that conventional sociology of religion could not do. For example, a typical questionnaire could ask if people believed in god, but it could not tell us which god a person accepted or rejected. In other words, the conventional social-science approach could not tell us the quality of the linkage to the sacred which is determined by one of our three gods. As a result, the data collected tells us almost nothing.

There is much more we can say as a result of seeing the religious quest from the perspective of the journey described above. We now know that there are no monolithic religious communities. Catholics, for example, are to be found in the service of all three gods. Therefore, a Catholic who journeys with the god of transformation has more in common with Hindus, Baptists, or Anglicans who travel with the same god than with a Catholic who is committed to the god of emanation. Furthermore, we can distinguish between three kinds of priesthood and ministry. A priest or minister is really a guide on the way, but they can only guide us to the sacred drama that they have experienced. Consequently, some will try to cover the fragmentation by leading us to give ourselves totally to Christ. This is to reduce Jesus to a fragment that attempts to cover our sense of loss regarding a worldview once holding the Catholic and/or Christian world together. This also incapacitates us because we take no action to incarnate the sacred through our own lives. These priests and ministers prepare us to ignore the incoherence by masking, repressing, and distorting our concrete problems. They urge loyalty to a fragment of the paradigm of emanation that is losing its ability to explain the whole of life. Other ministers preach an accommodation with the culture: we are urged to settle for less in this vale of tears and to pray for a better day. This integrationist or assimilationist approach is taken by many white ethnic clergy whose own ethnic group has been brought into the mainstream. We are urged to see god as the source of our mutual blessings and to pray to this god for further promotions. This is the god of incoherence who legitimizes the pursuit of power; it is this god who "helps those that help themselves." Irish Catholic clergy are prone to this approach. Moreover, Irish clerical academics often do not know how to reconcile their theological education that stresses love for individuals and their scientific social training that turns people into bloodless abstractions. In an attempt to blend love of neighbor with abstract social data they strive to develop studies that *neutrally* show patterns of discrimination or racism against Latinos. Some urge changes to let people into the system, while failing to critique the very foundations of a society that created and maintains a lower class based on racism, sexism, and classism. So, these ministers both in the ecclesiastical and academic pulpit teach us to live with incoherence. I personally witnessed Chicanos in South Texas in 1960 sitting in the back of a Catholic church while a white family sat alone in the front pew. There was no complaint by anyone, not even myself. All of us, both clergy and lay, Latino and Anglo, had come to accept living with incoherence. The outrage, when it did come, was over the refusal to let Latinos into the system but not the ill effects that a liberal, competitive society inflicts on all of us.

Our understanding of the sacred helps us to see how Pentecostals, Charismatics, Born-Again Christians, the Moral Majority, Jesus freaks, and other fundamentalists are essentially serving the same god regardless of institutional affiliation or previous interfaith antagonism. All of these groups for the most part are movements that try to deny that the web of life guarded by the god of emanation has broken. They appeal to a return to traditional values endowed with emanation; they seek to deny the modern world. All promise a return to a world of unity and security in a hostile world. Again, this is an example of returning to forms of emanation promising total security for complete loyalty. It cannot work, and when it does not, legislative violence might be used to force all to obey new laws that dictate a fixed morality based on the conscience of a powerful interest group. This creativity in the service of the dying paradigm of emanation is actually a form of regression because it cripples our ability to construct new and fundamentally better responses. Such attempts inevitably end as encounters in the way of life of incoherence.

In the realm of politics we can also see the basic affinity of a venerable revolutionary hero like Emiliano Zapata to the above groups. Zapata, like the guerrillas of the *Sendero Luminoso* movement in Peru, the Brown Berets of the late 1960s, the Young Lords, and the Black Panthers, all sought to answer the death of the god of emanation by the revival of this same old god in a new disguise. Zapata wanted to go back to a simple, rural, peasant landholding way of life. He did not understand the complexities of the new urban industrialized Mexico which displaced the peasant from the land.[33] For him the peasant was supreme, even though the seeds of Mexico's current problems were already there: scarcity of water and good soil, a growing population and foreign investment that increasingly created an urban class of *obreros*, workers. He wanted to ignore this reality. The *Sendero Luminoso* have killed in an attempt *not* to have to change; they want to preserve a way of life that they know is crumbling.[34] They failed because they had to organize a whole new way of life in order to prevent change; they changed but to preserve the old, so they enter into incoherence.

Some Brown Berets, Young Lords, and Black Panthers created a philosophy based on a romanticized and extreme nationalism that glorified Chicanismo, brownness, Puerto Ricanism, and blackness to the exclusion of all else. Thus, some Chicanos claimed that Anglos and, indeed, even the other minorities could teach them nothing because their historical and cultural experience was unique. Black Panthers and Young Lords echoed these sentiments. As recent as the late 1970s Chicanos who did not look Chicano, whatever that means, were being excluded from Chicano cultural seminars. Also, men and women who have identified themselves as Chicanos were suspect because one parent was Anglo. Such students were made to feel unwanted and were often pressured to choose between being Anglo or Chicano. Blacks in the early 1970s confronted Puerto Ricans with another either/or: either you are black or you are white, which also meant either you are with us or against us. Again, there was a lord involved in all this, but a hidden, rebel source under the shroud of nationalism that is an old lord with a new face, the lord of nothing, Satan, that deepens the incoherence, promising a world based on a lie of racial or ethnic superiority. It is a rebel lord, because it is a rejection of what whites have done to minorities, but the same consciousness, that of superiority, is now used against Anglos. We cannot attack racism by becoming racist. This is why I consider this kind of change not transformation but deformation. Black, brown, and white become polarized islands in a sea of mutual distrust and fear.

Our analysis also allows us to point out serious flaws in the pastoral letter of the U.S. bishops on Hispanics in the United States.[35] The religious rhetoric of commitment to Jesus, his Church, and his people is all there, and appropriately so. Yet there are different gods that are addressed within the same letter. For example, the letter appeals to the right of Latinos to be free from racism and economic exploitation, so that they might live a more human life.[36] Certainly this is the work of the god of transformation. But in relating to women there is another god present. The document reminds Latinos that "no culture is without defects or sins."[37] Then it goes on to strengthen one of the major failings of our culture by not even mentioning the ordination of women. This silence enhances and helps to legitimize the continuing subordination of Latinas in our culture.

> One of the glories of Hispanic women, lay and religious, has been their role in nurturing the faith and keeping it alive in their families and communities. Traditionally they have been the leaders of prayer, catechists and often excellent models of Christian discipleship.[38]

In short, Latinas exercise de facto priestly duties without the institutional recognition of their ministry. In this regard either the bishops are reinforcing male supremacy due to attempts to preserve the authority of a patriarchal hierarchy or they are asking women to live with the image of an all-male Christ because it is the way things have been. Most bishops view priests as extensions of their priesthood, will, and identity, usually in the way of life of emanation. Women do not make appropriate replicas of a male Christ and thus a male hierarchy.

What has been lost sight of is what priesthood is all about. The role of the priest or minister is to put people in contact with the sacred. But again we must ask which god. The priesthood of emanation and incoherence must constantly be on the lookout for heresy and must insist on a monopoly of officially mediating the sacred. That way people can be made secure or accommodated to changing realities by experts. But priesthood in the service of the god of transformation recognizes no such thing as gender, age, race, class, or formal education. Those who care deeply for others are thereby committed to transformative politics. To love others is to shape a society so that all might share in the fruits of human endeavor. To recognize one's own sacredness is to recognize the sacredness of my neighbor.

Furthermore, to put people in contact with their own self and sacred sources is to function as a minister of the sacred regardless of public or institutional ordination. In the way of life of transformation all of us are called to be priests, ministers of the sacred. So in fact we already have Latino and Latina priests who do the work of the god of transformation both as married or single persons. Nevertheless, I hasten to add that we need compassionate priests in the present situation. There is a political reality involved; the Catholic Church is a very powerful institution with enormous resources and influence in the world that still functions as a spiritual container for people who very much need the Church to prepare them for life. We must be sensitive to the needs of people who still require the nurturing of the Church.

The ministers of the god of transformation are ordained by the holy spirit. Their own priesthood is forged by responding to the sources within and by their own initiative to meet the needs of their own people. Gandhi understood his own ordination in this way. He felt that he had been raised up by the spirit to answer the call of the sacred *and* of his people. His own internal realization as a person was fulfilled by this act of service for others.[39] *El Payaso*, the clown in Federico Fellini's *La Strada*, ordains Gelsomina by placing a gold medal around her neck after urging her to love Zampano, a man dedicated to power "who will not love, you who cannot love." Gelsomina accepts her commitment to love as the meaning of her ordination. Many of us have intuitively understood this kind of ordination in our bones when we have witnessed our own elders, parents, grandparents, and others, take command at decisive moments of spiritual and emotional crises. We knew that the priests were not the only ones who could bring the Spirit or the transforming god into our situations.

Christians do a disservice to the priesthood by creating and preserving a privileged, clerical caste that is called the priesthood of Jesus. This reduces Jesus to a god of emanation or incoherence, when in fact Jesus' entrance into human history was a pivotal and grand moment because he was "one of the world's most profound and influential incarnations of the god of transformation."[40]

> His example gives us faith that any of us is capable—not of copying Christ's life: his human life was uniquely his own—but of living our particular life as a transforming life, which is also to say, to live it like Christ as the incarnation of the god of transformation.[41]

It is in this sense that Christians are priests in the ministry of Jesus Christ, as incarnations ourselves of the god of transformation. In our own community I think of people like Dolores Huerta, a Chicana woman who has consciously chosen a life of struggle and poverty on behalf of farmworkers. In this way Dolores fulfills her own vocation to be a full person in the very act of struggling for the humanity of others. Who can deny that she is in fact an ordained woman in the priesthood of the god of transformation. There are many others like Dolores, both Latino and Anglo, who labor with our people. Many Anglo parish priests have not taken refuge behind their clerical and institutional status to hide the realities spoken of here. They, too, have experienced the transforming sacred outside of their theological understanding. Popular forms of religiosity among Latinos, such as *santerismo*, the cult of the saints, and *espiritismo*, the appeal to benevolent and destructive sacred sources, must not categorically be rejected as many Christians do. We have to look to see which god is being served. After all, even the Catholic Mass or Protestant scripture service can be reduced to an act of superstition, a bargaining session with god, or a pious ritual unless it is intended to have us participate in the sacred drama of death and resurrection simultaneously in the personal, religious, and political aspects of our lives.

As mentioned above, Jesus is a crucial and axial event in human history. But Jesus is but one of many manifestations of the transforming god, even though he may be the highest manifestation of this god. Similarly, the priesthood of Jesus is but one priesthood of many that puts us in contact with the transforming god both within our own personal sources and to the Source of all. The refusal of many Christian priests and ministers to recognize this plurality of priesthoods of the transforming god makes them condescending and intolerant of each others' Christian priesthood and that of those who are non-Christian. There have always been holy men and women in all traditions who mediated the sacred in an extraordinary way. Indeed, transforming priests and ministers have recognized the validity of the priesthood of other denominations and faiths, as will be discussed below in the case of a Maryknoll missionary in Bolivia. Clergy of the god of emanation who co-opt Jesus, Buddha, LaoTse, Mohammed, and other holy men and women attempt to domesticate the sacred as *only* Christian, Buddhist, Confucian, Moslem, or Jewish. As a result, colleagues such as Virgilio Elizondo, who wrote an otherwise fine book on Mexican Americans, cannot cope with *mestizaje* on a broader theological plane.[42] *Mestizaje* is a blending of cultures. But Elizondo restricts the blending to European and American forms of culture and religion. The sacred was also indigenous to America, but he does not know how to distinguish true from false gods, having implicitly or unconsciously accepted the prejudice against all other gods as superstitious and pagan, that is, gods of emanation or incoherence. For example, Quetzalcoatl, the plumed serpent, is a symbol of the transforming god. He was for some centuries used as a god of emanation and now has to be rediscovered as a god of transformation. He is very similar to the god Mercury, who holds together the opposites of the world as sulphur and quicksilver, two of the main ingredients by which the alchemists dissolved and recoagulated the base metals of human personality in order to transform the dissolution of the old into the precious gold of a sacred self.[43] Both Mercury and Quetzalcoatl originally represented death and rebirth, incoherence and transformation, destruction and creation. Out of the struggle of opposites such as the human and the divine emerges the fundamentally new. Both gods represented the possibility of an infinite number of new forms, possibilities, and creations.

> Wherever the night sea voyage in pursuit of the sun is undertaken, by the gods of the human soul, it signifies this development toward the relative independence of an ego endowed with such attributes as free will. This tendency, which we have found in the Old World and in Malekula, can also be demonstrated in Aztec Mexico.
>
> It achieves its highest form in the myth of Quetzalcoatl, the Mexican hero figure. He is not a hero who transforms the outside world, but one who transforms himself by atonement. He is the dying and resurrected god, but he is also the hero king and the culture bringer, the earthly and divine representative of the principle of light and humanity. In his dual nature, he combines the western, deathly aspect and the eastern aspect of life: he is the evening star and the morning star. As morning star, he is the positive symbol of the ascending power belonging to the male-spiritual aspect of heaven and the sun. For this reason he is associated with the symbol of the east, the plumed serpent, i.e., the wind-ruach-spirit aspect. He is the god of knowledge and the ascending spiral tower is one of his attributes.[44]

There are many other gods and goddesses in the Latin American tradition that have to be rediscovered as possible guides and manifestations of the transforming god.

In a similar vein, Black Elk, a holy man of the Oglala Sioux, was ordained by the Spirit and received a vision given to him by the White

Buffalo Woman. For years Black Elk resisted his priesthood, his call to show the face of the sacred to the people, because he was afraid.[45] Even commercial television transcended itself and aired "The Mystic Warrior,"[46] the story of an American Indian who was given a vision and a message to redefine the traditional warlike warrior as a pilgrim warrior who is strong for peace, life, and new connections to previous enemies. He was also led by his own insights and the Spirit to redefine the culture of his people, especially sexuality and the relationship between men and women; he refused to take three sisters as his wives and further refused to accept a sister-in-law as his expected wife when his wife was killed. He resisted the code of warriors as that of being only the ability to kill the enemy; he sought new connections to old enemies. He wanted to transform the incoherence of the Sioux but was killed by a rival ethnic group of some of his own people who were still responding to the gods of emanation and/or incoherence. His message created great confusion even among his family and friends because he was responding to a different god, in a radically new ultimate paradigm of life. He was killed in his attempt to turn others around, literally convert them to a new god and vision of transformation. By refusing to accept his priesthood as a valid one, they also rejected his god and reaffirmed the old gods.

In *El Señor Presidente* by Asturias[47] and in Dostoevsky's "The Grand Inquisitor" of *The Brothers Karamazov*[48] we find the same struggle between old and new gods and priesthoods. Jesus as the transforming god brought freedom to the people; a Catholic cardinal as the Grand Inquisitor has accepted their freedom in exchange for bread or security. By reorganizing existence for the people based on a new-found security, freedom in exchange for passive obedience and bread, the Grand Inquisitor cheats them out of their humanity. He offers them the way of life of incoherence; he attempts to take them back to a golden age of happy serene peasants that never existed. For Dostoevsky he is, therefore, really the anti-Christ who leads them to the prison of incoherence. In this instance Dostoevsky pierces through the label or title of cardinal and shows us a priest of the god of emanation who has made an alliance with the god of incoherence, the state, in order to compel the people to obey. This very logic forces him to jail Jesus because even though the cardinal carries the title of priesthood of Jesus, it is merely to deceive the people. He must imprison Jesus because Christ as a god of transformation and the alliance of Cardinal and state as representatives of the god of incoherence and emanation are radically opposed gods who will link the Source of Sources to the people in mutually exclusive ways.

In *El Señor Presidente* Asturias gives us a drama again of the alliance between the two gods of emanation and of incoherence in a democratic system. The president, as priest and incarnation of the god of incoherence, of the state, is elected but seeks to devour and dominate the people as the old rulers did. He fails to possess the people as totally as the old priest/warrior class had done. He lacks the old legitimacy and for this reason uses the Church and the god of emanation to bless his regime. Asturias is also forewarning us of the future because he foresaw how the Latin American state with all of its democratic trappings was really the return of power and privilege for the few. The current national security state in Latin America is an indirect descendant of the ancient pyramid upon which the clerical/ warrior classes preserved the world with the blood of its citizens. It is indirect because the people no longer experience the truth or security of the web of life of emanation. The national security state therefore must revert increasingly to violence to dominate the people. Since the people do not accept its legitimacy, the state turns their confusion into a whole way of life, the paradigm of incoherence. It is precisely for this reason that the theology of liberation is so dangerous to both Church and state in Latin America. On the one hand, the advocates of liberation refuse to legitimize the power of the state and leave it naked in its ruthlessness and illegitimacy. On the other hand, the followers of the theology of liberation also refuse to allow the official Church to use the state as an instrument of power in order to force people back to the orthodoxy of the god of emanation. Thus the alliance of these two gods—the orthodox god of emanation and the god of incoherence of the state—is being undermined by an appeal to the god of transformation.

Knowledge of our three gods who connect us in qualitatively different ways to the Source of Sources also helps us to redefine sin, shame, and guilt and our traditional demons. The god of emanation uses sin or shame or both as traditional forms of repression so that we will control ourselves from within. There is no guilt, because guilt implies individual responsibility; guilt does not arrive until the paradigm of emanation breaks. The god of incoherence is the devil but not Satan. It is the devil who comes with incoherence in act II, scene I; the devil polarizes and divides and legitimizes fragmentation. The devil also makes it possible for us to turn the relationship of incoherence into a whole way of life so that we learn to live with incoherence in act II, scene II. But Satan is one of the main potential actors of act II, scene II; if Satan organizes, deepens, and creates false consciousness, so that people feel they have arrived in a new realm of security, then we are really trapped in the depths in deformation. Satan deepens our incoherence by giving false promises dressed as an old god. It is Satan who encourages and guides pseudoparadigms of emanation such as racism, fascism, and sexism. Satan wants us to overcome the fragmentation by making one fragment, such as racial purity, more powerful than the others.

Why do we call sexism, racism, and facism pseudoparadigms of emanation? Unlike the paradigm, or way of life, of emanation which began as a moment of truth that later became distorted—such as Jesus' view of the Church as discipleship turned into a hierarchial bureaucracy—the pseudoparadigm of emanation was never a moment of truth; it was a lie from the beginning. The transformation of a fragment such as religious orthodoxy or ideological purity into a whole way of life is the creation of something fundamentally new but worse; it is deformation. Any movement, ideology, or group that says that the individual is nothing and the state, or religious heritage, or racial group is everything is a deformation. In this sense Satan is the lord of nothing because this sacred source deepens and organizes a fundamentally worse life. During these historical moments the Source of Sources needs our participation together with the god of transformation to save the Source of Sources and ourselves.

The devil in our traditional religious language is really the god of incoherence who helps us to live with incoherence, to accept incoherence as a way of life. The devil stresses shame, because in a liberal society dedicated to power there is no morality except playing by arbitrary rules that are constantly rewritten by the powerful. Life is a war; there is no ultimate goal or value or meaning. This cynicism cannot take sin or guilt seriously, only shame: shame because not to make it, to obtain power, is to be seen by your peers and society in general as defective, as weak, as less than *macho*; poverty is, therefore, always your own personal fault. Yet in a liberal society everybody is *procedurally* equal: for example, all people have the right to defend themselves in court, but not all have the right to have the same money to be able to afford the best lawyer. In the paradigm of transformation the transforming god leads us to redefine sin, shame, and guilt, that is, as veering from the center of life to lose a transforming connection; sin means to deny the Holy Spirit who is the source of renewal, inspiration, and transformation. You have denied yourself access to new creation and therefore to lose one's self by your desire to dominate one's neighbor through various kinds of economic and political exploitation, which causes the neighbor to lose their humanity. Shame is experienced when you do not treat another human being as a person who is a face of god. The Source of Sources is impoverished because the gods of incoherence block any further emergence of the Source of Sources' creativity through human participation as incarnations of the god of transformation. This is why any kind of possession by a god—call it the state, a lover, a force like racism, an economic system, or a religion—is a sin: all of us are wounded: our self, our neighbor, our world, and our sources.

The *Comunidades de Base*, or basic Christian communities, found throughout Latin America, and especially in Brazil, together with the theology of liberation are extraordinary manifestations of the god of transformation. The BCCs represent an attempt to ground us in and return us to our deepest sources and origins. In their own language people like Gustavo Gutierrez and Juan Luis Segundo[49] speak of the economic system and the national security state as demonic instruments, which for us signifies the alliance of the gods of emanation and incoherence. Since the late 1960s certain groups of the Catholic Church in Latin America have taken a revolutionary step in choosing to identify with the poor. This conversion from the god of power to the god of compassion has cost many lives, including the clergy, even Archbishop Romero of San Salvador. There are many people, poor and rich alike, who serve the god of incoherence, the state, and who prove their loyalty by killing those who seek to organize so that all can share in the benefits of their societies. For this reason the basic Christian communities are feared by those of the Church and state who serve the interests of their own power. The basic Christian communities organize people as equal participants and use the scriptures as the basis for their acts of liberation. They form cooperatives to end the monopoly of merchants who exploit them. But they also speak as equals with the priests who work with them. It is the Spirit who speaks where it will and who is no respecter of titles. Priests earn their respect by meditating on and expressing the lived faith of the people.

This understanding of priesthood and its implications for hierarchical control threatens an element of the Church that wants to continue to treat the people as ignorant children so as to be able to control them. Many Catholic bishops are afraid of this kind of development among Latinos in this country. One of the bishops who participated in the writing of the pastoral letter on Hispanics in the United States mentioned the concern of the Latino bishops to avoid the language of liberation theology because it would antagonize many of the bishops. We live, then, in a period of religious, as well as political and social, history marked by the breakdown of the inherited traditions. The paradigm of emanation is dying and so is the god of emanation. This dying way of life strikes fear in the elites both clerical and lay, who now turn to the use of violence to force people back to the container. This is no longer possible. Incoherence, which meant breaking with the paradigm of emanation, is now turned into another whole way of life, the paradigm of incoherence that represses, masks, and distorts in order to dominate the people as property. Since all of the traditional values are dissolving, the powerful seek to build fortresses in a world that they cannot understand or control. Yet there is great potential for liberation. The people are free now to reexperience the Source without the traditional filters that excluded as much as they included. The personal experiences of people are of crucial importance, and we especially need people who are willing to participate in the very process by which the Source and ourselves will incarnate the fundamentally new.

This experience of breaking and searching for new answers helps to explain the phenomenal rise of groups such as the Pentecostal and Charismatic movements among Latinos. There is great fear of schism due to the heavy emphasis on personal conversion. Great pains have been taken to contain this movement by assigning bishops as spiritual directors and more importantly by reducing new insights into old categories. This is an attempt to neutralize the movement and to co-opt its impact. The choice of this example is not intended to approve of all *carismaticos*. It will depend on the quality of their connections to the Source and the faithfulness with which they participate in creating a new incarnation of the holy. Some may indeed be experiencing this Source. But others may be seeking another container to provide security. I fear that the Catholic Church has allowed the charismatic movement to grow so that it can compete with the various Protestant evangelical groups, especially the Pentecostals, for the loyalty of Latinos. This is an attempt to use the relationship of emanation in the paradigm of incoherence, or to provide security for Latinos searching for identity and the means of survival. The issue is for Latino Catholics who are the Church to redo, to recreate, to nurture another community not only because they are frustrated with tradition or angry with bishops but because it is demanded of them from within. If Latinos find that they cannot experience their own mystery due to certain Church teaching or structural authority, then they must question that teaching and authority. Also, we would ask as Latinos that neither the Catholic Church nor the evangelical groups use our vulnerability for their own institutional reasons. For either group to seek to embrace us in a new kind of security is to provide a false community and to profit from our incoherence.

We hasten to insist that we need the Christian churches as community. The community is neither an addendum nor an afterthought; it follows from the very essence of selfhood that can only emerge in creative relationship to self, other, world, and God. We need the community to test the quality of the gods that we are struggling with. The creation of the fundamentally new is not necessarily to the good; it can bring not only transformation but also deformation. An example in our own time is the phenomenon of facism, especially as exemplified in Nazism and Hitler. Fascism has also appeared in the form of right-wing death squads throughout Latin America. For the sake of *Orden*, order, the national security state will kill peasants who organize cooperatives. This is the kind of pseudoemanation which is really deformation that the Latin American Church has courageously resisted even to the point of martyrdom. We need to ask ourselves in which of our three ultimate paradigms the fundamentally new is emerging—emanation (keeping people from new consciousness), incoherence (preserving what is at the expense of mounting destruction), and transformation (the creation of alternatives that present new and better possibilities for all of human life). The Church as a community of transforming persons provides us with the initial container which we now know to be temporary. Following the new experience of the Source that breaks our previous container and sustains us through the chaos, we are in need to rest and build again, that is, to incarnate what we have seen in a new way. Because of this it is inconceivable that any Church in the future will ever be able to sustain the kind of permanent emanational embrace of its members that the Roman Catholic Church once did. The Catholic Church and all religious institutions are being asked to make a courageous institutional conversion that is based upon the full Gospel message which it has preached. This means participating in the birth, death, and resurrection of its founder and savior, Jesus, which must involve the Church's own death to power and her rebirth to embark anew on the journey of transformation.

As we ask these new questions, we come to see that there were indeed Catholic Christians who belonged to the countertradition, that is, that tradition of journeying with the transforming god that refused to be silenced in a time dominated by the god of the orthodox tradition; that sought to break through the veil to express the freedom of persons to contact their own god, and the Source. To live the tradition afresh then is to reexperience these Catholics in a new way: Ignatius Loyola, Nicholas of Cusa, Master Eckhardt, John of the Cross, St. Teresa of Avila, Peguy, and Teilhard de Chardin. They all realized that the traditions had begun as a revolution—the mystery of the

Source was revealed to us in a new incarnation as Jesus. But they also knew that the issue was to refuse to use Jesus as the magic man so that we could live in the age of the Spirit, who makes possible an infinite number of new incarnations with our participation. It was the risk of conversion that allowed Loyola and his colleagues to renew themselves and others through the *Spiritual Exercises*.[50] Through the yearly retreat the Jesuits were to seek the hidden *gnosis*, or knowledge of the process of transformation. Loyola practiced the heresy that God continues to reveal himself. Tradition, then, is not only what we remember but also what we forgot. We have to understand that tradition, too, is created, nourished, and destroyed by the persons living that tradition. We are free to continue what liberates us, to reexperience ourselves and the holy, *and* free to discontinue that which cripples by permanently fixing the holy and ourselves in formulas that either trap us in fixed faith or that repress any new insights.

This crisis of fixed faith and authority in the service of the god of emanation is especially deep and painful for Catholic missionaries. They are symbolic of an understanding of the crisis of an arrogant Church triumphant which seeks to give its truth by embracing the world through conversion. Conversion to what? To Jesus and to his Church is the usual answer. The name of Jesus is often used to mask the real god that is present, the gods of emanation or incoherence. But this is no longer a viable answer for many. Let us consider the example of the Maryknoll missionaries working in Latin America and more particularly in Bolivia and Peru. They came to baptize, teach, convert, and (for some) "save" the native population. Now they question the authority of their priesthood and sacraments. What has led them to such a crisis is a personal awareness that many suspected for a long time, that the sacred was here before them and goes on living side by side, and often in a hidden manner, with the Catholic faith. In an excellent documentary film, *El Curandero* (The Healer),[51] the Maryknoll Fathers told the story of one of their own. He baptized, preached, and said Mass and felt that he was making progress in strengthening the faith of the people. But one day almost by accident he discovered a hidden worship. He was shocked and dismayed and preached against this residual "paganism." It did not go away. The people ignored him. After 450 years Roman Catholicism was not the only religion. He sought out the meaning of the strange amulets and rituals. At first the Catholic priest was angry, then curious, and, finally, genuinely moved by what he discovered. Eventually he took an extraordinary step into the other world: he became an apprentice to an Aymara Indian *brujo* (male witch), or Shaman, who performed services for the people to an earth goddess, Mama Cocoa. The priest participated in the services. In the midst of this encounter the Aymara priest's son died. Both faiths were incapable of adequately explaining or soothing the harshness of death. That is to say, both religious expressions had to admit their inadequacies. It was a remarkable example of two men forced to leave behind their religious formulas in the face of incoherence. What is more noteworthy was the young priest's awareness that he no longer had the answers. His recognition of the validity of his friend's priesthood helped him to relativize the absolute claim of Catholicism. As the film ended, the Catholic priest narrated his determination to seek out how God has chosen to manifest himself.

Both the Aymara and Catholic religions had turned their gods into idols. Their gods were terrifying in their power and used it at their own whims. Marcellino, the Shaman, could see death only as a punishment from a god who would now make it up to them by giving them cattle. Father Salazar felt helpless in his attempt to console his friend. Some of the Indians in the film considered god cruel and death as a total end to everything. For almost five centuries the Catholic missionaries repeated and imposed their gods. An equal amount of time was spent by the indigenous population quietly resisting the gods of the white world by nourishing their threatened gods. The gods of the missionaries were turned into imperialists, and the Indian gods were cultivated as rebel gods. Missionaries and Indians were locked in a fruitless struggle which crippled both sides. Neither could reexperience self, other, or their gods. Catholic and Indian were possessed by their gods who began as authentic religious eruptions but now were reduced to idols.

> These gods, however, were able to engender and reiterate only a single act of transformation—a cycle of their own. They can therefore only connect themselves to our primitive consciousness. . . . These gods have also emanated angels and demons, spirits and matter of their own, but, left to themselves, they and their hosts and their works can only repeat themselves.[52]

But Jacob wrestled with the Angel; Job attacked Yahweh as unjust; Elie Weisel rejected a god who turned his back on innocent suffering; Jesus sought that the cup be removed; Prometheus stole fire from heaven; Antigone disobeyed Creon, the god of government; and Tevyev in *Fiddler on the Roof* transformed his traditional gods by responding to god's face in the concrete, his daughter's face. We do a disservice to ourselves and to the source by refusing to create conflict and change. To passively accept reality is to fail to recognize that reality, ourselves, and the source are unfinished. The concreteness of death and life provides us with ever-new opportunities to see hidden treasures, revealed anew at every moment. The concrete constantly shows forth the width and depth and breadth of the continuously creating underlying sources. We have to struggle with our gods, self, others, and the cosmos until we are blessed with a new face of god, seif, and history.

Father Salazar and his fellow missionaries must not end by romanticizing the Aymara and other Indian gods.[53] Perhaps the future of missionaries of all persuasions is to invite their hosts to a common struggle of seeking a new face of god in their own lives, the god of transformation.

Authority problems will immediately arise for such Catholics. The Latin American advocates of Liberation Theology such as Juan Luis Segundo of Uruguay, Gustavo Gutierrez of Peru, and Leonardo Boff of Brazil all recognize the role that fixed religion in the paradigm of emanation has played in freezing masses of people into permanent poverty as god's will. A theology based on a process of creation, nourishment, and destruction paralleled by a politics and sociology of liberation will call for a new ecclesiology, a new society, and a new kind of politics. One cannot be developed without the other. This entails calling down upon themselves the fury of Church and state. Segundo on one occasion gently but with great determination stated that any sacramental activity not directed to the transformation of the world was irrelevant.[54]

AUTOBIOGRAPHICAL WITNESS

We begin, then, by acknowledging at last our heresy. Not heresy, in its usual, limited meaning as a sharply dissenting version of a particular orthodoxy . . . I mean to acknowledge heresy in its original meaning, as choosing only what one can grasp one's self and thus opposed to any knowledge or practice imposed solely by the authority of others. It is the story of our unfinished relationship with an imperfect god. In the spirit of heresy, however, I am telling no myth except the one which I can grasp myself through the myth . . . but none of the tellers of this myth, nor I, are trying to establish the officially sanctioned canon of this story. There can be no final version of the story of continuous transformation. The task for each of us, including the reader, is to retell this myth of creation as he or she has learned to make their way on a consonant journey.[55]

I and other Latinos have a primary commitment to others and not to a fixed tradition or to the Church as permanent container. If we are the living members of our churches, then the traditions live in us. All religious groups are in process and constantly evolving because the members who compose those groups are continually redefining who they are in relationship to their sacred sources. It is only liberated individuals who can pose new questions as their consciousness of who they are grows. The most religious people in a time of crisis are those who can create new relationships to their underlying sources. Religious myths and symbols are intended to give access to the source of all mystery.

Robert McAfee Brown reminds us that we have to take our stand somewhere. Our religious traditions and communities are a rare blessing in such desolate times.[56] We do indeed need a concrete base from which to proceed. Furthermore, this is not an excuse for elitism. We owe an authentic response to our fellow Latinos; we have to relate to them where they are. The community as church can serve us all in the following ways depending upon our progress on the journey: it can protect those still coming to birth; provide a base for those who have unfinished work within it; be a home for those who have no strength to leave; offer a matrix to rediscover new symbolic meanings by reexperiencing the symbol as bridge to the source; function as a preparation for the next concrete step toward transformation; and, finally, it can serve as a liberated zone to evaluate and create a strategy by which to go beyond the container. We shatter the container in order to free the source within us. We choose to exercise the freedom to go beyond the fixed tradition in order to begin the journey to the center of the source.

Finally, allow me to end this chapter by giving an example of the kind of freedom open to Latinos and others to reinterpret their relationship to the sacred.

Our perspective allows us to recognize in the symbols of dogmatic faith frozen moments of transformation. . . . our relationship to symbols is a persistent test of how alive we are at each moment to the transformation of that unity which is ourselves, our yearning and our source. . . . As before, not all of us have the power to create symbols that inspire millions, but as never before, each of us will need to find out for himself and herself which symbols most inspire them along the way of transformation.[57]

As young men we were taught that the Eucharist was a cure for con-
cupiscence, that is, sexual passion. The Eucharist was reduced to being a guardian of a dispassionate chastity. Furthermore, communion
was a way of surrendering ourselves to Jesus as his followers. There
is another way of seeing the Eucharist. Participation in the life and
death of a god in primitive religions often involved a sacred banquet
in which the god was eaten. The strength passed from the god to the
person who ate the sacred food. Also, I came to learn that mandalas,
magic circles, or sun wheels were among the oldest religious symbols used to symbolize the unity of the whole of creation.[58] Black Elk
spoke of the circle at the center of creation that sustained the self,
the tribe, the world, and God simultaneously.[59] The Eucharist was
always represented by the symbolic mandala that archetypally pointed
to the self and God simultaneously. C. G. Jung and Hermann Hesse
both referred to Jesus as the symbol of the archetype of the self.[60]
Theologian Bernard Cooke spoke of the Eucharist as the cure for con-
cupiscence, which meant rejecting dishonesty. All these various in-
fluences had their convergence in my personal search for meaningful
symbols of transformation. I came to re-vision the Eucharist. It now
signified standing in the presence of someone who became a self by
being totally open to God as the source of all. He was the Saviour,
as D. H. Lawrence has said, because he was able to establish or initiate a new connection or way (TORAH) between humankind and
the universe.[61] He was the man for others who lived a life of creation,
nourishment, and destruction. By rebelling against the god of emanation in a fixed Mosaic Law, he participated in a new experience of
Yahweh *within* himself as the temple of the divine. He is the new
Adam, the Anthropos, the transforming god, the symbol of the new
humanity and incarnation divinized. Thus, for us as Latinos the issue
is not to give ourselves to Jesus but to save the saviour within ourselves, that is, the call to authenticity, the vocation to incarnate the
source again through our own humanity and thus, like Siddhartha,
become our own Buddha or Christ, or transforming god. Jesus is too
important to leave to the orthodox; He belongs to the artisans of a
new humanity. Finally, Jesus left us his Spirit, the god of transformation, as his legacy . . . known in the countertradition as the feminine principle of liberation who represents an infinite number of
new creations. The source did not begin by creating entities, neither
human nor spiritual, but by creating relationships—dialectical relationships that allow for encounters from opposing positions creating
the movement within which the new cosmos could emerge.[62] The
political and religious patriarchy in which we have lived has deprived

us of the creative dialectic of masculine-feminine.[63] To rediscover this in ourselves will be to rediscover women as concrete persons and end the frozen structures that violate us, both men and women.

Surely in all of this the Spirit, our transforming connection to the source, is leading us to the creation of new myths and symbols that will allow us not only to say Padre, Father, but also Madre, Mother, of us all. And this is now my image of a transforming church, a mother of us all who helps us to distinguish between the gods of emanation, incoherence, and transformation, even though in that very process she loses her identity as a vessel of emanation in order to rediscover herself as our guide beyond the god of incoherence to journey with the god of transformation.

As members of various religious traditions, and in my case, the Catholic Church, we must resist any church that seeks to possess us. We have to become mothers and fathers ourselves by conceiving and giving expression and struggling with the sacred impulses from the depths. We cannot become the means of revealing anew the source in our own incarnations unless we struggle against the primitive gods of emanation and incoherence and their representatives. It is in this way that we are the Church, the bearers of the sacred. Our sacred vocation is clear and urgent: to participate in the transformation of the source, our selves, our neighbor, and the world with all of its complexities.

6. The Politics of Liberation versus the Politics of Assimilation

Assimilation is a profound kind of poverty because it forfeits our uniqueness both personal and cultural. We can never be authentically Amerian and Latino but are forced to be either an excluded minority or an assimilated individualist. As Latinos we choose liberation, which means to be both Latino, who we are, and American, the promise of fulfilling the principles upon which this nation is founded. Perhaps our greatest contribution will be to witness to the right of each person to be a self in a community of equals that is commited to each other's advancement because they love others as themselves.

THE POLITICS OF LIBERATION VERSUS THE POLITICS OF ASSIMILATION

For Latinos to be political does not mean and is not constituted by their joining the Democratic party, the Republican party, or some other recognized national or local political organization—to think in these terms is to look to others to legitimize us and to give us permission to be political. To be political does not preclude joining or creating a political party, but it is not limited to this usual interpretation of politics. Political activity is a radical, fundamental human right that has always belonged to us but that was taken away from all of us, both minority and majority groups. To be political is to participate, to struggle with others on a plane of equality so as to be able to create, nourish, and destroy inadequate institutions and to build new ones. All of us have been violated to the point where politics has been reduced to legitimizing systems based on hierarchy that control us; so every two or four years we tell others that they can run our lives and shape our environment for us. Thus we abdicate our right to control our lives and world for the sake of being left alone to pursue individual dreams based on consuming more and better houses, cars, PhDs, appliances, and on and on.

Yet real work and real political participation is to re-create ourselves as species-being and the world according to our newly discovered selves. Political work means forging fundamentally new and better relationships to self, others, problems, and our sacred sources. Middle class or professional is defined not by status, power, or money but by where you stand in regard to the qualities of three kinds of work: preservation, creation, or destruction. The issue for us as Latinos is to discover individuals who share a common consciousness in regard to a particular kind of work, that is, are we interested in being opportunists or brokers for a system that will reward us with new positions of power so that we can help to police our own people; are we interested in creating movement in a system but only to the extent that it will open up new opportunities for a small group who then call for a halt to further change in order to protect newly acquired useful interests; are we individuals who hate, who are cynically bitter and so want to deprive all people of any movement; or, finally, do we identify ourselves as members of a much smaller group who are conscious and critical enough to participate in a constant process of breaking and remaking relations for the sake of the advancement of all our people?[1]

THE POLITICS OF ASSIMILATION

Education is political. Education has always been one of the most powerful socializing agencies of all societies. Socialization is never neutral or nonpolitical. Socialization may be defined as a process whereby a society, that is, the living members of a group who share values, prepares a person to desire what they, the society, wants them to desire. Thus, socialization acquires the same definition as repression: repression is an intrapsychic force that people use against their own desires.[2] Our desires are called subjective, that is, unreal, unfounded, so that we will concede to objective truths which are actually the subjective personal experiences of powerful others. These powerful others succeed in shaping all life according to their perceptions and interests. After generations of this kind of conditioning people are assimilated into an all-powerful, objective system. New generations now bow down before the system as a god that sustains them. But what they cannot do is question, conflict with, or destroy that god. We should not forget that Socrates was killed for political and religious reasons: poisoning the minds of the young by causing them to doubt and question the traditional gods and truths.

To assimilate is to make one's self over in the image of others, to immerse oneself and to fuse oneself. Why would anyone want to do that? To assimilate into power. The reason is that people with power have things, desirable things, security, travel, money, and respect. But to assimilate also presupposes discontent not only with what we lack but also with who we are. We begin to believe that we are powerless to influence and shape our lives, that this inability is our fault. Thus we have to become like the dominant: white, affluent, and powerful. Our background is poor, painful, and pitiful. So reject the past—which means reject our parents, our heritage, and ultimately crucial aspects of our own selfhood.

To assimilate is to choose a way of life of incoherence that strips us of spontaneity, vulnerability, emotional depth, creativity, imagination, which are all rooted in our sources. To assimilate is to acquire not only power but also anxiety; we see others as threats. Repression, competition, a fear of our inner desires is part of the bargain. We fragment ourselves and split ourselves off from feelings that might prevent us from gaining power. Is this really what we want? We should be grateful for this? Ultimately what the system wants is for us to choose our unfreedom by loving Big Brother, spontaneously to give our consent so that the will of the master and the will of the subject are one.[3]

Organized institutional religion in adjusting us to society also lends its power to the politics of conformity/assimilation, so that for us to attack social, political, economic, or religious practices or values results in our experiencing sin, shame, and guilt, the most primitive forms of people controlling or repressing themselves. This is the real power of civil religion, of the alliance of the ways of life of emanation and incoherence as represented by church and state.

Any person in this country faces these powerful forces. As Latinos we are members of a group that has been systematically excluded from participating in shaping our lives, and so the powers that oppress all Americans are even more deadly for us. Not only are we deprived of participating in our destinies, but the very core of authentic resistance—our selfhood—has been seriously wounded.

To be political, to shape our life, to plant, nourish, and uproot in the everyday fashioning of life, means to be a self, a person connected to one's self, to others, to problems, and to one's sacred sources. To suffer segregation, racism, and powerlessness is very damaging, but to suffer or be lamed in one's own identity is almost beyond repair. And yet, ironically, this very assault on our ethnic and racial self is the basis of our hope. To be white and blue-eyed is to be able to merge and fuse oneself into the dominant culture and to be accepted and rewarded. But it is a terrible trap—these people also have a self, a destiny; it is so completely bought off by the system's rewards that the repression is almost total. Whereas for us even if we try to be white, Anglo, Gringo, Spanish, or Irish Catholic, we know in our souls that we shall never be. It sticks in our throat; we feel it in our bones. We ultimately resist going under for good. At times the real pain of the memory of being called a dirty Mexican, greaser, or spic keeps us from integrating. At other times it is the legacy of struggle of our mothers and fathers and the generations before us. At such times of realization we are overcome with sadness that we have been ashamed of our own color, blood, language, heritage, and of our Spanish-speaking, poorly educated parents.[4] We then feel anger against the white people who have caused all the pain, while we realize that they too are victims of a society and system that does not want anybody to be a self—a participating, creating, nourishing, dismantling, and re-creating self. Powerful others want us to forget who we are. To refuse to do so is what constituted the black movement and the women's movement. We too are a people who resist, who want to be a part of a countertradition. But to belong to ourselves is to profoundly threaten those who have purchased their power by negating what they are and what they feel. It is so ironic that to be a self is such a radical, revolutionary, political decision.[5] It tells us something about the system of roles in which we are all involved; the one thing a society that is based on the *antiself* agrees on is that we can love others and sacrifice for them, but we must not love and desire ourselves.[6] What a beautiful and tender scene in Tom Robbin's novel *Even Cowgirls Get the Blues* when Sissy caresses and blesses her oversized thumbs because although they are a freak to others, they are the symbol and source of her unique mystery.[7]

THE ALTERNATIVE: THE POLITICS OF LIBERATION

The politics of liberation begin with you and I *reacquiring* who you and I are. We take ourselves back from greedy systems that hide behind the label of liberal democracy. They want us body and soul.

But just as you and I fought against our mothers and fathers who wanted us to feel guilty for leaving home, we are locked in the same archetypal drama with white society. We did not leave our families in the Bronx, Texas, California, Lima, Santo Domingo, Chihuahua, or Puerto Rico to give ourselves to a possessive system. We journeyed to find out who we are. We work not only to acquire skills but to put these skills at the service of our rediscovered self. Now we have an opportunity to take our psychic energy and our ego and the pleasure principle and to use it against the reality principle, that is, reality based on facticity, so-called neutral facts, that are really facts loaded with values for the sake of our own control and the control of others. The greatest pleasure that we can have is the pleasure of creating our own lives and refusing to live for the whims of others.[8]

The following are characteristics that constitute the shift from assimilation into systems, a colonial mentality, to the reacquiring of the self, or liberation:

> To create one's own life and environment is to cease to be an object (a thing to which something is done and which is defined by others) and to see oneself as a subject (a person who defines herself or himself and who acts on the world).

> To realize that there is no such thing as a dumb or neutral fact; the world is not given; it is created by men and women.

> People become conscious through separation; outside of the container of institutions and systems they can analyze, critique, and act.

> One begins to ask the key question: Who benefits from our lack of participation in regard to any particular problem?

> Economics and politics go hand in hand; an actual laissez-faire economics never existed but its idea served as a shield for the powerful to use the state for their own aggrandizement.

> Repression becomes oppression when the game is over and people refuse to control themselves out of love for the master; the master must turn to brute strength to force people back to normal, that is, to be docile and passive. Conscious people cannot go back to normal; something irrevocable has happened.

> Women and men recognize that they were not born dull and passive; they were made that way as the result of a particular historical and sociological situation. Thus people no longer blame themselves; they inherited a violent system.

Self-hatred and group hatred give way to structural analysis.

Latent racism is made manifest and is exposed; in its latent non-conscious form the dominant culture succeeded in socializing another group to believe in and to accept its own inferiority and incapacity for political action.

To take one's self back is to see the mystery in one's own life; no parent, system, god, or lover has the right to possess us. Now we are ready to be personal, political, and religious as three faces of the same journey of transformation.

THE ROLE OF RELIGION IN THE POLITICS OF LIBERATION

Freed through liberation from the demonic power of systemic enchantment, we can now journey with a new god, the god of transformation. We reject the god of orthodox systems and his by-product, institutionalized religion, as the final arbiter of life. We do not reject the sacred or true mystery that constitutes the goal of the journey of life. Nor do we forsake the true community of a pilgrim church. But where shall we begin? By going home in two ways: home within ourselves to rediscover our connection to our sacred sources, the god beyond god, and, second, home to our everyday relationships. Within our own persons we are locked in a struggle with different forces, voices, or gods. Richard Wagner tells us in his opera *Parsifal*, through the words of the chorus, that the purpose of the journey is "Erlosung dem Erloser!"—the redemption of the Redeemer or the salvation of the Savior.[9] The goal of the journey is twofold: to liberate one's own god or selfhood and, second, through the self, which is a spark of the divine, to free the Source of Sources who calls to us for help from the depths. In a similar vein Marguerite Yourcenar in a simple yet beautiful and stunning way redefines and stands on its head the traditional relationship between saved and Savior:

> What if we are mistaken in postulating that God is all-powerful, and in supposing our woes to be the result of His will? What if it is for us to establish His Kingdom on earth? I have said to you before that God delegates himself; now I go beyond that, Sebastian. Possibly He is only a small flame in our hands, and we alone are the ones to feed and keep this flame alight; perhaps we are the farthest point to which he can advance. How many sufferers who are incensed when we speak of an almightly God would rush from the depth of their own distress to succor Him in His frailty if we asked them to do so?

Such a notion ill accords with the dogmas of the Holy Church.

No, no, my friend; for I abjure in advance anything I have said which might further tear that Robe without Seam. God reigns omnipotent, I grant you that, in the world of the spirit, but we dwell here in the world of flesh. And on this earth, where He has walked, in what guise have we seen Him except as a babe on the straw, just like the innocents left lying on the snow when our moorland villages are devastated by the King's troops? Or as a vagabond, with no stone whereon to lay His head? Or as a man condemned and hanged at a crossroads, asking, in His turn, why God has abandoned Him? We are indeed weak, each one of us, but there is some consolation in the thought that He may be even weaker than we, and more discouraged still, and that it is our task to beget Him and save Him in all living beings.[10]

It is important to distinguish between these gods, the gods of emanation and incoherence and the god of transformation,[11] because the term "god" has usually carried a positive connotation for our people. But what is being pointed out here is the quality of our relationship to the sacred. The god of emanation breeds passivity, childishness, and loyal servants; one serves *under* the god of emanation. This is the god who presides over the paradigm of emanation that is now dying. This god of possession soon becomes the god of incoherence. The god of the service of emanation wants to prevent us from acting on what we know: we have to leave Egypt for good. Once we have left Egypt, the god of incoherence wants to trap us in the world of competition, the desert of an insatiable pursuit for power. The god of transformation is a guide who invites us to journey *with* her/him and together to participate in re-creating the face of the self, the earth, and the face of the Source. The gods of emanation and incoherence want us to remain committed to the pseudosacred outside of ourselves, to be stillborn, to become a transformed once-for-all believer, a repressed self who fears to hurt those who possess us. These are very powerful gods with all the necessary allies to help enforce their will. To struggle against these gods it is necessary to call upon a guide, the god of the transforming journey. By appealing to the god of transformation we ask to be accompanied by a creative spirit on our unique, personal journey. The gods of emanation and incoherence impoverish the Source of Sources, or God beyond god, because they either stress manifestations that are true for all time— there is nothing new; only affirmation of what already exists and is revealed—or declare that there is no ultimate truth. But the god of transformation leads us back beyond the morning star where the gods have their origin. Here human beings have to steal fire from heaven so as to give new form to self, cosmos, and Source. We and the Source create, nourish, and destroy.

When I was a boy, my mother used to say to me "*Eso es castigo de Dios*" (a punishment from God) to keep me in line, to force me to come back and beat my chest for daring to be something out of the ordinary or different from the norms. What my mother really meant was "¡Que Dios te castigue!" (May god punish you!) for daring to walk away from her. Terrible words but nevertheless true. Now what god was my mother appealing to? This was the god of the service of emanation who gave my mother security and buffered her suffering. The struggle with this god was over the degree of the intensity of accommodation to his will. My mother saw herself as an extension and agent of this god, so to break with her commandments was rupturing the relationship with god, culture, family, nature, or life as given. There was only one remedy: come back and ask for *perdon*, pardon or forgiveness ... make your peace with god, with me, with the Church, with reality so that the good feelings of unity and peace will be restored. But now more than ever before there can be no going back.

So the gods of possessive emanation will punish us, send us anxiety attacks, and condemn us as will the people who serve these gods. These false gods do not want us to save the Savior, or the sacredness within us, or to reveal the true Source of Sources in the depths. I love my mother and my culture, La Raza, but I dislike in myself and in our people the tendency, the desire, to run back to the god of emanation, there to commiserate with each other about the temptations of the world that threaten the container of orthodox truth. The new god of the system, the god of incoherence, wants us to be content with the world, that is, to settle for less by accepting as the meaning of life the acquisition of power. Religions that domesticate the sacred are merely one-act dramas of transformation. I ask not that we reject our parents but rather that we rediscover them and remind them that they gave us the tradition of journeying. They came to this country seeking a better life. So for Latinos to be tuly at home within themselves is to become cocreators with the Source of Sources of the world. It is to be like other Christs—incarnating again and again and making divinity concrete in ourselves and in the world. This is why we pray to the Spirit to free us from the god of the world so that we can leave secure assimilated flesh pots and journey into the desert for redefining and renaming ourselves. We earn the right to redefine our-

selves through struggling. This is the political significance of the term
Chicano or Boricua. Now rather than repeating worn-out prayers and
rituals, our lives become a new prayer. We are no longer transform*ed*,
defined, named, assimilated; rather we become transform*ing*, nam*-
ing*, defining, self-integrating persons; we are a sacred drama of relationships in motion.

Now to return from the struggle in our own depths to the everyday tasks of our concrete lives is to act out the truth that we learned
on the journey within. We are no longer the same. So we cannot continue to allow others to relate to us as if nothing had changed. We
are home, and yet our home is not the same because we have changed.
I am firmly convinced that if we act for the sake of transformation,
then it will also be for the good of all those who truly love us for
ourselves and for themselves. There will be suffering, but it will be
suffering with a purpose and with hope because out of it will come
our new selves. Now we are free to break or destroy relationships
that cripple all of us; we are not rejecting our mother or father,
abuelos, grandparents, the Catholic Church, or others who care for
us, but rather we reject the way they relate to us, and we reject the
false gods that bless our arrested personalities. We are calling those
related to us and ourselves to participate in a new drama of transformation. For example, when we go to church, we now celebrate the
sacredness of the Source of Sources within each of us and within the
community. This sense of our self-worth means that we can politically shape a world that manifests in its structure the reality of each
person's dignity and worth. Our Indian ancestors and the Catholic
Church were wrong to terrorize the population with an avenging god.
The God beyond god is not out there—a being to whom we construct
pyramids and cathedrals, but the sacred is the depth of our depths.
To seek and manifest our own mystery is to make real both ourselves
and the God that we reveal through our creation. For a jealous husband, or father, or lover, or Church, or state, or system to possess us
is to sin, to try to stamp out the spark of the divine within us. And
so we are free to re-create all our institutions: our marriages, schools,
economic, political, and social systems, to destroy systems that cripple us and to create again and again. At this point the political and
the religious meet and merge. The commandment not to create false
idols before Yahweh certainly applies to the greedy institutions and
systems that seek to demonize us by binding our demons, or selfhood.

Our task is to struggle with the gods that come up from the
depths to make sure that they are manifestations of the god of transformation. We have to test these gods and ourselves in a community

of people. What is inside us is both a terror and a promise. All of our repressed self's energies will come out in strange ways. We have to wrestle with these forces until they bless us. We are still in formation, in process. We are a people on the move. We are members of the countertradition, that is, men and women who have always believed that the world was unfinished, that they were unfinished, and that God was unfinished.

We are a people still growing our own Latinohood, naming ourselves constantly, creating, nourishing, destroying, always taking the next step. Our task is to help God into wholeness evermore often and covering an ever-larger network of life. So our God is not distant, perfect in his masculine aloofness, but our dios/diosa, God/Goddess is the god of transformation and is only perfect in relationship to our willingness to participate in the task of creation.[12] Thus, when we create political parties to enable us to confront racism, sexism, and classism, when we see women as equals, when we form unions to protect the dignity of our work, when we take control of our own school boards, then we *and* God are being political—shaping the world on a level of equality with others.

CONCLUSION

And so now we see the ultimate sin of assimilation into possessive and demonic systems. The only sin is to lose the self and to cause others to lose themselves. And what about our white/Anglo brothers and sisters and our brothers and sisters from other minority groups? We must not end with a narrow, stingy view of our ethnic and racial heritage that celebrates us at the expense of others. On the contrary, we owe it to our Anglo friends not to assimilate but to continue to resist a system that victimizes everybody. We have to step forward aggressively to remind them too that we do not identify them with this system, but we see them as concrete individuals who are sacred and unique. We have felt the worst of this system; thus we have earned the right to warn others. We must serve as a people who resist, who are part of that community of saints, the men and women of the countertradition who spent their lives witnessing to the creating of alternatives.

We cannot avoid moral decisions; we have to choose. Paulo Freire, the Brazilian educator associated with the movement *Conscientizacion*, or education as political consciousness, has taught us about a thematic universe, that is, the fundamental moral issues of our age. We live at a time in which the most fundamental issue is the confrontation between liberation and oppression.[13] As Latinos we have to take a stand, a political stand: we opt for either liberation or the control of others; either we help maintain a situation of systemic hierarchical inequality or we help to prepare our fellow Latinos and others to participate in shaping their own lives. Nor can we say that we shall wait until later when we have our credentials. We are all presently being socialized by our own educational institutions to take power, prestige, and status for granted, as our birthright *because* we have now been graduated, that is, moved up in society. We should remind ourselves always that all education is political; it is never neutral. We can allow ourselves to be prepared according to set roles, or we can shape ourselves and help others to determine their own lives. Plato saw the Academy as a preparation for political life. Plato sought to prepare his pupils for public service by having them contemplate the *Eidos*, or eternal ideas, that have to be made concrete in the world through political action. Moreover, no person could participate in this dialectic between contemplation and action without having a *daimon*, one's own fate that came from God, that is, one's own realization of self through pursuit of a particular life choice. This presence of a nonrational reality was the source of resistance against commercializing this gift of a life's calling that was intended to serve with particular skills the needs of others.[14]

Only persons connected to themselves, each other, and the sacred can create the vision to build a society of equal participation. Like the Invisible Man, we have to realize that our dilemma need not remain a private crisis of conscience. Even invisible Latinos who have been given visibility by the system have to come out of hibernation.[15] To continue to play the game as defined by official white America is to reinforce in their minds the stereotype that they have of us—mañana-oriented people who are perfectly happy with our occasional doctor or congresswoman. Our authentic invisibility is the self within that nobody sees. The only way that this invisible authentic self can become visible is in the concrete world around us if we decide to risk ourselves. Without the possibility of action all knowledge comes to nothing. In a very real sense our gifts have set us aside, dedicated us for others. I feel that we as Latinos have been ordained by history, that is, the Pilgrim god, the god of transformation, to take up the challenge of these times. Power, prestige, and money cannot fulfill our desires. We must heed Ralph Ellison, recently chosen as one of the best American novelists of the last twenty-five years, and refuse to make passive love to our sickness, the sickness that tells us there is nothing we can do, that the system with all of its gods is too big. But even restructuring an entire society can only be accomplished by transforming our daily particular, concrete relationships now, today, with those closest to us. No, there is no escape from the responsibility that we carry of participating in the journey of sowing the fundamentally new, uprooting destructive institutions and nourishing those which are conducive to justice. We as Latinos might not be interested in liberation, but liberation is interested in us.

7. Latino Professionals:

A Transforming Middle Class

We very much need skilled and competent Latinos. But we need Latinos who have skills for themselves and others and not for the sake of the market, where all of us are turned into commodities. We ask that our middle class be of a particular quality: a group dedicated to transforming institutions. This means to reserve the term "successful" to our Latino middle class who have learned how to create fundamentally new and better linkages to themselves, their work, and their community. Therefore, professional and middle class cannot be determined by income or prestige but by the character of a group who are passionately committed to a new wealth and quality of human work establishing new forms of justice that allow all to share and to benefit from the production of goods and services.

The terms "Chicano," "Boricua," and "Latino" are political statements; they represent an attempt by a people to redefine themselves as opposed to being defined by others, especially official, white Anglo-Saxon America, into Mexican Americans, Hispanos, or Spanish American. A "professional" is someone who should profess truth, justice, love, and wisdom and who stands passionately for life. The term "professional" was distorted and narrowed to signify a holder of a scarce technique—legal, medical, business administrative, bureaucratic—who can now sell his/her services on the open market.

In the metropolis, where men were both more and less equal than ever before, the most intimate relationships were determined by calculations of advantage. Marriage was seen as an instrument with which to acquire, consolidate and increase wealth and power. Young men and women were treated—and were taught to treat themselves—as commodities for speculation in a human market. "Has my father sold me, then?" Julie cried. "Yes, he had made his daughter into a piece of goods (merchandise) . . . and profited at my expense! He had paid for his life with mine!" (I.28,94) Thus marriage served to initiate innocent youth into the primary experience of modern society. They began their lives as adults by being sold; thrown into a universal market place, they would learn gradually to sell themselves. Modernity had liberated the self, only (it seemed) to transform it into capital. The modern development of individuality and of *sensibilité* opened up new dimensions of personal intimacy and love; yet any genuinely personal relationship was forced to go underground, and to define itself against all the institutions and values of modern society. Social relations were split into the dualism of "public" versus "private"; an individual could be himself only by leading a double life.[1]

MARKETABILITY

Too many of us have gotten to be marketable, that is, to the point of being or becoming professionals because the government and private industry made a concerted effort after the upheavals of the 1960s and 1970s to recruit the top members from all potentially troublesome racial and ethnic groups to help police their own people. "Police" is not used here necessarily in a repressive manner, but the science of "policing" consists in regulating everything that relates to the present condition of society. The aim of policing is to strengthen and increase the power of the state and likewise or thereby serve the public interest.

Latinos, especially Chicanos and Boricuas, are being recruited by some of the top universities. As a people, Latinos were for generations excluded and wounded by racism, classism and sexism. Now universities, government, and corporations compete with each other to placate the historical wound by giving *individual* therapy. Latinos with good grades and high SATs are, as individuals, considered to be some of the better, more literate, articulate, and functional Latinos.

So rather than professing a commitment to truth, justice, and love, there are those who want us to use Chicano or Boricua as a new power prefix to get ahead in the system. And some of us do, forgetting that there is a history of suffering that earned the right to create our opportunities. So we have new prefixes in the community: a Chicano lawyer, a Boricua policeman, a Latino doctor, a Boricua superintendent of schools; but too often it is the same old archetypal drama of individuals using their personal charms along with a group's history of past discrimination to get the cutting edge in a competitive society. The real meaning of assimilation is to choose to enact life in the way of life of incoherence.

It would be useful at this point to give a working definition of professional and to review the historical context of the professions.[2] Most social scientists speak of professionals in the following terms: a professional is a person who practices a skill that gives him or her a special power and prestige. Society grants these rewards because professionals are considered to have expertise in specialized bodies of knowledge linked to central needs and values of the social system, and because professionals are viewed as persons who are devoted to the public, above and beyond monetary gain. For the time being let us stay with this definition. Professionalization developed as an integral part of the bureaucratization and specialization characteristic of a mature nineteenth-century capitalism. The esoteric skill and knowledge of a particular group became a new kind of property. These special skills and expertise were translated into another scarcity— social and economic rewards. To enforce scarcity and thus control rewards, monopoly was essential. The rewards that could be demanded depended on the public's perception of the value of the skills. If this value perception was high, then the profession had a high degree of marketability. Thus professions consciously organized themselves to attain market power. Once a market was obtained, it had to be controlled. Yet such striving for monopoly based on marketable expertise is a crucial element in the structure of modern inequality. The professionalization movements of the nineteenth century prefigure a structural social inequality. Professions are the heart of an occupational hierarchy wherein legitimacy is founded on socially recognized expertise or on a system of education and credentialing. As Latinos we should not be naive about the very essence of professionalization—it is both effect and cause of a structure of inequality.

Professionalism and its growth is made possible by the openness of the American university to new areas of expertise and the widespread access to higher education in American society. Clearly our universities play an essential part in furthering and accelerating the hierarchical and unequal nature of United States society. Since the nineteenth century the professions have gone through a fundamental change. The predominant pattern is no longer a free practitioner in a market of services but that of the salaried expert in a large corporation. Yet the earlier model has been retained as a public relations gimmick, so that it constitutes a veil, a false image which obscures real social structures and power relations. This mystification has led to a false consciousness, so that even the poor or those on the lower-class levels of society accept the legitimacy of inequality by giving deference to people that they consider morally and intellectually superior to them. This superiority is founded on schooling and credentialing. Those who do not make it into the professions blame themselves, thus helping by their self-inflicted repression to justify inequality and closure of access to higher mobility. The professions have succeeded beyond their expectations in having an image of themselves fraught with ideology accepted as a value-free sociological ideal-type. This makes it easier for the professions to veil the element of power.

> Professions ultimately depend upon the power of the state, and they originally emerge by the grace of powerful protectors. The privileged position of a profession "is thus secured by the political and economic influence of the elite which sponsors it."[3]

POLITICAL ANALYSIS: STRUCTURAL VIOLENCE—THE POLITICS OF PROFESSIONALIZATION AND BOUNDARY MANAGEMENT

According to our theoretical perspective the process of carving out zones of autonomy based on competence is a relationship or institution of boundary management:

> In this form of encounter, the occupant of each pole claims an autonomous zone of jurisdiction based upon explicitly rationalized grounds of revelation, morality, law, power, or competence. . . . Boundary management is the dominant polarity of contemporary American society.[4]

By means of creating a boundary management or a professional expertise, a group shapes a zone of autonomy in which they are the experts and from which they can protect their interests and look toward the consolidation and enlargement of their area of jurisdiction. Such zones of autonomy give a group a power base by which to bargain with other jurisdictions in order to achieve benefits. This combination of bargaining power from a base of professional competence is the key for survival in official United States society.

Many other groups in our society that have not yet achieved a boundary management or a negotiating power of their own are locked into the two relationships of isolation and subjection. In isolation continuity is purchased at the cost of giving up the right to create change. Both parties agree to leave one another alone. The justice in this relationship allows persons the right to be left alone. The cost is the inability to effect change. In subjection a clear dominance is exercised by one person or group over another. Change takes place only with the wishes of the more powerful. Conflict must be suppressed, since the subjected do not have the ability to exercise options of which they may be aware. Not to be able to identify these relationships forces us into a rhetoric that is tantamount to giving systems a life of their own. Too many see the answer through simply defining themselves in terms of the present power relationships. For such people what is necessary to achieve the American Dream is to get out of isolation and subjection and achieve direct bargaining and boundary management. Those who cannot do so are considered to be either lazy, weak, or defective in some other way.

By applying this new political language, for example, to the health professions, we can see that organized medicine led by the American Medical Association is a formidable boundary management that has fused a coalition of boundaries with other groups such as pharmaceutical companies, insurance companies, legislators, and hospitals. Together this coalition has determined the cost, direction, and quality of the health delivery system. Within these boundaries such organizations exercise a total power over their personnel. Nurses among others were for a long time, and to a great extent still are, isolated from one another and therfore unable to create meaningful change or conflict. As a group and as individuals they were subjected by a coalition of largely white, male professionals who jealously guarded their prerogatives. There is no doubt that these men sincerely believe that what they were and are doing is in the best interest not only of themselves but also of the American public. What is at question here is not their sincerity but their narrow interpretations of what constitutes quality health care.

Institutions are essentially human relationships in motion. Politics is the ability to participate in the choosing of those human relationships which constitute the institutions in our society and which allow us to respond to problems. To be deprived of such a participation due to exclusion by others constitutes a violation of our human rights. It is an impoverishment that prevents people from taking the direction of institutions or their own human relationships into their own hands.

In United States society too many assume that the upward mobility by which one climbs out of isolation and subjection into negotiable positions and a competence of one's own is determined only by a willingness to work hard and seize the opportunities available. We often fail to recognize that there are organized groups, or boundary managements, that have a vested interest in preventing others from achieving their own autonomy. The autonomy and stability characteristic of the managerial class has been possible because it is prepared to defend its boundaries by restricting innovations to those that maintain the status quo. Thus violence does not have to be directly physical or overt to be violence—whatever prevents people from achieving the opportunity for a more human life, such as lobbying against legislation that regulates dangerous but profitable drugs, is violent.

Unfortunately this is the dominant relationship in United States society: boundary management in the service of incoherence, which constitutes the institutionalization and legitimation of institutionalized violence. Boundary management in the paradigm of incoherence means giving social and political approval to the pursuit of power after power. Persons caught in this chase refuse or are unwilling to stop violating others whose exclusion is necessary so that the few might continue to pursue wealth and power.

Because of their very position in the social hierarchy, the professions socialize us as competitive individuals. Too many of us believe that if we can get into positions of power through the professional ranks, we will be able to do something about the powerlessness of the Latino community. Again we must remind ourselves not to be naive. Professional education prepares us to give individualized service, which is a personal remedy for ills of a social nature. We, even as minorities, help to create a screen for the problems caused by bureaucratic systems. In this way we unknowingly become buffers for a brutal system that does not know or respect you or me as persons. So we ignore political action and analysis for more individual therapy. Our power as professionals is usually individual power to increase our status and prestige. Our very education emphasizes specialization to the neglect of the whole. The technocratic ideology of science and objectivity buffers those of us who are engineers and natural scientists from the political and social consequences of our work. We are always told that we cannot be responsible for the whole world, so we develop a sense of limited ethical responsibility. Further-more, we are badly wounded in our humanity by this fragmentation; our private self is allowed to muse about ethics, while the purposes of science are shaped by the dominant class. Ironically, we wake up one day and recognize that we have a great deal of the power of powerlessness.

> Paradoxically, the same ideology of the 'expert' which gives the technician a certain autonomy within his or her own specialty, simultaneously prepares the technician to execute blindly the designs of others.[5]

The universities are part and parcel of this fragmentation. In an increasingly credentialed society education serves as the central legitimation of the new forms of inequality. The dominant ideological apparatus of the system is the school.

> The various units in the system of higher education have themselves been relatively standardized and arranged in a recog-nized system of hierarchical prestige. This system operates as a switchboard to the world of work, but as a switchboard that would, at the same time, determine the distance and the speed of the trains. The trains are the different classes of colleges, uni-versities, and professional schools at which the passengers arrive after having been filtered by a number of other switchboards.[6]

The ivy-covered walls of academe provide a mystique of legitimate and superior authority for the professions within its embrace.

> The setting of the training process within the environment of an academic community with primary concerns in the dispas-sionate profession of knowledge itself serves to extend the range of legitimation, to add lustre and super-authority to the ideals of detachment, public rather than self-interest, service to an ideal and ethic. The universities have gained a legitimation of a util-itarian kind by the demonstrable needs which are met by those it certifies as competent—this allows the continued presence of many faculties whose contribution is demonstrably non-utilitarian in character.[7]

Thus the humanities that should provide us with a vision of how to re-create the world are turned into the poor relatives, the flunkies of the affluent practical professional courses of study.

The professional schools in the universities, in order to give a further cover of "all-aroundness," insist on courses in philosophy, ethics, history, and literature. They bow toward the rhetoric of creativity and the search for meaning in one's work and initiative. But all of these laudable goals are *defined* by education itself in such a way that it is compatible with the requirements of production in advanced industrial capitalism. All discontent is treated as an individual problem to be dealt with by the conflict resolution of still another professional, the industrial psychologist. The protests of subordinate professional workers can be managed by giving them more of the same: *individual* privileges. This approach coincides with professionalism's own ideological emphasis on individual career goals and individual solutions. The political is circumvented by a stress on individual malcontents.

> The ideology of professionalism deflects the comprehensive and critical vision of society which is necessary to reassess the social functions of professionalism. In this sense, professionalism functions as a means for controlling large sectors of educated labor and for co-opting its elites.[8]

Ordinary men and women, citizens find it difficult to challenge this privilege because society has convinced them that they must first become legitimate, must achieve power on society's terms before they can challenge the system. But, again, this individualizes the protest because the only solution is too often purely personal, that is, individual hard work so that you can make it to the top and change things. Once you are at the top, the system wins. The best of our people by getting to the top of their profession cannot help but legitimize inequality and elitism; they are living proof that knowledge is beneficent power. Latinos in the barrios unconsciously absorb this hierarchical vision of polity and society, thus making it easier for those in power to exercise privilege and power without even having to prove special ability.

CREATING ALTERNATIVES: THE MIDDLE-CLASS LATINO PROFESSIONAL AS POLITICAL INNOVATOR

Too often we see our education only as a preparation for a career goal. We establish priorities in relationship to a particular marketable profession. But we cannot afford to forget that education is political, that is, it is preparing us either to sustain a particular way of life, to dissolve it through responsible critique, or to create alternatives to what does not work. Unfortunately, most of us do not realize that education is a mirror of the culture, and so schooling prepares us to *preserve* rather than critique and re-create. Most of our education is therefore socialization, and university education is a more sophisticated level of preparing us to agree or to want what the society desires for us. This brings us close to a definition of repression: the dream of every state is to achieve a political victory over its subjects without the weapons of threats and promises. The aim of all political masters is to base their power upon the spontaneous consent of the governed. If the people can be made to duplicate spontaneously within themselves the society's will, so that what the system wills the people desire, then the will of the master and the will of the ruled are one, and now it is no longer necessary to base the power of the society on force but on the people's love for the master. This is why so much time and effort is spent on appealing to love of country, democratic principles, and nostalgic genuflections toward a glorious past.

Education also means a *critique* that presupposes a consciousness that separates us from the embrace of the society. It is this understanding of education that places us as Latinos who profess a vision of truth and beauty based on love on a collision course with the marketability of Latinos in the 1980s. White, liberal America often has good tendencies and wishes us well. But what they really want to do is to save their free-enterprise system by giving us access to the same tools that are available to them so that we can all legitimately and as equals compete with each other. But we know that not everybody will have equal access, and so we search and search for ways to rationalize our "privileges." We know that the great majority of our people will never make it in the system's understanding of success. We have to rationalize because we have accepted white, liberal America's understanding of professional, that is, an autonomous area of competence such as computer programmer, physicist, doctor, lawyer, or professor which now allows us to demand status, power, and money.

There is another path. A Latino professional middle class will play a critical role in our community. But what kind of middle class? What does it mean to be middle class? In keeping with our theoretical perspective it is possible for us to re-vision old and static concepts of the middle class. The poor are seen as the lower class or subclass of a hierarchical society. The middle class, usually the professional class, is considered as the climbing class who escaped poverty and who are on their way to the upper echelons of power and money. The middle class is often mistrusted as the group that advances at the expense of the poor. Many of our people either resent or envy the middle class. These feelings also have their roots in Latin America, where "la clase media" is looked upon as against the poor and Indian population. This view of society is based on stereotypes of class antagonism and therefore fails to analyze what is actually and potentially present. We may distinguish three kinds of middle class: that which seeks to maintain the status quo, another that wants to destroy a society with no alternatives to create another, and, finally, a group of men and women who share a common task—to create a more human community. Therefore, class, and especially middle class, must not be perceived merely on grounds of property or wealth, prestige, power or authority, or professional standing.[9] We cannot say that because people are poor or wealthy, they will be revolutionaries or conservatives. Regardless of what class people have been born into or have achieved, their *choice* in regard to helping in the creation, preservation, or destruction of a society is decisive. Rich and poor may at times have a common desire to preserve the status quo, with the poor hoping to be rich some day. This class of poor people considers reformers and revolutionaries alike as dangerous people who threaten their dreams. They will therefore resist change. On the other hand, those who want to quite literally bomb the system see it as evil and beyond repair. All their efforts are bent upon bringing down the system, with no other society in mind to replace it. Others who become conscious of the need for reforming society become aware precisely because of the opportunities afforded them by "middle-class" education and professional training that is supposed to make them defenders of the status quo. Instead they see fundamental injustices in their society. They hope to create or implement ways to reduce and eliminate human poverty *structurally*, that is, by changing the institutions and conditions of society so as to guarantee the incorporation of new generations of excluded people into the benefits of that society.

The threat and the promise are side by side. The danger is that as middle class, some Latinos will only be eager to embrace the goods, values, and styles of life characteristic of the middle class worldwide. The great potential is that a professional and salaried Latino middle class will occupy positions that provide the most effective leverage for transforming a society. Latino middle-class professionals will have to decide if they are interested in participating in the preservation, destruction, or transformation of a society. Within such a perspective of middle class, Latinos need not suffer from a success guilt or allow themselves to be called *vendidos*, or "sold out." To be successful or to make it can be transformed to mean men and women, regardless of background, who share the same vulnerability because they act to implement fundamentally new and better changes in all areas of life.

We spoke earlier of a professional who passionately speaks the truth, who cares about justice and love in the public as well as in the private realm. This pursuit must be made real and concrete in the everyday world. Plato taught us that the Academy had a practical meaning, that its goal was the condition of the state, not only the world of *ideals*.[10] In other words, the aim of education is to shape one's society, one's *polis* according to a vision. To be political is to know the dialectical relationship between the realm of *Eidos* and the concrete realm. After all, we can only dissolve the concrete and re-create if we have some understanding that humanity is rooted in the search for truth. For example, justice and compassion become concrete and therefore political when a Latina lawyer uses her skills to protect the right of children to a good education that will allow them consciously to shape their environment. Yet winning the case is not enough; what remains is to involve oneself in the quality of education, the preparation of teachers, the role of the community, and on and on. Here politics means always taking the next step to shape the ever-emerging newness of life. Such a lawyer together with other professionals can form task forces to create alternatives for others, that is, to help them become political so that they can sustain, dissolve, or give rise to new institutions. What is being shaped and broken in order to be molded again is human relationships or institutions which belong to all of us. In this sense politics is what we can and must do together. Latino professionals with this view of politics look to share their skills with others so that everybody will be able to *profess* their vision of the truth through skills. In this sense professional training enables us to protect ourselves and others from a system that feeds on powerlessness.

As Latino professionals and members of the transforming middle class, we need not perpetuate the same old, tired power relationships. Previously we used the term *inherited* boundary management to describe the usual search for zones of autonomy. We have already seen that there is another way to enact boundary management, and that is in the service of transformation. This is known as a strategy of subversion, a term taken from the Latin, which means to turn (*verto*) from below (*sub*). Rather than using a zone of autonomy to prevent change and preserve power, the professional can use her or his power to create liberated zones within which new approaches can be envisioned and fostered. But to believe that Latino professionals who have power will automatically be more loving than white professionals is naive. Power is power because it is scarce and comparative; often nothing has changed except the skin color of those who wield power. We do not so much need power as the capacity to transform our lives and our environment; this entails recognizing that we are not atomistic individuals but a community of people who need one another to realize our humanity. Capacity has five faces: a new consciousness, creativity, linked power in community, a shared justice, and a new connection to the sacred as the source of our capacity. To pursue power is to be driven by an insatiable individualism which makes others a threat. Freedom for rugged individualists means the right to be released from responsibility for others. Freedom in community entails the joy and suffering of creating new linkages with others.

The key for all Latino professionals is to separate the progressive human meaning of one's work from the ideological function inscribed in one's role by society. This begins as a task of personal salvation and liberation.

> Instead of the self remaining embedded unconsciously in the mysterious power of the other, incoherence breaks the spell and, in this case, leads to the free experience and analysis of opposing selves and their patterns of encounter within the individual and with others. Emanation itself is then transformed into an embodiment of the remaining true mystery of one's own self, and no longer of one's own unexamined self or the mysterious power of others.[11]

Challenging the structure of inequality requires a fundamental redefinition of the self. For professionals to succeed in this venture they cannot do it as fragmented individuals:

> Breaking with ideology, finding new norms for the social production of knowledge and the social uses of competence, demands passion, vision, and hard work. This major historical task can only be sustained by a solitary collectivity, aware of its past and of its place in the overall struggle for human liberation. In a historical perspective, abandoning the "subjective illusion" and the seduction of bourgeois individualism becomes the premise of personal freedom.[12]

Thus the passage from seeing problems in a purely personal perspective to an evaluation of their structural causes begins to heal the split between the personal and the political realm. This phase of political and social consciousness involves the development of new norms and new criteria that are alien to the logic of the individual pursuit of power.

> Institutionalized power that serves to maintain an enduring capacity to generate and absorb persistent transformation may take the form of procedures linking individuals in community as among scientists, or as between government and opposition in a legislative assembly. Individuals may be linked by commitments to common tasks of individual, social or political therapy, by intellectual collegiality, by love—always, by shared consciousness and creativity for collaborating in the world-wide task of transforming unintended, uncontrolled change into justice.[13]

For a professional to be rooted in this way in the community is to have a different concept of wealth. Rather than the zero-sum total, the bottom line, we can see wealth from a different perspective that allows a broader understanding of wealth based on human relationships. The joy of seeing people organize and change their environment because they are now actors is priceless. This is the real understanding of *respeto* that our culture insists upon. We want not a system that will respect our right to achieve power after power but a system that will respect our persons *as* persons. A system based on power is condemned to ambivalence toward personhood. Friends in a competitive situation are always prospective masters over each other, and victory will come to him or her who marshals the stronger weapons with greater skill. The other is the enemy. People in such a system cannot afford to love one another. Success in terms of power only serves to highlight their failure in terms of friendship. To cover such an emptiness and loneliness people strive for more power in order to make the suffering worth it. *Respeto* for Latinos means to give every man and woman his or her due, that is, to give deference because as a person they are sacred. A system, that is, organized ways of relating, that is incapable of ensuring this kind of respect for persons does not deserve to exist.

So we come to see that marketability means unceasing competition where others are the enemy. On the other hand, professing the hope that men and women can implement a new truthful vision through their insights and acquired skills is the alternative. For this reason we must see our education as being political. We have received our education largely *because* we are the members of an excluded group. It would be a supreme irony if we then allow the agenda of others to make us the policing role models for our people. What we have to do is to be persons *for* and *with* the community. This means creating strategies together with others to solve common problems on a plane of equality. To be a good leader in our community means to put ourselves out of business by leading people to connect to what made us different—our own authentic selfhood. For Rousseau the most important reason for citizen participation was not efficiency but authenticity: to be oneself meant to shape one's destiny, to unite thought and action, to guide the forces that shape one's life. Octavio Paz, a Mexican philosopher and poet, has argued that one of the characteristics that distinguishes us from Anglos is the cult of the festival. Paz sees the festival as a religious celebration because every true festival is communion. Festival for the Latino represents not separation but participation, not individualism but joining together.[14] Rousseau used the same image and reality of festival to signify a new politics, participatory democracy: the people in the festival become actors themselves.[15]

Finally, let us reflect on a deeper aspect of what it means to be a professional. Truth, love, beauty, and justice can be pursued and made concrete in the world in an infinite number of different ways—this is our human, political task. Some will do it as lawyers, nurses, teachers, or social workers. Underlying each of these helping professions is a calling. Plato and Socrates both stressed that a person had to find one's life's calling by being in touch with one's *daimon*, that is, fate or destiny.[16] As a professional connected to one's life's calling and not the manipulation of the market, a person is called by one's own *daimon* to serve as a guide for others. A guide is someone who assists others to come into contact with their own *daimon*, self, or mystery. Only those who are in touch with this source will be able to invoke it in others. Thus, the presence of *daimon* in Socrates was what determined his educational and political mission: to heal the split between possibility and reality. It is precisely the essential life choice, or *daimon*, of the professional that must protect our legal, medical, engineering, teaching tasks from becoming mere economic pursuit. This presence of a nonrational reality must be preserved because it maintains an element of mystery which is involved whenever persons hope to participate in one another's lives. Moreover, it is the presence of the *daimon* that gives professionals their authority. Thus, when they speak out on behalf of medical rights, legal abuses, building humane cities, or the protection of children, they do so not because of a desire to protect a vested interest but in the interests of others. The term "authority" taken from the Latin verb *augeo*, *augere*, means to give increase to the other, to lead a person to become their own author. Anybody not interested in this kind of transformative authority holds an illegitimate pseudoauthority based on degrees, laws, competence, or other justifying mechanisms.

Now it is precisely our *daimon*, our gift to reach out and shape the world, that is exploited by the present economic system. Responding to our inner fate through work is what constitutes our labor. This understanding of our labor as fulfilling our fate helps us to realize why the profit motive is really a kind of poverty. This profit-seeking economic system wishes to possess and dominate our labor, that is, our *daimon*, for its own profit. As an alternative we can create ourselves and the world through our labor, or the fulfillment of ourselves through shaping the world. This is the opposite of alienation, the loss of the self. Moreover, it was Marx who wrote that a human being became human or a species being to the extent that the other as a human being has become a need for him or her. In other words, people become human *because* of their necessary relatedness to one another, not in spite of or in competition with each other. Moreover, mutually fulfilling relationships constitute the new man and woman as wealthy or rich.[17] Authentic middle-class Latino professionals have an inner drive or necessity to create wholeness; by expressing this inner need they become truly free.

One might legitimately ask are there professionals who actually choose the commitment spoken of here. We have to know that this is possible. There are individuals who have decided to be a different kind of professional. Dr. Joseph Kramer had a lucrative medical practice in the suburbs when he realized how empty his life really was.[18] He moved quickly and established a new practice in a barrio in New York City, where his clients are almost all Latinos and blacks. The community has accepted him and trusts him. He makes home visits and treats his patients with respect and concern; he counsels people having emotional problems. Dr. Kramer, who has learned Spanish, cares deeply about people to the extent that he made a conscious decision to limit his income to one-half of what it had been before. We badly need stories of this kind with regard to the reality of transformation. People have to be asking the right questions and be open to seeing and creating alternatives. We need people to do this in all walks of life. Furthermore, Dr. Kramer is an Anglo, not a Latino. This forces us to face our tendency to speak about Anglos as a monolith of unconcerned people. Dr. Kramer is Anglo, but he does not have an Anglo attitude, that is, a belief of superiority. Furthermore, he serves as a hope to all of us that racial and ethnic wounds can be healed.

CONCLUSION

Latino professionals in the latter 1980s will be in a powerful position. As the welfare state is dismantled by powerful interests, there is a considerable lack of opportunity for our communities. Those who can take advantage of what is available will be at a premium because they will be a scarce commodity. To refuse to take advantage of this power for personal aggrandizement will demand a new kind of Latino/ Latina professional. Such professionals will have an opportunity to politicize themselves and others. Only persons connected to themselves can create the vision to build a society of equal participation in the way of life of transformation.

8. Choices for Latinos:

Creating the Present and the Future

Latinos have three fundamentally different ways by which to build the present and our future. Each of us must choose; we cannot be neutral. Furthermore, it is important to understand the underlying significance of how we decide to shape our lives. Two of our available paradigms, emanation and incoherence, no longer give us the capacity to confront problems. They are mortally flawed because they forbid the emergence of the new community: the self, our neighbor, and the transpersonal sacred. The only viable choice for Latinos, as well as others, is the transforming paradigm. Four models as choices for Latinos will be discussed: the traditional model, the assimilationist, the fragmented, and the transforming model. The traditional model corresponds to the way of life of emanation; the assimilationist and fragmented models are two different forms of the way of life of incoherence; and the transforming model parallels the ultimate way of life of transformation.

For some time now I have been concerned with helping to develop strategies for Latinos based on the theoretical view of life represented in this book: a theory of transformation, that is, reflection and action that allows us to deal simultaneously with the personal, the political, the historical, and the sacred faces of our lives.

Now that we know the theory and have seen its application in many dimensions of our daily lives, I would like to summarize our dialogue, our encounter of transformation, with some final reflections and symbols that point us toward the choices available to Latinos as they build a present and future. As we have seen, Latinos have three fundamental choices, three paradigms by which to enact all of our eight archetypal relationships. I would like to speak of four models that are another way of speaking about our three ultimate ways of life and that I believe will help us to understand where we have been, where we are, and what we can and must do together. These four models are the traditional, the assimilationist, the fragmented, and the transforming model.

THE TRADITIONAL MODEL

In discussions with fellow Latinos and non-Latinos we often used terms such as "traditional," "assimilated," or "transforming." I would like to reinterpret these concepts and to see them in the light of our theoretical perspective. The Latino traditional model points to a whole way of life that hangs together. Authority comes from God, to the head of state, through the father and elders to the family and community. Love, sin, the divine, death, meaning, virtue, marriage, and sex are all explained, understood, and lived as a total fabric of life. Everybody knows their place in such a scheme of life. Suffering and anguish are given meaning to the extent that they end by reconciling a person for successfully staying in their niche. It is truly a sacred canopy since everything is endowed with an overwhelming mystique. People outside of the canopy are outside of the pale of real life. Often the single household comes to symbolize in its architecture and authority patterns the whole cosmos. The customary high walls that surround the living quarters of Latin American countries protect *and* contain the inhabitants. Here you are safe and can enjoy the mystery of *Dios*, father, mother, and significant others. Outside is still a mystery, but a limited security that has to be buffered and bargained with. Beyond the pale of one's ethnic community is darkness, fear, and suspicion such that strangers from the North, even though they are Mexican or Chilean or Peruvian, are the subject of suspicion.

Within one's family, ethnic, or national container, persons are limited to the five relationships in which they were socialized: emanation, subjection, isolation, buffering, and direct bargaining within the sacred canopy of emanation. Sin, shame, and guilt are very powerful as containing factors. Conflict and change are severely limited and to be practiced only by the male guardians of the family, clan, and culture. This world works only as long as people do not raise fundamental questions based on their own experiences. You cannot question because you cannot even imagine an alternative world. The self is therefore absent as a source of resistance. Security is the hallmark of this model. To feel trapped is not necessarily painful if one simply sees it as fate or god's will. A sense of resignation can also provide one with great energy to work within the given limits. Moreover, what gives this model its flexibility and ability to survive are the two relationships of buffering and direct bargaining. If skillfully employed, these relationships constantly suppress potential breakdowns that could culminate in rebellion. Renewed appeals made to loyalty or god's love can buffer a person's despair. To give people greater benefits such as more affection, money, or freedom of movement is to mollify them before they get too far in their rebellion. Thus, women can heighten their ability to demand an increase in sharing the material wealth of their male guardians by becoming sulky, disobedient, or withdrawn. Such a subterfuge was reduced to being a ploy to get more of the same, not really a preparation to change radically their lives. But one never knew. So to keep emanation as both the dominant relationship and as the ultimate paradigm, the other relationships were used to eventually return the person to normal, being trapped in a golden cage.

Now when Latinos come to this country and have to face strangers outside of their world, they suffer incoherence: they really don't know what to do with them. To resort to the old relationships would be a disaster since these others do not share the same web of life. The Anglos do not respond to *respeto* except to see it as weakness and therefore to take advantage of us. How can traditional Latinos bargain with people who have fixed prices, laws, and boundaries for everything? In this context the web of life cannot be sustained. The children especially no longer feel secure and see their parents hesitant and silent in front of authority figures. Our parents often responded to this crisis by creating two worlds for us that caused great suffering. At home we were to speak Spanish and uphold the old patterns and way of life of emanation. In school we had to survive by being like the others, that is, learn new patterns of behavior, especially direct bargaining and boundary management and, more importantly, a new way of life, that of incoherence.

To escape this crisis some parents tried to enforce the traditional paradigm through physical intimidation. Subjection was used to try to shore up a way of life that was shattered forever. This is the use of subjection in the service of incoherence, because it constitutes a refusal or inability to deal with the breakdown of the old. Other of our parents romanticized the old world and tried to relive it, seeing it as the golden age of their lives. Again, we see here buffering and a *cariño* of emanation for a culture that is dying. The children look to authority for security. If they saw their parents relating them to a world and culture that did not in fact give them a sense of well-being, here and now, they began to call their parents old-fashioned. But more seriously, the children who needed security to grow were attracted to the symbols and persons of authority in the new culture. A quick comparison often led many of us to consider our Latino culture and parents as stigmas, as cause for embarrassment, and a heritage that perpetuated our lack of security.

The understanding of paradigms, or the underlying sources of life by which all of our relationships, feelings, values, and ideas are given ultimate meaning, helps us to understand much more profoundly classics such as *Five Families* and *La Vida* by Oscar Lewis[1] and *La Carreta* by Rene Marques,[2] as well as recent commentaries such as *A Welfare Mother* by Susan Sheehan.[3] When the families described left their rural birthplace and migrated to the cities of Mexico or Puerto Rico or to the United States, they did not simply exchange muddy roads for paved streets; they literally went from one ultimate way of life, emanation, to another, incoherence. These are two ways of life that are mutually exclusive in conflict: *el choque de las culturas*, the collision of cultures, is a radical confrontation, a grim struggle. People who are not restrained by seeing the world as resting in the hands of God see those who are still bound by such a moral ultimacy as naive. Even Latinos who have become cynical are more dangerous because they are recent victims and so understand how to exploit the incoherence. This is the situation poetically and yet painfully depicted in the film *El Norte*. A young illegal Guatemalan is betrayed by a "Pocho," a Mexican who is neither Mexican nor American but a perfect example of a fragmented, incoherent Latino who sought his identity through achieving power in this society. The Guatemalan *expected* loyalty because both were Latino victims in an Anglo world; the "Pocho" acted according to a new set of rules that negated the loyalty of emanation to be found among fellow Latinos, or *paisanos*. The new morality was based on defeating a competitor at any cost, and so he betrays the Guatemalan young man to the hated *migra*, the immigration authorities.

Elena Padilla in her excellent book, *Up From Puerto Rico*, of the late 1950s clearly understood in an intuitive manner the underlying thrust of a person's life. She knew that something had profoundly altered Puerto Ricans after living for a period of time on the mainland.

This change she was able to perceive by observing carefully the interaction between newly arrived Puerto Ricans and those who have been here for a long time or were born here.

> Soon after settling in New York, Puerto Rican migrants find that many of the expectations they have nursed about New York and their future lives here have begun to shatter. For example, the norms and values they hold concerning "proper" and "correct" behaviour are not the same as those held in New York—even among Hispanics. Individuals who left the island as adults and have been in New York for many years do not conform to their expectations either; they act differently and have learned to look at and weigh things differently from the ways in which such things are done in the island. . . . Puerto Ricans in New York do not help each other as they do in Puerto Rico and are not "united." New migrants speak frequently of the lack of consensus and solidarity among Puerto Ricans as reflected in the weakening and lack of recognition of mutual obligations among friends, relatives and countrymen.[4]

Puerto Ricans with a common heritage had become strangers to each other because they were relating to each other in the service of different ultimate paradigms of life. This is something for all of us as Latinos to keep in mind when we are automatically delighted to see a fellow Latino appointed, elected, or hired for a position. It depends on what ultimate service his or her life is oriented toward. Let us reserve the term brother and sister, *hermano* or *hermana*, for those who share with us a dedication to the creation of a new and fundamentally better life.

In *La Carreta, The Ox Cart*, a campesino family is torn by dreams of a golden future characterized by the good life in the cities and the pristine past which linked them to the sacred, the land, each other, and the common values of hard work, sharing, and love. The two sons, Luis and Chaguito, are eventually lost in the jungle of the cities, and it is the women, Doña Gabriela, the mother, and Juanita, who seek their sacred roots by returning to Puerto Rico *and* by going home within themselves to renew a world gone dead. This play is a contemporary reenactment of the journey of transformation that speaks poignantly to the experience of all Latinos who migrated to the United States. A generation later Tato Lavierra takes up the theme again in his provocative book of poetry *La Carreta Made a U-Turn*.[5] He rejects a romantic return to Puerto Rico as the answer and correctly points out that many Puerto Ricans are here to stay and so have to establish themselves here. However, he hedges by writing that a return to Puerto Rico is possible if return means to affirm one's Afro-Caribbean heritage and to reject the white upper-middle-class Hispanophile ideal. Certainly it is the three aspects, Afro-Caribbean-European, that the Puerto Rican must incorporate in creating an alternative here and now. We as Latinos cannot go back to the old web of life; we must not become cynical like the others and live fragmented lives, and we cannot become Anglo regardless of the efforts of some to assimilate. We cannot remain angry forever and allow it to lock us in confrontation after confrontation.

In *Five Families* the husband and wife are often at odds because the two are now living in different paradigms. A man who knows who he is in relationship to a particular woman quickly loses that identity when she acts according to the relationships of a different world. Thus men who controlled their wives on the *rancho* because the god of emanation, the culture, and society gave them the perennial right to do so are at a loss when a wife supports them. Her economic power, due to a move to the city, gives her not only direct bargaining power but actually endows her with a certain mysterious power. Husbands try to fight the inevitable but often give into a quiet passivity of their own. They try to preserve the web of life by accepting the new way but know that the old world is gone when a woman supports the family. Moreover, the wife sees the change in herself and might or might not like what she has become. But to survive they have to go on without understanding what is really happening to them.

THE ASSIMILATIONIST MODEL: LIVING WITH INCOHERENCE

As we discussed earlier, there are only three ultimate paradigms which shape our lives: emanation, incoherence, and transformation. The Latino traditional model corresponds to the paradigm of emanation. The assimilationist model destroys the loyalty characteristic of the traditional heritage; to assimilate is to accept the way of life of incoherence, that is, the constant shifting of alliances in the search for power. The pursuit of power cannot bring back the security that was lost with the breaking of the inherited container. In fact, it is not possible to be secure in a society based on liberalism. A liberal society is not intended to give security but its opposite, insecurity, so that people will continuously be "forced to be free" to compete for power. We soon learn that this system cannot provide security, so we are disillusioned. This failure of the assimilationist model in the public realm forces us to seek sources of emanation in the private realm. This inability to make our lives whole by being connected to our neighbors and to the transpersonal mystery in a new way is to live with incoherence.

Still many of us made the second choice, the assimilationist model. We wanted to be like the Anglos because they made things happen; they had power and a lot of nice things to prove their superiority. Of course the Anglos did nothing to discourage this attitude of superiority. We fed their prejudice with our need to belong, to be accepted, and, sadly, with our growing self-hatred. Lighter-skinned Latinos could always pass, intermarry, and merge into the other culture. The *morenitos*, or dark-skinned among us, had a more difficult time and always had to prove themselves by being better. Better at what? Better at the Anglo game, which meant it was still their game, their definition of life that dominated all of us. So we fought with Anglos on the school grounds, danced better than they did, and even took their girlfriends.

At home we argued that the Americans let their daughters go out to dances and to stay out later and to have boyfriends and on and on. Our parents called us *malcriados*, sassy children, because we lost the respect of emanation for the previous way of life. Some of us refused to speak Spanish and sometimes mocked our culture. Thus many of us, because we felt there were no choices, allowed ourselves to be assimilated into the Anglo patterns of living: competitive, individualistic, detached so that we could be upwardly mobile. We wanted to be somebody in this society. Some changed their name, others began to call themselves "Spaniards" or even "I'm American now." The sadness is that although we were moving toward greater personal autonomy by developing skills and pulling ourselves up by the proverbial bootstraps, it was now a new system giving us our identity. New roles were defined by a system in which occupational skills told us if we were somebody. Many of us were still high-school dropouts, blue-collar laborers, construction workers, and field hands. There were a growing number of professionals, but this created class differences among Latinos who were previously all poor. Upwardly mobile Latinos looked upon the others with contempt and felt that they were better. Self-hatred was now projected onto the group. Get out of the barrio if you want to make it because your people will pull you down was the slogan of teachers and counselors. You are one of the better Puerto Ricans, or Mexicans, or Latinos. Better because you are self-reliant, hardworking, and motivated. But really you are better because you are like us. Assimilation is really the search for power that will make us the envy of others. It is public opinion, society, that tells us who we are. But this is not like the traditional paradigm where we knew who we were and had security. Exactly. This search for power after power in its own way is a new search for total security but without the ability to ever achieve it. Liberal white society is a cheat because it is really trying to tell us that a system called free enterprise can give everybody a good life. The cost of this way of life of incoherence is repressing the fact that many will never make it, are *intended* to never make it, so that the game of running in the same spot will continue.

Nor does life hang together in this assimilationist model. It is really living with incoherence. Security is gone: How can I be sure of anything when the upward climb has caused me to be disconnected from myself, my community, my past, my parents, and a loving God? Again, many of us realized this but felt that there was no other choice. Some Latinos did resist as we can see from the various nationalistic movements such as the Chicano Brown Berets and Puerto Rican Young Lords. These groups at times responded to the disillusionment with a nationalism that intended to go back to the old ways. Yet, this is the creation of a pseudoparadigm of emanation because it takes an aspect of our life, racial and ethnic identity, and invests it with total meaning. It is another embrace promising security because life in the system of power is so precarious. There were many shades of meaning and disagreements, but I think that many Latinos were looking for a kind of purification or redemption, a justification by asserting our past. This was a kind of rebellion because we knew what we did not want, Anglo culture, but we did not know what to put in its place except a vague sense of returning to our *raices*, or roots. In response to an attempt on the part of Anglos to give us a competitive system that did not work for us, we retreated to a total way of life that once gave meaning to the cosmos but which since had been shattered. We could not go back but tried to do so. This approach deepened our incoherence and threatened us with deformation.

THE FRAGMENTED MODEL

The guilt arising out of this dilemma gave rise to another form of the paradigm of incoherence that many Latinos experienced, fragmentation. To be fragmented is characterized by an attempt to live in two different worlds. People now decide to live with incoherence

as a given of life. A fragmented people act as if they are in control
by acting out the role that is given them to play as determined by
the situation. Here Latinos are still impoverished because we are cut
off from others and from our transpersonal sources. However, there
is a development in becoming "streetwise." For example, we basically
decide after having figured out the system that we are going to tell
people what they want to hear so that we can live a life of promotions with a minimum of hassle. That is our public, competitive,
public life. In the private realm Latinos attempted to hold on to a
way of life that connected them to their past. Often there was a contempt for the *Gringos* and their culture, but it could not surface. There
was also a begrudging respect based on a doubt about our own ability. At times we felt superior because we were surviving and even
doing well in spite of the Anglos. But again it was all a defensive comparison with others to tell us if we were making it and therefore a
tacit assumption that the Anglo way was superior. People cannot live
this kind of fragmentation without also severing their very souls. It
means that we still cannot be who we are; roles dictate who we are,
and this situation determines the limited choice of roles. Latinos are
caught between two worlds, one promising security by holding on
to fragments of the dying way of life of emanation and the other the
insecure rewards of power in the way of life of incoherence. The Anglo
world provides the opportunity for power that is sometimes made
more acceptable by rewarding people with consumer well-being, while
the Latino world promises a stable environment, the remnant of a
golden age that we can live within to find security in a world of dis-
continuity. So many of us try to juggle these two worlds—feeling uneasy and defeated when we cannot reconcile the two. It is really a
trade-off between accepting a dying way of life of emanation and living with incoherence to survive. Both ways of life want to possess
us, and we are caught having to keep both happy, never being able
to give ourselves to either because in our bones we are warned to hold
back that final commitment.

A Welfare Mother is an excellent study of fragmentation. It
dramatically and graphically portrays the attempts of a Latina to survive through welfare "cheating." It is fragmentation because bits and
pieces of a past rural web of life exist to give her respite from the
guilt she feels in having had to become like the rest of society in order
to protect herself and her children. But there is no ultimate direction
or grounding to her life anymore. Initially she is embarrassed to cheat
but then cheats because "everybody cheats." Her life is further fragmented by having to travel from one agency to another simply to stay

housed and fed. Whole days are consumed in visiting and waiting for case workers. She is not angry or impatient, merely sullen and more passive to protect herself from anger. She is very affectionate toward her children, but it is a losing battle because the society at large does not care about them. She lights candles to favorite saints and asks for help. Yet throughout the book there is evidence that Mrs. Santana holds onto loyalty to the family. It is her one, if not only, bulwark, an island in a world of betrayal. Her affection and love for family is a desperate act surrounded by relationships devoid of caring, compassion, or concern.

Such a situation is in reality the paradigm of incoherence because an alternative world still cannot be built. A professional, middle-class Latina also finds increasing incoherence in her attempt to juggle the two worlds of mutually exclusive ways of being. She might have accepted all the necessary patterns of behavior to be a professional such as a doctor. Deep down she at times feels guilty and finds it difficult to be a male version of a doctor. Her culture, which is still deeply embedded in her, both personally and historically, pulls her back to being a woman *because* she is married, has a man to complete her, has children to justify her life and a home in which she can be herself, that is, the self given to her by her past. If her husband responds to this nostalgic need, trouble will be inevitable. A professional woman is given respect if she is aggressive, independent, and confident. To go home and suddenly become a deferring, covertly manipulative, and pouting wife to achieve concessions cannot work. To continue to deny aspects of oneself is to invite more and more conscious suppression of what we know to be true. Sooner or later this kind of conscious suppression, because it cannot become repression, or an unconscious denial of self, will explode into confrontation. These explosions for the sake of maintaining two false worlds will continue to take place with no resolution because there is no ultimate meaning in the paradigm of incoherence. It is incoherent precisely because of the inability of people to be wholly present to themselves, others, their transpersonal sources, or situations. Thus, what began as a calculating way to face the demands of two worlds, the liberal Anglo society and the traditional Latino past, is doomed to failure. There simply is nobody home except a fragmented self that continues to create a fragmented world running from one fragment to the next.

This is no longer a rational, coldly calculated strategy of living, but a life out of control that leads to more irrational striving to force a scheme of things to work. Many Latinos, I feel, are stuck here. They have not really figured out the system, because they are still running without being able to transform their lives. Incoherence is a reality regardless of salary or status; this kind of poverty affects the rich and poor alike. This inability to shape our lives leads to anger and ambivalent feelings about what we are really loyal to. So we get caught up in rhetoric about "the damn system," the need for cultural pluralism, playing the game, and so on. Others of us do not want to change our lives. There is a satisfaction in being numb and ignoring the cost of either illusion: the pursuit of power or looking for security in powerful others. It is almost as if the two illusions feed each other in a sadomasochistic manner. When we are weary of being aggressive and competitive, we can always retreat to the home front to be indulgent with others and feel the security of possessing and being possessed. Conversely, if a person cannot exercise domination on the job, they will seek it over others at home. This kind of dualism allows the mutual violence of both worlds to continue because we can always escape to the other side, thus never having to ask what the whole system is doing to us.

THE TRANSFORMING MODEL

A growing number of Latinos are looking for a way, for good talk, to help them to go beyond the shattered container of the traditional, to overcome the temptation of assimilation and the dilemma of living in a fragmented world. The only viable response to the growing despair is the model or paradigm of persistently transforming ourselves and our relationships with others and with the sacred. For the first time, as our symbol indicates, the participatory self is at the center of her or his life. This is no longer mere subjectivism as in the incoherence of liberalism, where people are freed from obligations to one another. The participatory self is a self related to one's self, to one's neighbor, and to the transpersonal in a fundamentally new way. Relationships in the other two paradigms possess the person, whereas in this drama the self is free *because* each cares for his or her neighbor due to a new linkage to the sacred. This is a very important point. It helps to explain why even though a Latina might have achieved the relationship of boundary management on the personal level as a doctor, she is still not free to care for others as a priority since the A.M.A. defines who she is as a professional, what kind of fees she can charge, and what her upward mobility depends upon.

Many follow this kind of definition without being aware of it.

Moreover, United States society with its emphasis on status and power wants us to be in emanation to the role of doctor or lawyer such that we are an extension of a mysterious knowledge that gives us identity and power. Thus assimilation is to be absorbed into power. When Latinos realize this, they work for a compromise between their identity and the system's demands, which creates the fragmentation. But a person knows that no system of inherited or officially sanctioned relationships can give her an identity. Thus, as was described earlier, the person can realize that the sacred transpersonal is the source of her mystery. Now all eight relationships are available to shape daily living. Rather than the system, the tradition, or dual worlds at the center, the participatory self is present to decide what to do with legal skills; legal skills do not possess a Latino lawyer; the Latino who has chosen to acquire legal competence can now help to defend Latinos seeking to organize their own unions, women who are establishing health clinics, to protect undocumented workers from exploitation, and to incorporate a coalition of other professionals to create a scholarship fund. There is no end to what can be done once people are connected to a community of three: one's neighbor, one's own selfhood, and the sacred transpersonal.

Let me give some examples of what it means to be free to relate to others in the service of transformation. One day at home I noticed that my youngest son, Matthew, was sad. I asked him if he was one of my best friends, and he said, "I'm not a friend; I'm a son." What Matthew was telling me was that he still needed a lot of protection, affection, and security before he could be a friend, an equal, a strong person on his own. He still needed the relationship of emanation enacted in the way of life of transformation to prepare him to participate in a wider range of life. Later that same day I met with a young man who was refusing to write a paper because he did not like to write. I told him that he would fail the course. This is clearly subjection, but it must be employed for the purpose of teaching him to write, so that he can walk away from me and the university with skills that prepare him to participate with others in shaping a different world. This is what the transforming model is all about: persons connected to self, their neighbor, and to sacred sources can participate in creating, nourishing, destroying, and re-creating whole networks of life.

Knowledge and practice of the process of transformation in relation to some issues is not enough; it has to be done again and again. Furthermore, it is important to indicate that persons do not choose one paradigm or model once and for all and then win the revolution for good. From one moment to the next we might relate ourselves to a person in the polarity of subjection but in the paradigm of in-coherence, so that we mask the real reason for asserting ourselves. But in a moment of silence we *know* that we have been destructive; there can be no hidden agenda or fudging of the issue, such as "I did not realize what I was doing." So in regard to particular issues or per-sons, a person may be in different relationships in two different para-digms. Thus I may be very well connected in a transforming way to my mother but in a real constraint of incoherence as regards my father. Yet the authentic relationship that allows for mutual growth between my mother and me stands as a constant reminder of what transforming relationships are all about. Similarly, I believe that al-though we are in fact in different relationships at a particular point in our life, some of which are clearly destructive, still I believe that there is an underlying bent or life's choice, a whole way of life, spoken of above, that ultimately points us toward one of the three paradigms or models as our life's choice. The fundamentally new always begins as an overwhelming source of joy and fear, a paradise of fright. We can only know what the Source wants of us when we struggle to dif-ferentiate or to give concreteness to the undifferentiated.

Having a new relationship to ourself, to our neighbor, and to a loving God liberates us to use all eight relationships in regard to any problem in the service of transformation. The paradigm of trans-formation allows us to preserve what is best in our tradition, while we can critique and disallow whatever contradicts the right of all Latino men and women to be compassionate and loving persons. Thus, unlike the assimilationist/fragmented Latino, who rejects the traditional relationships and replaces them with the power relations of official United States society, the Latino or Latina who is now liberated to create new concrete forms of the eight relationships can also reject the *inherited* forms of the traditional model—emanation, subjection, isolation buffering, and direct bargaining—without reject-ing the archetypal patterns themselves, that is, the potential of each relationship. But the way of life of transformation also allows us to refuse to be limited to the inherited or created forms of the power relations of Anglo society that assimilate/fragment us in the way of life of incoherence.

So what do we end up with? Latinos who, as a result of being radically linked to others and to the sacred, can be *cariñosos*, affec-tionate, can employ their skills, exercise authority in demanding obe-dience, but who also know how to protect when necessary, know when to withdraw, who are aware when they do not know, and who are open to transforming their lives and situations. Within such a paradigm the public realm can become the realm of life renewed by the private realm and vice versa. Whatever strategies we create to solve issues on the personal or political level are also available to the other. Thus, love is restored to its proper place in *all* of life. This allows us to use all relationships because we care deeply about the people who walk into our lives. In this way we mutually fulfill each other. In contrast, the other ways of life commit us to possessing, using, and manipulating others for personal gain in security or power.

Our goal in relating to others must always be to lead them to a new kind of participation with their neighbors and the god of transformation. This is true empowerment. Anything else would be the perpetuation of dependence. To illustrate this point, I would like to recount a session with a group of welfare workers, many of whom were minorities and Latinas. They were speaking of how they helped people week after week so that many became perpetual clients. This set up a dangerous relationship based on power, so that the clients buffered their true feelings, exchanged the required docility necessary to receive benefits in the mode of direct bargaining, felt subjected by late or uncaring case workers, and generally felt trapped in a poverty that was endless. Burnt-out social workers merely processed the people, which meant that they perpetuated relationships that kept the clients in their place—dependent, poor, and humiliated. This kind of bureaucratic treatment has often led to angry encounters, because minority people and the previously quiet Latinos are experiencing a sense of injustice. They feel that they are being paid off by the system in exchange for good behavior. This awareness of manipulation has led many to question why there have to be poor people. Not to accept a sense of inherited inferiority is to ask where did our powerlessness come from and whom does it benefit? Such feelings lead to tensions that cannot be addressed by more money and quicker services; some people are rejecting a whole system. This is incoherence; there is only angry conflict, no justice, no sense of direction, and no agreement with the agents of the system. Caring but efficient bureaucrats protest that they are only doing their job, but they refuse to or cannot see that their job includes detaching themselves from their feelings, so that they can process people and turn their clients' hurt into an abstraction. The welfare worker is angry because he or she is fragmented since the bureaucrats' caring cannot be translated into effective action, as it is blocked by their professional code and hope for advancement. Some bureaucrats have been betrayed by slick and cynical people who have figured out the system and merely want to destroy by ripping it off. To these officials all welfare people are now

considered suspiciously as potential cheaters. People on each side turn
themselves and the others into an abstraction: us and them. In the
meantime the poor sink deeper into becoming an underclass, another
abstraction, and the incoherence deepens.

Many welfare workers are genuinely continuing to reach the people for whom they are responsible. We spoke of how we wanted welfare clients to take charge of their lives. But we are speaking of Latinos
recently arrived from Latin America who have little or no skills or
money and who are not aggressive. The strategy has been to work
on providing job training, welfare subsidies, and bilingual education.
Still the Latinos are unassertive. The treatment was perpetuating the
illness. Nobody thought of the importance of their sense of selfhood,
of being a people in need of being related to others and to a source
of mystery within themselves. Nobody had thought of building a
sense of confidence and of skills as extensions of who they were and
what they wanted to do. This is because gaining empowerment in
official United States society is acquiring competitive skills so you
can be independent, and caring agencies can be free of you. That is
how the social workers saw their own lives. So they sought to make
others tough and independent by providing skills; the goal was not
to lead a person to participate in shaping one's life environment. As
a result, the poor become "successfully socialized" when they learn
conforming behavior or how to compete, hold a job, be suspicious
of others, and gain power. This is assimilation into the way of life
of incoherence.

In the dialogue that ensued many of the social workers were surprised when it was insisted that they look at their own lives and
values and ask themselves what they were doing. How could they
counsel, assist, or guide others unless they knew where they were
leading people. Success has too often been identified as helping a person to assimilate into the values of power or to cope by accepting
payments. Whereas before he or she was considered to be a produc-
tive member of society, that very society at one point caused them
to lose their job because it was part of the acceptable cost of fighting
inflation. Unemployment can be created by small groups of people
making political decisions that affect all of our lives. Given this vast
system, how do social workers prevent a sense of powerlessness and
cynicism in themselves and in their clients? There is no other place
to start except to see the self as part of a larger group of people who
can link with others to create new forms of justice. As the conversation continued, some of us came to recognize that personal awareness of how systems work—that is, the particular relationships needed

to keep the combine going—are specifically dependent upon the roles that people unquestioningly follow. A conscientious person asking questions and caring deeply about others can indeed accept responsibility for dismantling a system, keeping in mind that a system is always relationships. To dismantle also carries the opposite task of creating an alternative lifestyle. This is not difficult once one accepts the risk. Certainly a social worker can organize with other colleagues, administrators, lawyers, members of the legislature, and especially the entire community, to replace regulations that hurt the poor. This is using one's skills, office, connections, and obligations owed, not for personal gain, but to change the quality of peoples' lives. This is an example of creating institutions that bind us in a common task in the service of transformation and substituting this for the power that disconnects us in the way of life of incoherence.

Finally, to be vulnerable as a self is to allow the constant emergence of new consciousness, creativity, new linkages to others, new forms of justice by staying in contact with the transpersonal source in the depths. To be a participatory self is also to be able to continue to collaborate yet to disagree and change for the sake of remaining open to the demands of new life. To organize life in this manner is to be at one and the same time personal, political, historical, and religious. To persistently shape life in the paradigm of transformation means to leave open the chain of creation as it enters through the realm of the sacred emanating the new. This emanation is then transcended through the mutual struggle between the human and the divine. This is what transformation is all about.

Notes

1. A Theory of Transformation

1. D. H. Lawrence, *The Plumed Serpent* (New York: Vintage Books, 1972).

2. Manfred Halpern is presently preparing his own study, *Transformation: Its Theory and Practice in Personal, Political, Historical, and Sacred Being*. In writing this book I have gained greatly from having read the various chapters of his manuscript.

3. Manfred Halpern, "Notes on the Theory and Practice of Transformation," Unpublished manuscript, 1980, p. 5.

4. Much of the summary above and the quotes from Halpern's theory are taken from "Four Contrasting Repertories of Human Relations in Islam: Two Pre-modern and Two Modern Ways of Dealing with Continuity and Change, Collaboration and Conflict and Achieving Justice," *Psychological Dimensions of Near Eastern Studies*, ed. L. Carl Brown and Norman Itzkowitz. (Princeton: The Darwin Press, 1977), p. 62.

5. Ibid., p. 64.

6. Ibid.

7. Ibid., pp. 64-65.

8. Ibid.

9. Ibid. pp. 77-78.

10. Ibid., p. 65.

11. Halpern, "Notes on the Theory," p. 1.

12. Ibid.

13. Halpern, "Four Contrasting Repertories," pp. 78-79.

14. Harry J. Brill, *Why Organizers Fail* (Berkeley: University of California Press, 1971).

15. Halpern, "Four Contrasting Repertories," p. 83.

16. Halpern, "Notes on the Theory," p. 10.

17. Halpern, *Transformation*, chapter three, "The Student Rebellion of the 1960's," or "A Diagnostic as Well as Critical Application of the Initial Movements of the Theory of Transformation," pp. 30-31.

18. Halpern, "Notes on the Theory," p. 10.

185

2. *The Search for Latino Identity*

1. Octavio Paz, *El Laberinto de la Soledad* (Mexico City: Fondo de Cultura Economica, 1959), p. 21.

2. Gabriel Garcia Marquez, *One Hundred Years of Solitude* (New York: Harper and Row, 1970).

3. Rolstan Adams, "The Search for the Indigenous," in *The Analysis of Hispanic Texts*, ed. Beck *et al.* (Jamaica, New York: Bilingual Press, 1976), p. 76.

4. Ibid., p. 85.

5. Octavio Paz, "Reflections: Mexico and the United States," *The New Yorker*, September 17, 1979, p. 140.

6. Ibid.

7. Octavio Paz, "Twilight of Revolution," *Dissent*, vol. 21, no. 1 (Winter 1974).

8. Philip Slater, *Earthwalk* (New York: Bantam Books, 1975).

9. Octavio Paz, *The Other Mexico: Critique of the Pyramid*, trans. Lysander Kemp (New York: Grove Press, 1972), p. 105.

10. Ralph Ellison, *Invisible Man* (New York: Random House, 1952), pp. 567-68.

11. See the study by Joan V. Bondurant, *The Conquest of Violence* (Berkeley: University of California Press, 1965).

12. See Ashley Montagu, ed., *The Concept of Race* (New York: The Free Press, 1964), especially the chapter "The Concept of Race."

13. Manfred Halpern, "Applying a New Theory of Human Relations to the Comparative Study of Racism." A paper presented for publication by the Graduate School of International Studies, University of Denver, June 1969.

14. See William I. Thompson's essay "Of Physics and Tantra Yoga," in *Passages About Earth: An Exploration of the New Planetary Culture* (New York: Harper and Row, 1974). In this essay Thompson brilliantly states the case that the consciousness of the scientist is crucial: "We no longer have a science of nature, but a science of the mind's knowledge about nature" (p. 91).

15. Shlomo Avineri's analysis of Marx's understanding of human relationships is superb. *The Social and Political Thought of Karl Marx* (Cambridge: Cambridge University Press, 1968).

16. In regard to my awareness of Liberia I am indebted to Mr. Moses Duopu, a Liberian student at Seton Hall University.

17. David Gordon, *Women of Algeria: An Essay on Change* (Cambridge, MA: Harvard University Press, 1968).

18. I learned much about this ability to affirm one's own ethnic and racial origins in order to move to a more inclusive sense of humanity from Gandhi's struggle with his identity. See Erik Erikson, *Gandhi's Truth: On the Origins of Militant Nonviolence* (New York: W. W. Norton, 1968).

19. After Malcolm X had given a talk at an eastern university, a young white woman was so moved by his remarks on racism that she followed him

to New York City to ask him if there was anything that she could do. He answered: "Nothing." He later regretted this response. See *The Autobiography of Malcolm X*, with the assistance of Alex Haley (New York: Grove Press, 1966), pp. 286 and 376.

20. In this regard see Michael Novak's book *The Rise of the Unmeltable Ethnics* (New York: Macmillan, 1973).

21. This has been the role of such men as Malcolm X, Martin Luther King, Jr., Cesar Chavez, and Gandhi.

22. Manfred Halpern, "Transformation and the Source of the Fundamentally New." A paper prepared for a Caucus for a New Political Science Panel on Archetypal Epistemology in the section on Epistemological Alternatives to Behavioralism, Annual Meeting of the American Political Science Association, Chicago, September 1, 1974, p. 42.

23. Halpern, "Applying a New Theory of Human Relations," p. 34.

3. The Politics of the Latino Family

1. David C. Gordon, *Women of Algeria: An Essay on Change* (Cambridge, MA: Harvard University Press, 1972).

2. Gregory J. Massell, "Law As an Instrument of Revolutionary Change in a Traditional Milieu, The Case of Soviet Central Asia," *Law and Society Review*, vol. 2, no. 2 (February 1968).

3. See Christopher Lasch, *Haven in a Heartless World* (New York: Basic Books, 1979).

4. On this point of the family as bastion of the *status quo* see the conversations between Daniel Berrigan and Charles Coles. *Geography of Faith* (New York: Bantam Books, 1971).

5. See C. J. Jung, *Collected Works*, Bollingen Series, vol. 8 (Princeton: Princeton University Press, 1969).

6. In this regard see the following: A. B. Ulanov, *The Feminine* (Evanston: Northwestern University Press, 1972), and Mary Daly, *Beyond God the Father Toward a Philosophy of Women's Liberation* (Boston: Beacon Press, 1973).

7. By Latino here is meant persons from the Caribbean, Central and South America, and their descendants now living in the United States. However, there are groups in Latin America such as some of the various white ethnics in Costa Rica, and Germans in Argentina, who would not be described by the analysis given here. The main thrust of this paper is of the Spanish/Mestizo Catholic strain in Latin America. Given these individual differences, it is still important and necessary to be able to generalize as long as it is recognized that there will be exceptions even among the Spanish, Indian, Mestizo element.

8. Oscar Lewis, *Five Families* (New York: New American Library, 1959).

9. See Mao's discussion of the authority patterns operative in the tradi-

tional Confucian family in Edgar Snow, *Red Star Over China* (New York: Grove Press, 1961), pp. 131-32.

10. As stated in a conversation with a Mexican father.

11. For excellent discussions of the Mother archetype see Erich Neumann's two books: *The Origins and History of Consciousness*, Bollingen Series (Princeton: Princeton University Press, 1971), and *The Great Mother*, Bollingen Series (Princeton: Princeton University Press, 1974).

12. In this regard see Joseph E. Kerns, *The Theology of Marriage: Historical Development of Christian Attitudes Towards Sex and Sanctity in Marriage* (New York: Sheed & Ward, 1964), as well as works previously cited by Harding, Ulanov, and Roszak.

13. For a further description of these myths see Alfonso Caso, *The Aztecs, People of the Sun*, trans. Lowell Dunham (Norman: University of Oklahoma Press, 1959), and Irene Nicholson, *Mexican and Central American Mythology* (London, New York, Sydney, Toronto: Paul Hamlyn, 1967).

14. Nicholson, *Mexican and Central American Mythology*, p. 28.

15. Betty and Theodore Roszak, eds., *Masculine/Feminine* (New York: Harper and Row, 1969), foreword, p. 8.

16. See, for example, Marilyn French, *The Women's Room* (New York: Harcourt Brace Jovanovich, 1978).

17. Ulanov, *The Feminine*, pp. 277-85.

18. Jolande Jacobi, "Symbols in an Individual Analysis," *Man and His Symbols*, ed. C.G. Jung (New York: Dell, 1973), p. 327.

19. James Olney, *Metaphors of Self* (Princeton: Princeton University Press, 1972), p. 17.

20. An archetype is the necessary form in which concrete relationships manifest themselves. We cannot experience the archetype directly; we come into contact with it through symbols in dreams, visions, and fantasies. Although universal, it is imperative that individuals constellate the archetype in a personal concrete manner. Every archetype has a negative and positive aspect. For this reason the issue is not to reject one's mother or father but to transform the possessive relationship into one of mutual liberation. Thus, a young man's mother and a young woman's father can become their friends in the process of their individuation. Similarly, the internal mothers, our sources in the unconscious, instead of being our enemy can creatively be related to our conscious self.

21. Leo Tolstoy, *Ann Karenina*, trans. David Magarshack (New York, Toronto, London: New American Library, 1961), pp. 154-55.

22. Ulanov, *The Feminine*, pp. 241-68.

23. Ibid., pp. 284-85.

24. I am very much aware of the current crisis that Latino families, especially the Puerto Rican family in the New York City area and the Chicano family in the California area, are facing. The growth of single, female parent families is cause for deep concern. In addition, the pregnancy rate for unmarried teenage women from these specific groups is alarmingly high.

Therefore, the family politics described in this chapter is even more important. The inability or refusal of Latino men and women to create new and better relationships is partially responsible for the breakdown of many families. The strong family unit is what empowered us to survive the racism that affected our well-being in this society. We have to struggle with each other as men and women, husband and wife, father and mother, in order to protect and nourish the next generation.

25. As quoted in Armando B. Rendon, *Chicano Manifesto* (New York: Collier, 1971), p. 189.

26. June K. Singer, *The Unholy Bible* (New York: G. P. Putnam's Sons, 1970).

27. In this regard see Alan W. Watts, *Myth and Ritual in Christianity* (Boston: Beacon Press, 1968).

28. John Neihardt, *Black Elk Speaks* (Lincoln, NB: University of Nebraska Press, 1961).

29. For an excellent story that portrays the struggle of the human/divine man, Jesus, see Nikos Kazantzakis, *The Last Temptation of Christ* (New York: Bantam, 1971).

4. The Politics of Transformation in the Latino Community

1. Manfred Halpern, "A Redefinition of the Revolutionary Situation," *Journal of International Affairs*, vol. 23, no. 1 (1969), pp. 58-59.

2. For an excellent insight into the similarities between all traditional family units regardless of race or country see Mao's account of this struggle with his traditional Confucian father and family in Edgar Snow, *Red Star Over China* (New York: Grove Press, 1961), pp. 132-33.

3. Especially see Oscar Lewis, *Five Families* (New York: New American Library, 1959).

4. For a penetrating insight into this dilemma see Piri Thomas, *Down These Mean Streets* (New York: Alfred A. Knopf, 1970).

5. One of the better critiques of American culture is Philip Slater, *Earthwalk* (New York: Bantam Books, 1975).

6. See Robert McAfee Brown, *Religion and Violence* (Philadelphia: Westminster Press, 1973).

7. Ken Kesey, *One Flew Over the Cuckoo's Nest* (New York: Signet Books, 1962).

8. Alan Paton, *Too Late the Phalarope* (New York: Charles Scribner and Sons, 1953).

9. For an explanation of this archetypal relationship see James Hillman, *Re-visioning Psychology* (New York: Harper and Row, 1975) and Adolf Guggenbuhl-Craig, *Power in the Helping Professions* (Zurich: Spring Publications, 1976).

10. I owe this example to Jim Rebhan, one of the finest students whom I have taught, who participated in the conference at New York University during the spring semester 1977.

11. For an excellent analysis of the empowerment of Latinos see John Shockley, *Chicano Revolt in a Texas Town* (Notre Dame, IN: University of Notre Dame Press, 1974).

12. See Alan Pifer, The Annual Report of the President, Carnegie Corporation of New York, *Bilingual Education and the Hispanic Challenge* (New York: Carnegie Corporation, 1979), p. 16.

13. As reported in *Data Note: On the Puerto Rican Community* (Institute for Puerto Rican Policy, 114 East 28th Street, New York, N.Y. 10016), no. 3 (June 1984), p. 1.

14. Mario Barrera, *Race and Class in the Southwest* (Notre Dame, IN: University of Notre Dame Press, 1979), pp. 54-57.

15. Pifer, *Bilingual Education*, p. 9.

16. Ibid., pp. 9-10.

17. Erich Neumann, *The Origins and History of Consciousness*, Bollinger Series XLII (Princeton: Princeton University Press, 1971), p. 165.

18. Carl Gustave Jung, *Memories, Dreams, Reflections* (New York: Vintage, 1973), pp. 252-53.

19. Gerald McDermott, *Arrow to the Sun* (New York: Viking Press, 1974).

20. C. G. Jung, *Memories . . .* p. 256.

21. Joseph G. Jorgensen, *The Sun Dance Religion: Power for the Powerless* (Chicago and London: University of Chicago Press, 1972), p. 1.

22. J. E. Brown, *The Sacred Pipe* (Baltimore, MD: Penguin Books, 1971), p. 95.

23. Jorgensen, *The Sun Dance Religion*, pp. 226-27.

24. C. G. Jung, ed., *Man and His Symbols* (New York: Dell, 1973), p. 230.

25. Herbert Silberer, *Hidden Symbolism of Alchemy and the Occult Arts* (New York: Dover, 1971), p. 319.

26. *Historia Cultural de Puerto Rico 1493-1969* (San Juan: Editorial Universities, Universidad de Puerto Rico, 1975), p. 48.

5. Latinos and the Sacred

1. Manfred Halpern, "Archetypal Dramas: The Realm of the Sources," chapter four of a book to be published by Princeton University Press: *Transformation: Its Theory and Practice in Personal, Political, Historical, and Sacred Being*, p. 177.

2. Ibid., p. 175.

3. Emile Durkheim, *The Elementary Forms of the Religous Life*, trans. Joseph W. Swain (New York: The Free Press, 1969). Max Weber, *The Religion of China: Confucianism and Taoism*, trans. and ed. Hans Gerth (Glencoe, IL: The Free Press, 1951); *The Religion of India: The Sociology of Hinduism and Buddhism*, trans. Hans H. Gerth (Glencoe, IL: The Free Press, 1958); *The Protestant Ethic and the Spirit of Capitalism*, trans. Talcott Parsons (Lon-

don: Allen and Unwin, 1930; New York: Scribner, 1958); *The Sociology of Religion*, trans. Ephraim Fischoff, intro. Talcott Parsons (Boston: Beacon Press, 1963); *The Methodology of the Social Sciences*, trans. and ed. Edward A. Shils and Henry A. Finch, with a foreword by Edward A. Shils (Glencoe, IL: The Free Press, 1949). Karl Marx and Friedrich Engels, *On Religion*, intro. Reinhold Neibuhr (New York: Schocken, 1964).

4. Sigmund Freud, *The Future of an Illusion*, trans. W.D. Robson-Scott, rev. and ed. James Strachey (Garden City, NY: Anchor, 1964).

5. Ernest Troeltsch, *The Social Teaching of the Christian Churches*, trans. Olive Wyon (New York: Macmillan, 1931).

6. Wilfred Cantwell Smith, *The Meaning and End of Relgion: A New Approach to the Religious Traditions of Mankind* (New York: New American Library, 1964).

7. Bernard Lonergan, S.J., "Theology in Its New Context," in *Theology of Renewal*, vol. 1, ed. L.K. Shook, C.S.B. (Montreal: Palm Publishers, 1968).

8. For another study that takes the religious seriously see Ninian Smart, *The Science of Religion and the Sociology of Knowledge* (Princeton: Princeton University Press, 1973).

9. See W.I. Thompson's book *Passages About Earth* (New York: Harper & Row, 1974) for an excellent application of this threefold process.

10. For a discussion of alchemy as a sacred process of transformation symbolized in the work with metals see Titus Burckhardt, *Alchemy* (Baltimore: Penguin, 1971).

11. For the significance of the moon as a symbol of woman's mysteries as well as a symbol of transformation see M. Esther Harding, *Woman's Mysteries Ancient and Modern* (New York: Bantam, 1973).

12. See Joseph Epes Brown, ed., *The Sacred Pipe* (Baltimore: Penguin, 1971), n. 10, p. 23; pp. 80-83.

13. This is also Bernard Lonergan's conclusion in his own epistemological studies. See his article "Cognitional Structures," in *Studies in Honor of Bernard Lonergan, S.J.*, ed. Frederick E. Crowe, S.J., *Continuum*, vol. 2, no. 3 (Fall 1964).

14. Werner Heisenberg, *Physics and Beyond* (New York: Harper & Row, 1971), and Thomas S. Kuhn, *The Structure of Scientific Revolutions*, 2nd ed. (Chicago: Chicago University Press, 1970), p. 89.

15. W.I. Thompson, *Passages About Earth*, p. 91.

16. Halpern, "Transformation and the Source of the Fundamentally New," pp. 23-24.

17. Ibid., p. 20.

18. An old Muslim proverb attributed to Al Ghazzali (d. 1111) as quoted in Halpern, ibid., p. 10.

19. Arthur O. Lovejoy, *The Great Chain of Being: A Study of the History of an Idea*, William James Lectures delivered at Harvard University, 1933 (Cambridge, MA: Harvard University Press, 1950).

20. For a good treatment of archetypes see the *Collected Works of Carl Gustave Jung*, ed. Sir Herbert Read, Michael Fordham, Gerhard Adler, William

McGuire, trans, R.F.C. Hull, Bollingen Series IX (Princeton: Princeton University Press, 1970), especially vol. 9, part 1; and for a good introduction to Jung see Calvin S. Hall and V.J. Nordby, *A Primer of Jungian Psychology* (New York: Mentor, 1973).

21. Halpern, "Transformation," p. 25.

22. Lonergan, "Theology," p. 41

23. Halpern, "Transformation," p. 24.

24. Ibid., p. 22.

25. Halpern, "The Countertradition," *Transformation*. This is an earlier version of the manuscript, chapter 20.

26. The author wrote a doctoral dissertation as a personal statement describing the process as discussed here—i.e., creation, nourishment, destruction—in his own life and as shared by other Catholics. *The Breakdown of Authority in the Roman Catholic Church in the United States*, Princeton Theological Seminary, November 1971.

27. Erich Neumann, *The Great Mother*, trans. Ralph Manheim, Bollingen Series XLVII (Princeton: Princeton University Press, 1974), pp. 8-9.

28. Erich Neumann, *The Origins and History of Consciousness*, trans. R.F.C. Hull, Bollingen Series XLII (Princeton: Princeton University Press, 1971).

29. Halpern, "The Human Being in the Image of God: A Cosmos of Creative Participation," chapter five of Halpern's forthcoming book, *Transformation*.

30. Ibid., p. 24.

31. Ibid., p. 29.

32. Ibid., p. 62.

33. For fine historical analyses of the displacement of peasants from the land in order to create a permanent, cheap, and plentiful labor class, see the following works: Mario Barrera, *Race and Class in the Southwest* (Notre Dame, IN: University of Notre Dame Press, 1979); Frances Fox Piven and Richard A. Cloward, *The New Class War* (New York: Pantheon, 1982); and Penny Lernoux, *Cry of the People* (Baltimore, MD: Penguin, 1979).

34. See the article by Mario Vargas Llosa, "Inquest in the Andes," *New York Times Magazine*, Sunday, July 31, 1983.

35. All references to the pastoral letter are taken from the edition published by *Origins*, N.C. Documentary Service, January 19, 1984, vol 13, no. 32, published by the National Catholic News Service, 1312 Massachusetts Avenue, N.W., Washington, D.C. 20005.

36. Ibid.; see especially pages 537-39.

37. Ibid., p. 531, section 5, paragraph 2.

38. Ibid., p. 532, section 9, paragraph 2.

39. See Erik Erikson's *Gandhi's Truth*, pp. 253, 395-423.

40. Halpern, "The Human Being in the Image of God," p. 35.

41. Ibid., p. 35.

42. Virgilio Elizondo, *Galilean Journey: The Mexican American Promise* (Maryknoll, NY: Orbis Press, 1983).

43. See Burckhardt, *Alchemy,* pp. 133-38.

44. Neumann, *The Great Mother,* pp. 203-4.

45. Neihardt, *Black Elk Speaks,* pp. 48-49.

46. An ABC program aired on May 20 and 21, 1984, and based on the novel *Hanta Yo.*

47. Miguel Angel Asturias, *El Señor Presidente,* trans. Frances Partridge, Nobel Prize Library, vol. 2 (New York: Alex Gregory; Del Mar, CA: CRM Publishing, 1972), pp. 9-168.

48. Fyodor Dostoevsky, *The Brothers Karamazov* (New York: New American Library, 1958), chap. 5, pp. 222-44.

49. Gustavo Gutierrez, *A Theology of Liberation,* trans. and ed. Sister Caridad Inda and John Eagleson (Maryknoll, NY: Orbis, 1973); Juan Luis Segundo, S.J., *A Theology for Artisans of a New Humanity,* in collaboration with the staff of the Peter Faber Center in Montevideo, Uruguay, trans. John Drury (Maryknoll, NY: Orbis, 1974). In this latest series Segundo makes it clear that the methodology that he has employed, namely, dialectical and archetypal analysis, demands a reformulation of all the basic theological issues: God, Church, sacraments, history, person, grace, and the world.

50. *The Spiritual Exercises of Saint Ignatius Loyola,* trans. with a commentary and a translation of the *Directorium in Exercitia* by W.H. Longridge (London and Oxford: A.R. Mowbray, 1950). For a good explanation of the *Exercises* see Karl Rahner, S.J., *Spiritual Exercises,* trans. Kenneth Baker, S.J. (New York: Herder and Herder, 1965).

51. Made for and distributed by the Maryknoll Fathers, Maryknoll, NY, 1973, directed and produced by Thomas Cohen.

52. Halpern, "The Countertradition," p. 48.

53. Conversations held in Chaclacayo and Lima, Peru, between June 28 and July 3, 1975, with Maryknoll missionaries.

54. Lecture delivered at Chaclacayo, Peru, July 1, 1975.

55. Halpern, "The Countertradition," pp. 28-29.

56. See Robert McAfee Brown, *Religion and Violence* (Philadelphia: Westminster Press, 1974).

57. Halpern, "The Countertradition," pp. 93-94.

58. See C.G. Jung, ed., *Man and His Symbols* (New York: Dell, 1973), pp. 266-85.

59. Brown, *The Sacred Pipe,* chap. 5, "The Sun Dance," pp. 67-100.

60. Hermann Hesse, *Demian* (New YorK: Bantam, 1966), p. 94, and C.G. Jung, *Collected Works,* vol. 9, Bollingen Series (Princeton: Princeton University Press, 1968).

61. D.H. Lawrence, *Phoenix II, Uncollected, Unpublished and Other Prose Works,* collected and ed. Warren Roberts and Harry T. Moore (New York: Viking Press, 1970). See especially his short story "Reflections on the Death of a Porcupine," pp. 460-74, where he has a superb discussion of the Holy Spirit as the restless wind that transforms chaos into incarnation.

62. Halpern, "The Countertradition," p. 34.

63. Ann Belford Ulanov, *The Feminine in Christian Theology and*

Jungian Psychology (Evanston, IL: Northwestern University Press, 1971); see also Mary Daly, *Beyond God The Father: Towards a Philosophy of Women's Liberation* (Boston: Beacon Press, 1973).

6. The Politics of Liberation versus the Politics of Assimilation

1. For an excellent reinterpretation of middle-class and salaried professionals see Manfred Halpern, "Toward a Transforming Analysis of Social Class," in *Commoners, Climbers, and Notables,* ed. C.A.O. Van Nieuwenhuijza (Leiden: E.J. Brill, 1977).

2. For a provocative study of repression see Norman O. Brown, *Life Against Death* (New York: Vintage, 1959). Also Herbert Marcuse, *Eros and Civilization* (New York: Vintage, 1955).

3. George Orwell's *1984,* following Rousseau's insight, illustrates how modern society reduces all passion to loyalty for the state.

4. Richard Rodriquez never realizes or at least does not acknowledge this sadness but rushes to be like the others. See his *Hunger of Memory: The Education of Richard Rodriquez* (New York: Bantam, 1983).

5. This is the theme of Ken Kesey's book, one of the best American political novels, *One Flew Over the Cuckoo's Nest* (New York: Signet, 1962).

6. The systematic nurturing of the antiself in both traditional and modern society is brilliantly outlined by Marshall Berman in his *Politics of Authenticity* (New York: Atheneum Press, 1972).

7. Tom Robbins, *Even Cowgirls Get the Blues* (New York: Bantam, 1976), pp. 114-15.

8. Brown, *Life Against Death* pp. 23-67.

9. Richard Wagner, *Parsifal*, libretto English version by Stewart Robb (New York/London: G. Schirmer), p. 22.

10. Marquerite Yourcenar, *The Abyss,* trans. Grace Frick (New York: Farrar, Straus and Giroux, 1976), pp. 221-22.

11. I am greatly indebted to Manfred Halpern for much that follows. These ideas are expressed in his chapter four, "The Human Being in the Image of God: A Cosmos of Creative Participation," an unpublished manuscript entitled *Transformation: Its Theory and Practice in Personal, Political, Historical, and Sacred Being.*

12. Ibid., p. 62.

13. Paulo Freire, *Pedagogy of the Oppressed* (New York: Continuum 1970).

14. This insight into Plato's view of education as political I owe to Paul Friedlander, *Plato,* trans. Hans Meyerhoff, Bollingen Series LIX (Princeton: Princeton University Press, 1973), especially chapters one, two, and four.

15. Ralph Ellison, *Invisible Man* (New York: Vintage, 1972), epilogue, pp. 559-68.

7. Latino Professionals: A Transforming Middle Class

1. Marshall Berman, *The Politics of Authenticity* (New York: Atheneum Press, 1972), pp. 217-18.

2. For much of my analysis regarding the professionalization of the professions I am indebted to Magali Sarfatti Larson's excellent study *The Rise of Professionalism*: A Sociological Analysis (Berkeley: University of California Press, 1977).

3. Ibid., p. xii of the introduction.

4. Halpern, "A Redefinition," p. 64.

5. Robert Merton, "The Machine, the Worker, and the Engineer," as quoted in Larson, *The Rise of Professionalism*, p. 237.

6. Larson, *The Rise of Professionalism*, p. 201.

7. J.A. Jackson, ed., *Professions and Professionalization* (Cambridge: Cambridge University Press, 1970), pp. 4-5.

8. Larson, *The Rise of Professionalism*, p. 237.

9. Manfred Halpern, "Toward a Transforming Analysis of Social Class," in *Commoners, Climbers, and Notables*, ed. C.A.O. Van Nieuwenhuijza (Leiden: E.J. Brill Publishers, 1977).

10. For an excellent explanation of Plato's political vision see Paul Friedlander, *Plato*, trans. Hans Meyerhoff, Bollingen Series LIX (Princeton: Princeton University Press, 1973), esp. chap. 4, pp. 85-107.

11. Halpern, "Toward a Transforming Analysis," p. 74.

12. Larson, *The Rise of Professionalism*, pp. 243-44.

13. Halpern, "Toward a Transforming Analysis," p. 72.

14. Octavio Paz, "Reflections: Mexico and the United States," *The New Yorker*, September 17, 1979, p. 140.

15. Rousseau's Letter to d'Alembert, section 126, as quoted in Berman, *The Politics of Authenticity*, p. 215.

16. I am greatly indebted for my understanding of *daimon* in Plato and Socrates to Friedlander's *Plato*, pp. 32-58.

17. See Shlomo Avineri's article: "Marx's Vision of Future Society," *Dissent*, 20 (Summer 1973), pp. 323-31.

18. As reported on *Sixty Minutes*, CBS, "Pillar of the Community," Sunday, November 27, 1983 and again April 29, 1984.

8. Choices for Latinos: Creating the Present and Future

1. Oscar Lewis, *La Vida* (New York: New American Library, 1959).

2. Rene Marques, *La Carreta* (Rio Pierdas, Puerto Rico: Editorial Cultural, 1963).

3. Susan Sheehan, *A Welfare Mother* (Boston: Houghton Mifflin Company, 1976).

4. Elena Padilla, *Up From Puerto Rico* (New York and London: Columbia University Press, 1969), pp. 28-29.

5. Tato Lavierra, *La Carreta Made a U-Turn* (Houston: Arte Publico Press, University of Houston, 1981).

Index